CITIES
AND CLIMATE
CHANGE

The Urban Development Series discusses the challenge of urbanization and what it will mean for developing countries in the decades ahead. The series delves substantively into the core issues framed by the World Bank's 2009 Urban Strategy, *Systems of Cities: Harnessing Urbanization for Growth and Poverty Alleviation.* Across the five domains of the Urban Strategy, the series provides a focal point for publications that seek to foster a better understanding of the core elements of the city system, pro-poor policies, city economies, urban land and housing markets, urban environments, and other issues germane to the agenda of sustainable urban development.

Cities and Climate Change: Responding to an Urgent Agenda is the first title in the Urban Development Series.

CITIES
AND CLIMATE
CHANGE
Responding to an Urgent Agenda

Daniel Hoornweg, Mila Freire, Marcus J. Lee,
Perinaz Bhada-Tata, and Belinda Yuen, editors

THE WORLD BANK
Washington, D.C.

This volume is a product of the staff of the International Bank for Reconstruction and Development / The World Bank. The findings, interpretations, and conclusions expressed in this volume do not necessarily reflect the views of the Executive Directors of The World Bank or the governments they represent.

The World Bank does not guarantee the accuracy of the data included in this work. The boundaries, colors, denominations, and other information shown on any map in this work do not imply any judgement on the part of The World Bank concerning the legal status of any territory or the endorsement or acceptance of such boundaries.

ISBN: 978-0-8213-8493-0
eISBN: 978-0-8213-8667-5
DOI: 10.1596/978-0-8213-8493-0

Cover photo: ©Atlantide Phototravel/Corbis

Library of Congress Cataloging-in-Publication Data

Cities and climate change : responding to an urgent agenda / edited by Daniel Hoornweg ... [et al.].
    p. cm.—(Urban development series)
    Collection of papers prepared and presented at the World Bank's Fifth Urban Research Symposium.
    Includes bibliographical references and index.
    ISBN 978-0-8213-8493-0—ISBN 978-0-8213-8667-5 (electronic)
    1. Urban ecology (Sociology—Congresses. 2. Greenhouse gases—Congresses. 3. Climatic changes—Congresses. I. Hoornweg, Daniel A. (Daniel Arthur), 1961- II. Urban Research Symposium (5th Marseille, France 2009)
HT241.C555 2011
307.76—dc22

2011007569

Contents

Foreword

The 5th Urban Research Symposium on Cities and Climate Change—Responding to an Urgent Agenda, held in Marseille in June 2009, sought to highlight how climate change and urbanization are converging to create one of the greatest challenges of our time. Responding to this challenge effectively and sustainably is a key objective for governments, authorities, institutions, and other organizations involved in urban development processes. The World Bank, the French Ministry of Ecology, Sustainable Development, Transport and Housing, and the French Development Agency were therefore particularly committed to the co-organization of the symposium.

Cities consume much of the world's energy, and thus produce much of the world's greenhouse gas emissions. Yet cities, to varying extents, are also vulnerable to climate change impacts, with poor populations facing the greatest risk. Thus, adaptation and increased resilience constitute priorities for every city, and cities have a key role to play in mitigating climate change. Climate change mitigation and adaptation in cities has emerged as a new theme on the global agenda, creating a strong desire among governments, the private sector, and the academic community worldwide to learn from experiences and good practice examples.

The 5th Urban Research Symposium made an important contribution to the growing body of knowledge and practice in the area of cities and climate change. During the three-day symposium, approximately 200 papers were presented to more than 700 participants representing more than 70 countries. As co-organizers, we found it very rewarding to have such an audience and to see the wide range of topics discussed, from indicators and measurement to institutions and governance.

The symposium was made possible through the commitment and contributions of a wide range of partners and cosponsors, as well as through the interest and participation of the wider community of urban researchers and practitioners. We were encouraged by the symposium's success, which exceeded many expectations, and therefore wish to further disseminate its results. This publication is comprised of an edited selection of the many papers submitted to the symposium and gives a flavor of the questions asked and possible answers. (The entire collection of symposium papers is available as an online resource for interested readers.) We look forward to the benefits that the knowledge gained and the partnerships forged during the symposium will have for global efforts on cities and climate change.

Inger Andersen
Vice President
Sustainable Development Network
The World Bank

Michèle Pappalardo
General Commissioner for Sustainable Development
Ministry of Ecology, Sustainable Development, Transport and Housing

Rémi Genevey
Executive Director (Strategy)
French Development Agency

Acknowledgments

The 5th Urban Research Symposium was co-organized by the World Bank, the French Ministry of Ecology, Sustainable Development, Transport and Housing (MEDDTL), and the French Development Agency (AFD). The symposium's Steering Group included Abha Joshi-Ghani, Mila Freire, and Daniel Hoornweg of the World Bank; Aude Vermot-Gaud and Anne Charreyron-Perchet of MEDDTL; and Nils Devernois and Laureline Krichewsky of AFD. The symposium's Scientific Committee comprised Yves Crozet, Mila Freire, Pierre-Noel Giraud, Bernd Hansjuergens, Sylvy Jaglin, Andrew Norton, and William Solecki.

The symposium Secretariat was led by Jean-Jacques Helluin and Perinaz Bhada at the World Bank. Many World Bank colleagues provided helpful comments at every stage during the symposium's development, from the initial concept note review through to the symposium itself. Excellent organizational and administrative support for the symposium was provided by Adelaide Barra, Viviane Bernadac, Louis Blazy, Laura de Brular, Vivian Cherian, Xiaofeng Li, Maria Eugenia Quintero, and Berenice Sanchez. Thanks also go to Zoubida Allaoua and Kathy Sierra of the World Bank, and to Robert Peccoud and Veronique Sauvat at AFD, for their guidance and leadership.

The institutional and strategic partners who generously contributed to the symposium included the French Environment and Energy Management Agency (ADEME), Caisse des Dépôts, the Cities Alliance, the Dexia Group, the Euromedina Urban Network, the European Commission, the Fonds Français pour l'Environnement Mondial (FFEM), the French Ministry of Foreign Affairs, GDF Suez S.A., the German Federal Ministry of Education and Research, the Global Environment Facility (GEF), the German Company for Technical Co-operation (GTZ), ICLEI (Local Governments for Sustainability), Institut des Sciences et des Techniques de l'Equipement et de l'Environnement pour le Développement (ISTED), the International Development Research Centre (IDRC), the International Society of City and Regional Planners (ISO-CARP), the Lincoln Institute of Land Policy, the City of Marseille, Metropolis, the Organisation for Economic Co-operation and Development (OECD), United Cities and Local Governments (UCLG), the U.K. Department for International Development (DFID), the United Nations Environment Programme (UNEP), the United Nations Human Settlements Programme (UN-HABITAT), the United Nations Population Fund (UNFPA), the Urban Climate Change Reseach Network (UCCRN), and Veolia Environnement S.A. The World Bank's Energy Sector Management Assistance Program (ESMAP) commissioned some researchers and produced a related publication.

Much appreciation is due to the authors of all papers submitted and presented at the symposium, as well as to all symposium participants whose ideas and contributions provided for rich and lively discussions during the various sessions. The authors of the eight commissioned research papers helped to synthesize and strengthen the knowledge presented at the symposium, including through the preparatory workshop for commissioned researchers.

This publication was prepared by a team from the Urban and Local Government Unit of the World Bank composed of Christa Anderson, Mila Freire, Daniel Hoornweg, Marcus Lee, and Belinda Yuen, with assistance from Adelaide Barra. Technical and substantive editing was ably undertaken through a team comprising Anu Ramaswami, Sebastian Carney, Elliot Cohen, Shobhakar Dhakal, Enessa Janes, Christopher Kennedy, Cynthia Skelhorn, and Joshua Sperling. Useful comments were received from the peer reviewers, Ellen Hamilton, Susan Parnell, and Federica Ranghieri. The Office of the Publisher provided editorial and production services.

Contributors

Rimjhim Aggarwal, Arizona State University, USA

Andrea Armstrong, Durham University, U.K.

Jonathan Barton, Pontificia Universidad Católica de Chile, Chile

Alain Bertaud, urban planner, independent consultant, USA

Erach Bharucha, Bharati Vidyapeeth Institute of Environmental Education and Research, India

Harriet Bulkeley, Durham University, U.K.

Carsten Butsch, University of Cologne, Germany

Sebastian Carney, University of Manchester, U.K.

Shu Yi Chu, University of Oxford, U.K.

Edoardo Croci, IEFE–Bocconi University, Italy

Shobhakar Dhakal, National Institute for Environmental Studies, Japan

Michail Fragkias, Arizona State University, USA

Shibani Ghosh, University of Oxford, U.K.

Dirk Heinrichs, Institute of Transport Research, German Aerospace Center, Germany

Katy Janda, University of Oxford, U.K.

Peter Johnston, University of Cape Town, South Africa

Christopher A. Kennedy, University of Toronto, Canada

Frauke Kraas, University of Cologne, Germany

Kerstin Krellenberg, Helmholtz Centre for Environmental Research–UFZ, Germany

Andrea Lampis, Universidad de los Andes Bogotá, Colombia

Benoit Lefèvre, Iddri, Sciences Po, France

Mark P. McCarthy, Met Office Hadley Centre, U.K.

Sabrina Melandri, IEFE–Bocconi University, Italy

Tania Molteni, IEFE–Bocconi University, Italy

Caroline Moser, University of Manchester, U.K.

Ooi Giok Ling (deceased), Nanyang Technological University, Singapore

Anu Ramaswami, University of Colorado Denver, USA

Michael G. Sanderson, Met Office Hadley Centre, U.K.

Heike Schroeder, University of Oxford, U.K.

Johanna Vogel, Helmholtz Centre for Environmental Research–UFZ, Germany

Toby Warden, The National Academies, USA

Belinda Yuen, The World Bank, USA

Jimin Zhao, University of Oxford, U.K.

Abbreviations

AFOLU	agriculture, forestry, and other land use
BAU	business as usual
BRT	bus rapid transit
CBD	central business district
CBO	community-based organization
CCAR	California Climate Action Registry
CCP	Cities for Climate Protection
CDM	Clean Development Mechanism
CER	certified emissions reduction
CHP	combined heat and power
CNG	compressed natural gas
CO_2	carbon dioxide
CO_2e	CO_2-equivalent emissions
CRZ	coastal regulation zone
CVCA	communitywide vulnerability and capacity assessment
DDR	disaster risk reduction
DMRC	Delhi Metro Rail Corporation
DRM	disaster risk management
EU	European Union
FAR	floor area ratio
GCM	global climate model
GHG	greenhouse gas
GRIP	Greenhouse Gas Regional Inventory Protocol
GURC	Global Urban Research Centre
GWh	gigawatt-hour
IC	integrated circuit
IEA	International Energy Agency

IPCC	International Panel on Climate Change
JNNURM	Jawaharlal Nehru National Urban Renewal Mission
kWh	kilowatt-hour
LCA	life cycle assessment
LCCA	London Climate Change Agency
LPG	liquefied petroleum gas
LTO	landing and take-off cycle
MFA	material flow analysis
MTA	Metropolitan Transportation Authority
MWh	megawatt-hour
NGO	nongovernmental organization
OECD	Organisation for Economic Co-operation and Development
PCCAA	Participatory Climate Change Adaptation Appraisal
PIA	participatory impact assessment
PKmT	passenger kilometers traveled
PNA	Policy Network Analysis
PPP	parity purchasing power
PTW	pump to wheel
PVA	participatory vulnerability assessment
RCM	regional climate model
SOV	self-operated vehicle
UHI	urban heat island
UNFCCC	United Nations Framework Convention on Climate Change
USCOM	U.S. Conference of Mayors
USMCPA	U.S. Mayors Climate Protection Agreement
VKmT	vehicle kilometer traveled
WBSCD	World Business Council for Sustainable Development
WRI	World Resources Institute
WTP	wells to pump

1

Introduction: Cities and the Urgent Challenges of Climate Change

The Challenge of Cities and Climate Change

Climate change is among the most pressing challenges that the world faces today. Given current atmospheric concentrations of greenhouse gases (GHGs), the world is already committed to significant warming. This is a serious challenge, given the wide range of expected climate impacts on natural systems, as well as on human societies, as assessed in the most recent report of the Intergovernmental Panel on Climate Change (IPCC 2007). The severity of these impacts will depend in part on the outcomes of global efforts to mitigate climate change. Yet developing countries and poor populations everywhere remain the most vulnerable to the impacts of climate change. Even as poverty reduction and sustainable development remain at the core of the global agenda—as emphasized in the *World Development Report 2010: Development and Climate Change*—climate change threatens to undermine the progress that has been achieved to date (World Bank 2010a).

Urbanization is a defining phenomenon of this century. Developing countries are at the locus of this transformation, as highlighted in the World Bank's 2009 Urban Strategy. It is often repeated that more than half of the world's population is now urban. Most of the population of industrialized countries is urban, with numerous developing countries, particularly in Latin America, also highly urbanized (UN 2010). Many developing countries in other regions of the world are following the same path. This transformation represents a challenge, but also a huge opportunity. The *World Development Report 2009: Reshaping Economic Geography* (World Bank 2009) framed this in a new paradigm: to harness the growth and development benefits of urbanization while proactively managing its negative effects.

Cities concentrate wealth, people, and productivity, but they also concentrate vulnerability to natural disasters and to long-term changes in climate. Rising sea levels will affect millions of people living in coastal cities. Similarly, migration, changes in land use, and spatial development are likely to increase the vulnerability of populations to changes in weather and climatic conditions. Adaptation to climate change is therefore an imperative for cities, as it is for the world at large. The urgency of this challenge is also evident when considering the massive investments in buildings and infrastructure that cities in developing countries will undertake in the coming years, which will lock in urban form and structure for many decades thereafter.

The 5th Urban Research Symposium

The links between cities and climate change were the subject of the 5th Urban Research Symposium held in Marseille in June 2009. Under the main theme, *Cities and Climate Change—Responding to an Urgent Agenda,* the symposium aimed to advance the state of knowledge on cities and climate change from an applied research perspective. Attended by more than 700 people from more than 70 countries, the symposium featured eight teams of commissioned researchers and approximately 200 research papers selected from more than 500 initial proposals. The symposium was a groundbreaking event, given its scale and its focus on cities and climate change.

The symposium's research topics were organized around five clusters. The first dealt with *models and indicators to measure impact and performance of cities.* The complexity that characterizes climate change at the global level is heightened at the city level by the need to define boundaries, to identify consumers and producers, and to understand intercity flows. This is also the area where progress has been the most visible, with international partnerships and committed local governments working together to harmonize concepts and improve data collection. In turn, the increased availability of data and indicators stimulates research to test and apply global models at the city level.

The second cluster focused on *infrastructure, the built environment, and energy efficiency.* This area received the largest number of papers, covering issues from urban heat islands to urban transport policies and energy conservation. The insights from this cluster are important given the massive investments that cities in the developing world are expected to make in coming decades. Cities are also eager to share progress and discuss solutions that have worked elsewhere. Complementing this volume, the Energy Sector Management and Assistance Program at the World Bank has published selected papers from this cluster on energy efficiency in cities (Bose 2010).

The third cluster dealt with *finance and the economic incentives related to climate change*. The papers in this cluster focused more on financing requirements and the difficulties that cities may face in meeting these requirements and less on the use of market-based instruments and policies such as carbon finance, taxes, or incentives to change behaviors or encourage intercity collaboration.

The fourth and fifth clusters were concerned with the areas of *institutions and governance* and the *social aspects of climate change*. Both clusters produced important papers demonstrating the value of early commitment and participation in cities, as well as the potential to use local development initiatives for mainstreaming climate change concerns in cities.

The eight commissioned research papers are representative of the five clusters and cover issues such as the measurement of GHG emissions, city indicators, energy efficiency in buildings, and the importance of urban form. Papers were commissioned to ensure that leading, cutting-edge research was the organizing principle of the symposium and to provide better coverage of climate risk assessment and resilience, the role of institutions and governance, and the social aspects of climate change.

The symposium was an intense and research-rich three-day learning event. It became clear that experts and academics have differing views on any number of questions, but the areas of consensus are far greater than the areas of divergence. Although researchers continue to improve our knowledge of the world, decision makers cannot wait for all doubts or differences to be resolved. Moving forward, there is increasing urgency to get cities involved in climate change, not only in taking greater leadership roles but also in contributing to cutting-edge research at the city scale, defining practical solutions for urban and periurban areas, and ensuring that research is translated into local policy options. The symposium represents a start on this longer-term journey in understanding the links between cities and climate change—the body of research and projects on cities and climate change continues to grow rapidly.

This publication presents an edited selection of eight papers from the symposium that cover both climate change mitigation and adaptation. Examples and case studies from cities in industrialized and developing countries are included, and attention is paid to the perspectives of the poor in adapting to climate change. Of necessity, these papers represent only a small segment of the vast and rich range of knowledge brought together by the symposium. Abstracts of a further selection of symposium papers are included in the appendix to this volume. The complete set of symposium papers is available on the symposium's website, accessible through www.worldbank.org/urban.

The rest of this introduction presents the main conclusions and key messages emerging from the symposium from across all five clusters. These are organized broadly into sections on mitigation and adaptation, with a final section on priorities for future work.

Cities and Climate Change Mitigation

Cities are critical in global efforts to mitigate climate change. Although questions remain about how exactly GHG emissions should be attributed geographically, most of the world's GHG emissions are ultimately attributable to cities, which are centers of economic activity. Cities are responsible for two-thirds of global energy consumption, and this proportion is expected to grow further (IEA 2008). Yet, because of their density, efficiency, and adoption of innovations and new technologies, cities can also provide solutions for reducing emissions.

Measuring City GHG Emissions

A fundamental step for cities when it comes to climate change mitigation is to quantify the GHG emissions attributable to cities. Emissions must be measurable to be manageable; cities will otherwise not be able to set meaningful targets for emissions reductions, to track progress toward achieving such targets, or to obtain financing readily. In response to this need, much has already been achieved at the city level. ICLEI's (International Coalition for Local Environmental Initiatives, now known as Local Governments for Sustainability) Cities for Climate Protection (CCP) campaign, for example, features a five-milestone process that includes establishing a baseline emissions inventory. In 2009, CCP had grown to include more than 1,000 local governments worldwide (ICLEI 2010).

Various methodologies for measuring city GHG emissions have been developed in Europe and North America—such as Bilan Carbone, the Greenhouse Gas Regional Inventory Protocol, the International Local Government Greenhouse Gas Emissions Protocol, and Project 2 Degrees—raising questions of consistency and comparability. Although most efforts have sought to follow IPCC guidelines, considerable variation is found among these methodologies, for example, in terms of the GHGs covered and of the sectors (such as energy, waste, transport, and embodied emissions in food and other materials consumed) included (Bader and Bleischwitz 2009). Significant questions exist with regard to the treatment of emissions associated with transport to and from a city and of emissions embodied in materials consumed within a city but produced outside it. Another basic methodological issue lies in the definition of the city for the purpose of measuring emissions, whether based on administrative borders, a defined metropolitan area, or a functional economic space. In many developing country cities, the availability and reliability of data also present a challenge.

The chapter in this volume by Kennedy and others, "Greenhouse Gas Emissions Baselines for Global Cities and Metropolitan Regions," addresses these issues directly and reviews existing methodologies and available published results for various cities. Using a consistent, harmonized methodology, the authors have calculated per capita emissions for more than 40 cities around the world. This demonstrates that consistency and comparability are possible and constitutes a seminal contribution to the joint effort among the United Nations Environment Programme (UNEP), the United Nations Human Settlements Programme, (UN-HABITAT), and the World Bank to advance an open, international standard to measure GHG emissions from cities. Unsurprisingly, the results reveal that per capita emissions tend to be higher in the cities of industrialized countries compared with developing country cities. Furthermore, although these results show that per capita emissions in cities are generally lower than corresponding national per capita emissions, recent research on U.S. cities suggests that when emissions embodied in materials consumed in cities are taken into account, city per capita emissions are in fact very close to national per capita emissions (Hillman and Ramaswami 2010).

Factors Influencing City Emissions

A variety of factors influence a city's emissions profile in complex ways. These factors include urban form and land use patterns, climate, building design and technology, transport modes, and income levels. One would naturally expect lower per capita emissions in a city with more energy-efficient buildings, higher rates of public transport use, or lower income levels. The relative importance of such factors is explored by Croci and others in their chapter, "A Comparative Analysis of Global City Policies in Climate Change Mitigation," which includes case studies of London, New York City, Milan, Mexico City, and Bangkok. The authors identify income levels as a major factor in explaining the level of city emissions, while also noting a number of methodological issues in calculating emissions—Bangkok, for instance, estimates transport emissions from fuels consumed within the city, whereas the other cities use vehicle-kilometers traveled.

The emissions profiles of cities can be very different depending on specific city contexts. Croci and others point this out clearly in their comparison of cities across industrialized and developing countries. The largest contributor to emissions in Bangkok is the transport sector, but in London and New York City it is the buildings sector—specifically energy consumption in residential and commercial buildings, with transport coming second. Bangkok's climate, income level, urban form, and transport systems are all factors that explain this difference. The implication for mitigation in cities is that although cities can certainly learn from one another when developing and implementing mitigation strategies, specific solutions and mitigation measures may not be easily transferable or directly relevant for other cities.

The Importance of Urban Form for Emissions

Perhaps of greatest interest for urban planners and managers is the issue of urban form and density. It has long been known that denser cities tend to have lower per capita energy consumption (see, for example, Newman and Kenworthy 1989) and therefore lower per capita emissions, and within a given city, per capita emissions are lower in the denser parts of the city. Although this received wisdom has been questioned (Mindali, Raveh, and Salomon 2004), these correlations have been confirmed in recent work, including from the symposium papers and from research cited in the *World Development Report 2010* (World Bank 2010a). Yet urban form is shaped over longer time horizons, through planning, policy, and investment decisions.

In the chapter "GHG Emissions, Urban Mobility, and Efficiency of Urban Morphology," Bertaud and others use the examples of Mumbai, New York City, and Singapore to show how price signals—including energy prices and carbon market–based incentives—are a key factor in reducing GHG emissions from urban transport, in combination with land use and transport planning and policies. They suggest that monocentric cities and density can be managed with the right policies and that emissions from monocentric cities can be reduced if demand for transport between suburbs and the center increases. In their examination of the factors explaining differences in demand for urban transport, the authors consider how significant reductions in GHG emissions from urban transport can be achieved through technological change to reduce carbon content and through a shift in transport mode from private cars to public transit. The use of energy pricing based on carbon content would promote both of these changes.

The demand for urban transport also depends on urban spatial structures. Bertaud and others go on to show how in all three cities, spatial policies, including floor area ratios (FARs), have played an important role. New York City and Singapore have been able to maintain a high level of transit share by mandating high FARs, prioritizing and improving connections to public transport, ensuring high levels of amenities that make downtown areas attractive, and promoting mixed-use developments located at integrated transport hubs.

Governance Matters for Climate Mitigation in Cities

Armed with a growing understanding of their GHG emissions, many cities are already at the forefront of the mitigation challenge, with subnational efforts in these communities proceeding even as global climate change negotiations have made limited progress. Cities are leading and positioning themselves as a significant part of the solution. Although cities in the industrialized world such as Chicago, London, or New York City are oft-cited examples, cities across various developing countries, such as Cape Town, Mexico City, and São Paulo, are also rising to the challenge. Climate change mitigation plans and responses do vary among cities, as shown in the examples studied by Croci and others—London has adopted a long-term emissions reduction goal with intermediate steps, New York City and Milan have chosen medium-term targets, and Bangkok and Mexico City have shorter-term targets for 2012. All of this is encouraging, because cities offer humanity the best way to efficiently provide critical services and allocate increasingly scarce resources.

The importance of governance for climate action in cities is demonstrated clearly by Bulkeley and others in their chapter, "The Role of Institutions, Governance and Planning for Mitigation and Adaptation by Cities." The authors provide a comprehensive global review of the current state of mitigation and adaptation action by cities, focusing mainly on cities in the global South. Selected case studies include Beijing, Cape Town, Hong Kong, New Delhi, Melbourne, Mexico City, Mumbai, São Paulo, Seoul, and Yogyakarta. They examine how these cities are taking action in three key sectors: buildings, transport, and urban infrastructure. Issues of governance are dominant when it comes to regulating GHG emissions, providing services, and working with other jurisdictions. Key factors that shape responses to mitigation at the local level include effective policy making, access to additional finance, the congruence between jurisdictional areas and the spatial scale at which problems present themselves, and municipal competencies in key areas such as energy, planning, and transport. Governance at the city scale matters, as do the links and relationships with institutional and governance arrangements at other spatial scales.

Fast-growing cities offer enormous opportunities for investments in new energy-efficient technologies and for increasing the amount of energy from alternative and renewable energy sources. As demonstrated in the chapter by Croci and others, the energy sector usually offers the greatest potential, with cities' mitigation efforts accordingly focused on promoting energy efficiency (particularly through standards and regulations for buildings) and striving for lower carbon intensity in the energy supply. Across most cities, transport is the second most important sector, with policies focused on encouraging public transportation instead of the private automobile. Many symposium papers reflected the wide-ranging body of research on green buildings and energy efficiency. These include low-energy redevelopment in Rotterdam (van den Dobbelsteen and others), options for increasing energy efficiency in Nigerian buildings (Akinbami and Lawal), rainwater harvesting and evaporative cooling in Germany (Schmidt), and sustainable house construction in France (Floissac and others).

The motivations of cities and city stakeholders for engaging in climate mitigation also need to be understood. Warden's chapter, "Viral Governance and Mixed Motivations," describes some of the factors that led to American cities committing to address climate change and to the launch of the U.S. Conference of Mayors' Climate Protection Agreement (USMCPA) in 2005. The USMCPA has been very successful in motivating mayors in the United States, with more than 1,000 mayors signed on in 2010 (USCOM 2010). Growing public awareness, a flexible framework agreement, and having participants as proponents all contributed to the "viral" spread of climate engagement among U.S. cities. The USMCPA remains valuable because of its ability to generate awareness and engage a large number of cities on the issue of climate change. Although focused on the U.S. experience, Warden's analysis indirectly helps to advance our understanding of the engagement of cities worldwide on climate change issues through international networks such as ICLEI and the C40 cities.

A key observation is that, globally, climate change action among cities is focused more on mitigation than on adaptation. This is a point advanced by Bulkeley and others and reinforced by the analyses of Croci and others and Warden. The broad field of proposals submitted to the symposium also reflected a bias toward mitigation. This is the case even among cities in developing countries, even though these cities tend to have lower per capita emissions and thus would have relatively fewer mitigation opportunities. These cities' vulnerability to the impacts of climate change would also suggest an urgent need to focus on adaptation issues. Although various explanations have been advanced, such as the need for greater institutional capacity in developing countries, further research exploring this relative emphasis on mitigation is needed, as is strengthened understanding of how and why cities are motivated to undertake action on adaptation.

Cities and Climate Change Adaptation

Given that cities are concentrated centers of population and economic activities, any impact or disruption, whether natural or human induced, has the potential to affect vast numbers of people. The expected impacts of climate change pose a massive challenge to cities. These impacts will vary from city to city, as well as within a city. For instance, coastal cities are vulnerable to rising sea levels, to more intense precipitation that increases the likelihood of flooding in low-lying areas and landslides on steep slopes, and to extended heat waves that threaten cities unaccustomed to very hot summers. In every city, the poorest populations are the most vulnerable, because they have the least adaptive capacity and often occupy areas that are more exposed to hazards. Building resilience and adapting to climate change are therefore a high priority for cities. Yet city managers and practitioners serving the urban poor often point out that the multiple competing priorities of today are challenging enough; paying attention to uncertain future climate impacts is thus seen as a lower priority. In light of this, better appreciation of the cobenefits from urban poverty reduction and adaptation to climate change is needed.

Cities Responding to the Adaptation Challenge

In spite of the emphasis on mitigation thus far, and the many existing pressing needs faced by city managers and practitioners, there is a growing body of research and practice on adaptation in cities. Again, cities in industrialized countries are commonly cited as examples of good practice in adaptation planning, but cities in developing countries are also increasingly interested and active in this area. Heinrichs and others present findings from eight cities (Bogota, Cape Town, Delhi, the Pearl River Delta, Pune, Santiago de Chile, São Paulo, and Singapore) in their chapter, "Adapting Cities to Climate Change: Opportunities and Constraints." The full collection of symposium papers also reflected this trend of increased activity in climate adaptation among developing country cities, for example, in the papers by Carmin and others, which examined the cases of Durban and Quito, and by Dodman and others on community-level responses in the Philippines. Together, these papers show that far from being laggards, in many cases developing country cities are the ones turning out to be the first movers and innovators when it comes to preparing for, and adapting to, future climate impacts.

Several key enabling factors can be identified among those cities that are already responding to the adaptation challenge. The importance of identifying these enabling factors cannot be overemphasized, because these are essential for ensuring that cities are able to adapt. Bulkeley and others argue that these factors largely fall under the area of institutions and governance, which suggests that efforts to strengthen institutional and governance capacities in general at the city level would have the cobenefit of enabling better responses for adaptation. Heinrichs and others highlight several factors that also emerge across the wider collection of studies, including the availability of information, the need for higher levels of awareness, synergies with existing priorities and programs, the existence of strong leadership, availability of dedicated resources, and adequate technical and financial capacities.

Understanding Climate Impacts in Cities

One basic requirement for adaptation planning in any city is a sound analysis of possible climate impacts. In itself, this is a challenge of substantial complexity—there is considerable uncertainty on what future climate impacts might be for a given city, although our knowledge and modeling capabilities are constantly improving, for example, with downscaling climate models. In "Urban Heat Islands: Sensitivity of Urban Temperatures to Climate Change and Heat Release in Four European Cities," McCarthy and Sanderson show how urban areas can be included in regional climate models, using the cases of Athens, Cairo, London, and Moscow. The authors focus on the "urban heat island" effect, which arises from heat released through human activity in cities, such as the heating and cooling of buildings, traffic exhaust, and even human metabolism. Urban buildings and structures absorb heat during the daytime and release it at night, leading to an increase in nighttime temperatures. The authors caution that future heat waves may be underestimated if finer features at the urban scale are not included in model simulations. The potential for applying this analysis to other cities is considerable and would enable individual cities to fine-tune their knowledge of potential changes in local temperatures.

In general, modeling efforts are well situated within a broader field of work on assessing climate risks in cities. Bulkeley and others and Heinrichs and others analyze how cities are already anticipating and planning for future climate impacts. One of the symposium's commissioned research papers by Mehrotra and others also addressed this need: It presented a framework for climate risk assessment in cities and emphasized the importance of distinguishing among the different types of risks faced by different cities. The forthcoming Urban Risk Assessment, an approach for assessing disaster and climate risk in cities, is being developed by the World Bank with UNEP and UN-HABITAT and proposes a unified methodology for this purpose. It represents another important step in bringing the fields of disaster risk management and climate change adaptation closer. Although both communities of practice have the common aim to support decision making under uncertainty, they have largely operated in isolation from each other until recently (Tearfund 2008).

Climate Adaptation and the Urban Poor

An important issue when considering climate change adaptation, especially in developing countries, is to ensure adequate focus on the urban poor. Significant literature can be found on the economic impacts and costs of adaptation to climate change (see, for example, World Bank 2010b). Evidence is also available that the number of people affected by disasters is on the rise, and within cities, most disaster-related injuries and deaths occur among low-income groups (UN-HABITAT 2007). Moser and Satterthwaite (2008) clearly demonstrate that the main driver of increasing loss of life is poverty, which limits individual and household investments, and exclusion, which limits access to public services. In this context, not only does climate change exacerbate the existing vulnerabilities of the poor, but it also creates new risks as more areas in a city are exposed to climate-related hazards. The urgency is increased in those cities in developing countries with high concentrations of vulnerable urban poor.

A framework for focusing on the urban poor is provided by Moser in "A Conceptual and Operational Framework for Pro-Poor Asset Adaptation to Climate Change," which shows how the vulnerability of the urban poor's assets can be analyzed and offers examples of asset-based adaptation responses. Vulnerability varies depending on hazard exposure and the capacity to cope and adapt; these in turn depend on factors such as settlement quality and infrastructure provision. At the individual level, factors such as age, gender, and social status also matter. Greater assets (both intellectual and physical) reduce vulnerability and improve the capacity of the individual and community to react and adapt to disasters, including post-disaster reconstruction.

A closer understanding of specific vulnerabilities is also useful for taking concrete actions. Because many poor settlements are located in vulnerable places or lack protective infrastructure, long-term resilience can be increased by identifying better locations, increasing property ownership, and improving infrastructure. At the community level, improving community capacity and resilience is essential. The paper by Bartlett and others on the social aspects of climate change in urban areas, together with the paper by Dodman and others, reveals how community-based organizations and initiatives can be very effective in enabling adaptation among disadvantaged city dwellers.

An emerging conclusion is that the key to adaptation among the urban poor is to continue to address the basic poverty reduction and sustainable development agenda in cities to improve the livelihoods and resilience of the poor—ensuring adequate and effective delivery of services such as health, education, water, energy, public transport, and waste management; providing safety nets and increasing food security; upgrading facilities and infrastructure in slums and other informal settlements; and providing security of tenure and property rights.

Priorities for Future Work

Although the foregoing discussion has distinguished clearly between mitigation and adaptation to climate change, responding to the complex challenges of climate change in cities does not always lend itself to distinct categorizations in terms of mitigation or adaptation. Comprehensive and integrated approaches, which include both mitigation and adaptation strategies and the synergies between them, are needed to fully address this challenge. They also offer opportunities for cities to identify and take advantage of cobenefits; for example, investments in energy efficiency in buildings can both reduce GHG emissions and increase resilience in the face of more extreme weather conditions. Although much work is already taking place on integrated approaches that deliver cobenefits, greater awareness of these is needed, as is broader implementation in the field, beyond demonstration and piloting.

The symposium—its papers, presentations, and discussions—reveals numerous areas in which further research is required to strengthen diagnosis and policies at the local level, building on what is already under way. Several of these are highlighted here. First, the advances made to measure and analyze city GHG emissions need to be consolidated and eventually lead to internationally accepted methodologies used with the same rigor and accountability by cities in both the global North and South. This will ensure that mitigation efforts are well targeted within cities with progress toward mitigation targets properly tracked, and this clarity and consistency will facilitate access to additional finance. Second is the need to continue to expand work on adaptation in cities, in terms of both understanding future climate impacts and implementing the most effective adaptation actions in response to specific risks including disasters. Third, we need to increase our knowledge of the unique circumstances of developing country cities, because considerable variation is found among these cities across regions and across different city sizes and locations. Fourth is the need to undertake further economic and social analyses of all aspects of climate change in cities; this was especially apparent from the relatively small proportion of papers at the symposium on economic and social issues: Only a handful of papers addressed the crucial issue of financing climate actions in cities. The costs and benefits of (non)action, social influences, and behavioral studies are central to understanding the basis of public attitudes and behavior for effective climate change action. Last but not least, data availability is a critical constraint, for which continued efforts in data collection and utilization are needed.

The overwhelming response to the symposium far exceeded initial expectations. It is clear that the field of research on cities and climate change is growing and rapidly evolving, which bodes well to ensure that the best knowledge and analysis is applied to the urgent challenges that cities face in responding to climate change. The World Bank and its partners are committed to working with cities, researchers, and other agencies to improve the well-being of cities and their residents, especially the poor and the vulnerable.

References

Bader, N., and R. Bleischwitz. 2009. *Study Report: Comparative Analysis of Local GHG Inventory Tools.* Bruges: College of Europe; Paris: Institut Veolia Environnement.

Bose, R. K., ed. 2010. *Energy Efficient Cities: Assessment Tools and Benchmarking Practices.* Washington, DC: World Bank.

Hillman, T., and A. Ramaswsami. 2010. "Greenhouse Gas Emission Footprints and Energy Use Benchmarks for Eight U.S. Cities." *Environmental Science and Technology* 44 (6): 1902–10.

ICLEI. 2010. "Cities for Climate Protection (CCP) Campaign." http://www.iclei.org/index.php?id=10829.

IEA (International Energy Agency). 2008. *World Energy Outlook 2009.* Paris: IEA.

IPCC (International Panel on Climate Change). 2007. *Climate Change 2007: The Physical Science Basis. Contribution of Working Group I to the Fourth Assessment Report of the Intergovernmental Panel on Climate Change,* ed. S. Solomon, D. Qin, M. Manning, Z. Chen, M. Marquis, K. B. Averyt, M. Tignor, and H. L. Miller. Cambridge, U.K.: Cambridge University Press.

Mindali, O., A. Raveh, and I. Salomon. 2004. "Urban Density and Energy Consumption: A New Look at Old Statistics." *Transportation Research Part A: Policy and Practice* 38 (2): 143–62.

Moser, C., and D. Satterthwaite. 2008. "Towards Pro-Poor Adaptation to Climate Change in the Urban Centres of Low- and Middle-Income Countries." Human Settlements Working Paper Series Climate Change and Cities 3, International Institute for Environment and Development, Global Urban Research Centre, London.

Newman, P., and J. Kenworthy. 1989. *Cities and Automobile Dependence: A Sourcebook.* Aldershot, U.K.: Gower Technical.

Tearfund. 2008. *Linking Climate Change Adaptation and Disaster Risk Reduction.* Teddington, U.K.: Tearfund.

UN (United Nations). 2010. *World Urbanization Prospects: 2009 Revision.* New York: UN Department of Social and Economic Affairs.

UN-HABITAT (United Nations Human Settlements Program). 2007. *Enhancing Urban Safety and Security: Global Report on Human Settlements 2007.* London: Earthscan Publications.

USCOM (U.S. Conference of Mayors). 2010. "Mayors Leading the Way on Climate Protection." http://www.usmayors.org/climateprotection/revised/.

World Bank. 2009. *World Development Report 2009: Reshaping Economic Geography.* Washington, DC: World Bank.

———. 2010a. *World Development Report 2010: Development and Climate Change.* Washington, DC: World Bank.

———. 2010b. *The Economics of Adaptation to Climate Change. Final Synthesis Report.* Washington, DC: World Bank.

2

Greenhouse Gas Emission Baselines for Global Cities and Metropolitan Regions

Christopher A. Kennedy, Anu Ramaswami,
Sebastian Carney, and Shobhakar Dhakal

Increasing urbanization, globalization, and expected climate change will necessitate new forms of urban management in the twenty-first century. New urban metrics will be required, including measures of urban competitiveness (Duffy 1995; Llewelyn-Davies, Banister, and Hall 2004), gross metropolitan product (BEA 2009), urban greenhouse gas (GHG) emissions (Dodman 2009; Harvey 1993; Kates and others 1998; Satterthwaite 2008), material flows (Kennedy, Cuddihy, and Yan 2007), and vulnerability to climate change (Rosenzweig and others 2009). Such measures will also inform assessment of risks that may be used to guide investment in cities. In other words, many of the metrics that are currently recorded for nations are now needed and can be developed for urban areas.

This chapter is concerned with the establishment of baseline measures of GHG emissions attributable to urban areas (cities and metropolitan areas). Over the past two decades, several entities have been active in establishing methodologies for estimating urban GHG emissions. One example is ICLEI (International Coalition for Local Environmental Initiatives, now known as Local Governments for Sustainability), which is a worldwide coalition of local governments (ICLEI 2006). More than 500 of ICLEI's member cities have established GHG baselines using software developed by Torrie-Smith Associates, under the Partners for Climate Protection program. Several larger cities, including, for example, London, Paris, and Tokyo, have developed their baselines using their own methodologies. Eighteen European urban areas, including eight capital regions, have been studied using the Greenhouse Gas

GHG Regional Inventory Protocol (GRIP; Carney and others 2009); GRIP has also been used for Scotland and Sacramento, California. Additional urban areas have been studied by academics (Baldasano, Soriano, and Boada 1999; Dhakal 2009; Dubeux and La Rovere 2007; Kennedy and others 2009; Ramaswami and others 2008) and at meetings such as those hosted by IGES/APN (2002) and Nagoya University/NIES/GCP (2009). The approaches used to establish GHG emissions in these studies are essentially adaptations or simplifications of the Intergovernmental Panel on Climate Change (IPCC) guidelines. However, minor differences in methodology need to be resolved—and clearer reporting mechanisms need to be established.

This chapter first reviews the types of methodology that have been used to attribute GHGs to urban areas. We begin by broadly describing the approaches used to determine GHG emissions for nations (IPCC 2006) and for corporations (WRI/WBCSD 2009), both of which inform the attribution of emissions to urban areas. We then discuss in more detail the specific differences in methodology between various studies of urban GHG emissions. The approaches used to establish emissions for more than 40 global urban areas (table 2.1) are used to demonstrate where differences in methodology occur (table 2.2).

TABLE 2.1
Definition and Population of Cities and Metropolitan Regions in This Chapter

Abbreviated name used in this chapter	Definition	Study year	Population
Europe			
Athens	Metropolitan region	2005	3,989,000
Barcelona	City	2006	1,605,602
Bologna	Province	2005	899,996
Brussels	Capital region	2005	1,006,749
Frankfurt	Frankfurt/Rhine-Main	2005	3,778,124
Geneva	Canton	2005	432,058
Glasgow	Glasgow and the Clyde Valley	2004	1,747,040
Hamburg	Metropolitan region	2005	4,259,670
Helsinki	Capital region	2005	988,526
Ljubljana	Osrednjeslovenska region	2005	500,021
London	Greater London	2003	7,364,100
Madrid	Comunidad de Madrid	2005	5,964,143
Naples	Province	2005	3,086,622
Oslo	Metropolitan region	2005	1,039,536
Paris I	City	2005	2,125,800
Paris II	Île-de-France	2005	11,532,398

TABLE 2.1, *continued*

Abbreviated name used in this chapter	Definition	Study year	Population
Porto	Metropolitan region	2005	1,666,821
Prague	Greater Prague	2005	1,181,610
Rotterdam	City	2005	592,552
Stockholm	Metropolitan region	2005	1,889,945
Stuttgart	Metropolitan region	2005	2,667,766
Turin	Metropolitan region	2005	2,243,000
Veneto	Province	2005	4,738,313
North America			
Austin	City	2005	672,011
Calgary	City	2003	922,315
Denver	City and county	2005	579,744
Los Angeles	County	2000	9,519,338
Minneapolis	City	2005	387,711
New York City	City	2005	8,170,000
Portland	City	2005	682,835
Seattle	City	2005	575,732
Toronto	Greater Toronto area	2005	5,555,912
Washington, DC	District of Columbia	2000	571,723
Latin America			
Mexico City	City	2000	8,669,594
Rio de Janeiro	City	1998	5,633,407
São Paulo	City	2000	10,434,252
Asia			
Bangkok	City	2005	5,658,953
Beijing	Beijing government-administered area (province)	2006	15,810,000
Kolkata	Metropolitan area	2000	15,700,000
Delhi	National capital territory	2000	13,200,000
Seoul	Seoul City	1998	10,321,496
Shanghai	Shanghai government-administered area (province)	2006	18,150,000
Tianjin	Tianjin government-administered area (province)	2006	10,750,000
Tokyo	Tokyo metropolitan government–administered area (Tokyo-to)	2006	12,677,921
Africa			
Cape Town	City	2006	3,497,097

Source: Studies as cited in table 2.2.

TABLE 2.2
Comparison of Greenhouse Gas Studies for Selected Cities and Metropolitan Regions

City or metropolitan region[a] Source	ENERGY	Electrical line losses	Gasoline use from sales data	Gasoline use scaled	Gasoline use from model or traffic counts	Aviation: all fuels loaded at airports	Aviation: all domestic; intl LTO only	Marine: all fuels loaded at ports
Europe								
Athens Carney and others 2009	✓	✓	?	?	?		✓	
Barcelona Kennedy and others 2009	✓	✓			✓	✓		?
Bologna Carney and others 2009	✓	✓	?	?	?		✓	
Brussels Carney and others 2009	✓	✓	?	?	?		✓	
Frankfurt Carney and others 2009	✓	✓	?	?	?		✓	
Geneva Kennedy and others 2009	✓	✓	✓			✓		n.a.
Glasgow Carney and others 2009	✓	✓	?	?	✓		✓	
Hamburg Carney and others 2009	✓	✓	?	?	?		✓	
Helsinki Carney and others 2009	✓	✓	?	?	?		✓	
Ljubljana Carney and others 2009	✓	✓	?	?	?		✓	
London Kennedy and others 2009	✓	✓			✓	✓		neg.
Madrid Carney and others 2009	✓	✓	?	?	?		✓	
Naples Carney and others 2009	✓	✓	?	?	?		✓	
Oslo Carney and others 2009	✓	✓	?	?	?		✓	
Paris I Mairie de Paris 2009	✓	✓	?	?	?	?	?	?

Marine: inland or near-shore (12 mile) only	Railways	Biofuels (fuel wood, dung cakes)	INDUSTRIAL PROCESSES	AFOLU	WASTE	Landfill: scaled from national data	Landfill: EPA WARM model	Landfill: total yield gas	Waste-water	UPSTREAM FUELS	EMBODIED FOOD OR MATERIALS
?	✓		✓	✓	✓	✓			✓		
	?				✓			✓		✓	
?	✓		✓	✓	✓	✓			✓		
	✓		✓	✓	✓	✓			✓		
	✓		✓	✓	✓	✓			✓		
	?				✓			✓		✓	
✓	✓		✓	✓	✓	✓			✓		
?	✓		✓	✓	✓						
?	✓		✓	✓	✓	✓			✓		
	✓		✓	✓	✓	✓			✓		
	✓				✓			✓		✓	
	✓		✓	✓	✓	✓			✓		
?	✓		✓	✓	✓	✓			✓		
?	✓		✓	✓	✓	✓			✓		
?	?		✓	✓	✓	?		?	?	✓	✓

continued

TABLE 2.2, *continued*

City or metropolitan region[a] *Source*	ENERGY	Electrical line losses	Gasoline use from sales data	Gasoline use scaled	Gasoline use from model or traffic counts	Aviation: all fuels loaded at airports	Aviation: all domestic; intl LTO only	Marine: all fuels loaded at ports
Paris II *Carney and others 2009*	✓	✓	?	?	?		✓	
Porto *Carney and others 2009*	✓	✓	?	?	?		✓	
Prague *Kennedy and others 2009*	✓	✓			✓	✓		n.a.
Rotterdam *Carney and others 2009*	✓	✓	?	?	?		✓	
Stockholm *Carney and others 2009*	✓	✓	?	?	?		✓	
Stuttgart *Carney and others 2009*	✓	✓	?	?	?		✓	
Turin *Carney and others 2009*	✓	✓	?	?	?		✓	
Veneto *Carney and others 2009*	✓	✓	?	?	?		✓	
North America								
Austin *Hillman and Ramaswami 2010*	✓	✓			✓	✓*		
Calgary *City of Calgary 2003*	✓	?	?	?	?			n.a.
Denver *Ramaswami and others 2008*	✓	✓			✓	✓*		n.a.
Denver *Kennedy and others 2009*	✓	✓			✓	✓*		n.a.
Los Angeles *Kennedy and others 2009*	✓	✓		✓		✓		✓
Minneapolis *Hillman and Ramaswami 2010*	✓	✓			✓	✓*		
New York City *Kennedy and others 2009*	✓	✓			✓	✓		✓

Marine: inland or near-shore (12 mile) only	Railways	Biofuels (fuel wood, dung cakes)	INDUSTRIAL PROCESSES	AFOLU	WASTE	Landfill: scaled from national data	Landfill: EPA WARM model	Landfill: total yield gas	Waste-water	UPSTREAM FUELS	EMBODIED FOOD OR MATERIALS
	✓		✓	✓	✓	✓			✓		
?	✓		✓	✓	✓	✓			✓		
	?		✓	✓	✓			✓		✓	
?	✓		✓	✓	✓	✓			✓		
✓	✓		✓	✓	✓	✓			✓		
	✓		✓	✓	✓	✓			✓		
?	✓		✓	✓	✓	✓			✓		
?	✓		✓	✓	✓	✓			✓		
					✓		✓			✓	✓
				✓	✓			?			
			c		✓		✓			✓	✓
					✓			✓		✓	
			✓		✓			✓		✓	
					✓		✓			✓	✓
					✓			✓		✓	

continued

TABLE 2.2, *continued*

City or metropolitan region[a] *Source*	ENERGY	Electrical line losses	Gasoline use from sales data	Gasoline use scaled	Gasoline use from model or traffic counts	Aviation: all fuels loaded at airports	Aviation: all domestic; intl LTO only	Marine: all fuels loaded at ports
Portland *Hillman and Ramaswami 2010*	✓	✓			✓	✓*		
Seattle *Hillman and Ramaswami 2010*	✓	✓			✓	✓*		
Toronto *Kennedy and others 2009*	✓	✓	✓			✓		neg.
Washington, DC *DC Dept. of Health 2005*	✓	?	?	?	?			
Latin America								
Mexico City *Secretaria del Medio Ambiente 2000*	✓	?	✓					
Rio de Janeiro *Dubeux and La Rovere 2007*	✓	✓	✓			✓		
São Paulo *SVMA 2005*	✓	?	✓			✓		
Asia								
Bangkok *Kennedy and others 2009*	✓	✓			✓			
Beijing *Dhakal 2009*	✓	✓	✓					
Delhi *Mitra, Sharma, and Ajero 2003*	✓	?	?	?	?			
Kolkata *Mitra, Sharma, and Ajero 2003*	✓	?	?	?	?			
Seoul *Dhakal 2004*	✓	?	?	?	?			
Shanghai *Dhakal 2009*	✓	✓	✓					

Marine: inland or near-shore (12 mile) only	Railways	Biofuels (fuel wood, dung cakes)	INDUSTRIAL PROCESSES	AFOLU	WASTE	Landfill: scaled from national data	Landfill: EPA WARM model	Landfill: total yield gas	Waste-water	UPSTREAM FUELS	EMBODIED FOOD OR MATERIALS
					✓		✓			✓	✓
					✓		✓			✓	✓
			✓		✓			✓		✓	
			✓	✓	✓	?			✓		
	✓		✓		✓	?		?		✓	
			✓	✓	✓			✓	?	✓	
			✓	✓	✓			?		✓	
					✓			✓			
	✓			✓‡	✓‡						✓
	✓			✓‡	✓‡						✓

continued

TABLE 2.2, *continued*

City or metropolitan region[a] *Source*	ENERGY	Electrical line losses	Gasoline use from sales data	Gasoline use scaled	Gasoline use from model or traffic counts	Aviation: all fuels loaded at airports	Aviation: all domestic; intl LTO only	Marine: all fuels loaded at ports
Tianjin *Dhakal 2009*	✓	✓	✓					
Tokyo *Tokyo Metropolitan Government 2006*	✓	?	?	?	?		§	
Africa								
Cape Town *Kennedy and others 2009*	✓	✓	✓			✓		✓

Source: Authors' analysis using information from studies as cited in sources listed in first column.

Note: The table displays only emissions subcategories for which there are differences between studies. AFOLU = agriculture, forestry, and other land use; LTO = landing and take-off cycle; n.a. = not applicable neg. = negligible; ? = uncertain/indeterminate; * = aviation emissions are apportioned across co-located cities in the larger metropolitan area; † = AFOLU emissions were estimated and found to be less than

This is followed by an extended discussion of critical cross-boundary emissions most relevant to urban areas. A few cities have, independently, quantified their cross-boundary emissions, so called because their emissions occur outside the geographic boundary of the city of interest but are directly caused by activities occurring within the geographic boundary of a city (such as with ecological footprinting). For example, airline travel has been included in GHG accounting for Aspen, Colorado, and Seattle, Washington, in the United States; some foods (rice and milk) and cement have been included in emissions for Delhi and Kolkata, India (Sharma, Dasgupta, and Mitra 2002); food, cement, and freight transport have been included for Paris (Mairie de Paris 2007); and key urban materials such as food, water, transport fuels, and cement are accounted for in Denver (Ramaswami and others 2008). This chapter discusses how these emissions can play a role in augmenting baselines for urban area, the policy implications, and the methodological approaches that have been used.

Baseline GHG emissions are presented for 44 urban areas, including those in developed and developing nations. Although total emissions have been reported for urban areas since the late 1980s (Baldasano, Soriano, and Boada 1999; Harvey 1993), this chapter primarily presents baselines from recent studies (such as Carney and others 2009; Dhakal 2004, 2009; Kennedy and others

Marine: inland or near-shore (12 mile) only	Railways	Biofuels (fuel wood, dung cakes)	INDUSTRIAL PROCESSES	AFOLU	WASTE	Landfill: scaled from national data	Landfill: EPA WARM model	Landfill: total yield gas	Waste-water	UPSTREAM FUELS	EMBODIED FOOD OR MATERIALS
✓	✓	?	✓	✓?	✓				✓#		

0.1 percent and hence not reported; ‡ = AFOLU and waste emissions for Delhi and Kolkata are given in Sharma, Dasgupta, and Mitra (2002); § = includes only aviation emissions within the urban region; # = also includes electricity.

a. See table 2.1 for definitions.

2009; Ramaswami and others 2008). These emission baselines reflect the methodologies employed and emissions sources considered. Therefore, the baselines are presented either with or without emissions from industrial processes (which may be incomplete),[1] waste (where methods differ), and aviation and marine (which is subject to debate).

Overview of National, Corporate, and Subnational GHG Inventorying Procedures

The IPCC (2006) Guidelines for National Greenhouse Gas Inventories are the international standard for national reporting under the the the United Nations Framework Convention on Climate Change (UNFCCC). The guidelines describe procedures for determining annual (calendar year) inventories of more than 10 categories of GHG emissions (and removals) that occur as a result of human activities. The aim with national inventories is to include GHG emissions that occur within the territory and offshore areas under each nation's jurisdiction, although some special issues are found with transportation emissions, as discussed later. Emissions are categorized under five broad sectors: Energy; Industrial Processes and Product Use; Agriculture, Forestry, and Other Land Use; Waste; and Others (which includes precursor and indirect N_2O emissions).

The methodology for determining most emissions entails multiplication of data on a level of human activity by an emissions factor. The IPCC guidelines include substantial guidance on collecting data, managing uncertainty in calculations, conducting quality assurance procedures, and identifying the key categories of emissions. With respect to the accuracy of calculations, the concept of *tiers* is particularly important. The tier indicates the level of complexity in methodology, with Tier 1 being basic, Tier 2 intermediate, and Tier 3 the most complex. Higher-tier methods have greater data requirements and are generally more accurate. The tier concept can apply to both activity data and emissions factors, where for example, an emissions factor may be nationally specific or a general one.

Volumes 2 to 5 of the IPCC guidelines provide detailed procedures for determining emissions from various subsectors, using Tier 1, 2, and 3 methods. In the next section, we will highlight a few specific procedural details from the IPCC guidelines, where they differ from approaches used to determine GHG baselines for urban areas.

First, however, we outline procedures that corporations have adopted for reporting GHG emissions because many municipal governments, given their level of jurisdiction, have resorted to tackling their corporate emissions (street lighting, for example, has emerged as one possible area of intervention in municipalities).

The World Resources Institute/World Business Council for Sustainable Development (WRI/WBSCD) procedures have arguably become the best practice for reporting GHGs by corporations (and other institutions). The WRI/WBCSD procedure applies standard accounting principles of relevance, completeness, consistency, transparency, and accuracy. Business goals served by conducting GHG inventories include managing GHG risk and identifying reduction opportunities. Although the standards are in themselves policy neutral, they have been adopted by many GHG programs, including voluntary reduction programs, GHG registries, national and regional industry initiatives, GHG trading programs, and sector-specific protocols (WRI/WBSCD 2009).

Two approaches for attributing GHG emissions to a corporation are provided: the equity share and control approaches. By the *equity share* approach, a company accounts for emissions based on its share of equity in operations. By the *control approach,* a company accounts for all (100 percent) of the emissions from operations over which it has control, whether financial or operational (WRI/WBSCD 2009).

The WRI/WBCSD procedures make particular efforts to be supportive of national-level reporting programs. First, the procedures use emission factors that are consistent with the IPCC. The WRI/WBSCD also recognize that official government reporting often requires GHG data to be reported at a facility level, rather than at a corporate level. So whether a company uses an equity share approach or a control approach to establish its corporate inventory, it is also encouraged to itemize emissions from facilities that it operates. Governments typically require reporting on the basis of operational control, either at the facility level or at some consolidation over geographic boundaries.

The WRI/WBCSD also introduced the concept of *scope* of emissions, enabling companies to distinguish between emissions from facilities that they own or control and emissions that result from broader company activities (table 2.3). Scope 1 emissions are those from sources such as boilers, furnaces, and vehicles that are owned or controlled by the company (producer). Emissions from electricity consumed by the company are in Scope 2 (consumer), whereas other emissions that are a consequence of the company's activities, such as extraction and production of purchased materials, transportation, and product use, are in Scope 3 (consumer). These Scope 3 emissions do not necessarily entail a full life-cycle assessment; they are a practical determination of the main indirect emissions attributable to the company's activities.

The WRI/WBCSD Scopes 1–2–3 framework has been adopted widely, with small variations, by several organizations that seek to establish standards for carbon accounting with a view toward future carbon trading. Examples of some of these organizations include the California Climate Action Registry (CCAR), the Chicago Climate Exchange, the Colorado Carbon Fund, and the

TABLE 2.3
Definition of Scope 1, 2, and 3 GHG Emissions

Scope 1: Direct GHG emissions

Direct GHG emissions occur from sources that are owned or controlled by the company, such as emissions from combustion in owned or controlled boilers, furnaces, and vehicles or emissions from chemical production in owned or controlled process equipment. (Direct CO_2 emissions from combustion of biomass and GHGs not covered by the Kyoto Protocol are not included in Scope 1.)

Scope 2: Electricity indirect GHG emissions

These are emissions from the generation of purchased electricity consumed by the company. Scope 2 emissions physically occur at the facility where electricity is generated.

Scope 3: Other indirect emissions

Emissions in this optional reporting capacity are a consequence of the activities of the company but occur from sources not owned or controlled by the company. Examples of Scope 3 activities are extraction and production of purchased materials, transportation of purchased fuels, and use of sold products and services.

Source: Adapted from WRI/WBCSD 2009, 25.

North American Climate Registry. Many cities and states are participating in one or more of these registries, although it is often the municipal government and not the government emissions that are being reported. For example, participants in the Chicago Climate Exchange include U.S. cities such as Aspen, Boulder, Chicago, and Portland; U.S. states such as Illinois and New Mexico; and Melbourne, Australia. The North American Climate Registry notes that its participants include several large privately owned utilities, as well as local governments from Austin, San Francisco, Seattle, and provinces in Canada.

Thus, as we seek to develop community-wide GHG accounting protocols at the city scale, adapting the WRI/WBCSD Scope 1–2–3 framework (already consistent with IPCC) with relevant modifications necessitated by the smaller spatial scale of cities, would provide consistency with other GHG accounting protocols. Ramaswami and others (2008), in developing a hybrid demand-based method for GHG emissions accounting in Denver, articulated a set of five Scope 3 items that provide a holistic account of the material and energy demand in cities (discussed further later in this chapter).

Procedures for attributing GHG emissions to urban areas lie somewhere between those used for national inventories and those for corporate inventories. Like the IPCC's national guidelines, the procedures for urban areas aim to attribute emissions to a spatially defined area, such as that within a municipal boundary in the case of a city's (community) emissions. The ownership of land within the area, public or private, is of no relevance. Similar to the WRI/WBCSD Scope 2 and 3 emissions, however, GHG emissions attributed to urban areas can include those that occur outside of the area as a consequence of *activities* within the area. The main challenge in developing a single global methodology for urban areas is deciding which (if any) emissions that occur outside of urban boundaries should be allocated to the urban area (Satterthwaite 2008).

ICLEI's recently revised (draft) protocol for local government (community) emissions adopts the concept of scopes, similar to the WRI/WBCSD. Under Scope 2 emissions, ICLEI (2009) includes indirect emissions from consumption of electricity, district heating, steam, and cooling. All other indirect or embodied emissions resulting from activities within the geopolitical boundary are classified under Scope 3, although a consistent set of relevant Scope 3 activities are not yet explicitly defined by ICLEI for the city scale.

Care must be taken in interpreting Scope 1, 2, and 3 emissions under ICLEI's protocol. Some emissions from utility-derived electricity and heat combustion may be accounted as both Scope 1 and Scope 2 emissions, if they occur both within and outside the geopolitical boundary. Similarly, emissions from landfill waste may be accounted for under Scope 1 and Scope 3. To avoid double counting, ICLEI's final reporting standard includes all Scope 1 emissions, plus additional emissions from electricity, heat, steam, solid waste, and waste water that occur outside of the geopolitical boundary.

Moving to a slightly larger scale, the GRIP methodology, developed at the University of Manchester, has primarily been applied to European regions (although it is also being applied in the United States), typically consisting of a large urban center with surrounding industrial and agricultural lands (see definitions in table 2.1). GRIP reports emissions from the six main GHGs (the Kyoto basket): carbon dioxide (CO_2), methane (CH_4), nitrous oxide (N_2O), hydrofluorocarbons, perfluorocarbons, and sulfur hexafluoride (SF_6). The methodology closely follows the IPCC guidelines by reporting, for example, energy and industrial process emissions by detailed subsectors. Indeed, results are developed so as to be comparable with national inventories as well as other regions. The GRIP methodology is also consistent with approaches used to study other cities or city regions. For example, it does assign electricity emissions associated with electricity generation to the end user (for example, GRIP reports Scope 1 and 2 emissions and some Scope 3 emissions).

A particular strength of the GRIP methodology is its ability to recognize and manage differences in data quality. GRIP has a three-level reporting scheme, where level 1 (green) is for the most certain data, level 2 (orange) is for intermediate-quality data, and level 3 (red) is lower-quality data; the last example usually is scaled from information in national inventories. (The levels have some similarities with IPCC tiers but are not the same.) The color coding is used in the reporting procedure to provide a clear indication of uncertainty in the results.

Overall, the urban GHG methodologies used by ICLEI and GRIP, as well as the academic studies, are fairly consistent with one another. All draw upon IPCC guidelines, with many incorporating out-of-area Scope 2 and Scope 3 emissions. The main differences lie with which emissions, particularly Scope 3, are included in final reporting.

Review of Methodology for Urban Baselines

This section identifies the specific differences in methodology between selected urban GHG studies and explains how the approaches taken relate to the IPCC and WRI/WBCSD procedures. Table 2.2 shows the emissions subcategories for which there are differences between studies. Emissions are discussed under the four main categories of the IPCC: Energy; Waste; Industrial Processes and Product Use; and Land Use, Agriculture, and Forestry.

Energy

The energy sector, including stationary combustion, mobile combustion, and *fugitive* sources, is by far the greatest contributor to GHG emissions from urban areas.

The determination of emissions from stationary combustion in urban areas follows the IPCC guidelines, with the exception of emissions from electricity use and district heating systems. Of the sectors considered under stationary combustion, the residential and commercial/institutional sectors are consistently important in urban areas. Emissions from these sectors can be determined with high certainty where fuels are metered, such as with natural gas. There may be some uncertainty with fuels that are delivered by multiple market participants, such as fuel oils, or where many different fuel types are used.[2]

The extent of emissions from stationary combustion in the industrial sector varies considerably by urban region. In some studies, fuel use is not distinguished by sector. Under GRIP, however, emissions from energy combustion in the manufacturing industries are reported according to IPCC's subcategories. In the inventory for Glasgow and the Clyde, for example, emissions from combustion are reported for the following industries: iron and steel; nonferrous metals; chemicals; pulp, paper, and print; food processing; beverages and tobacco; nonmetallic minerals industries; and other. (In GRIP, emissions from industrial energy combustion may be presented under "other industry" where data are not sufficient to distinguish between different industrial types.) Such detailed reporting is perhaps more important in wider metropolitan regions for which industrial energy use is typically more prevalent than in central cities.

For GHGs from electricity and heat production, all the urban areas considered in table 2.2 include Scope 2 emissions. From our studies, it appears to be conventional to allocate emissions from electricity consumption to the consumer of that electricity. Moreover, in most studies, the transmission and distribution line losses have been included in the determination of emissions attributable to urban areas (table 2.2). The motivation for including emissions from electricity production is that the size of these emissions is dependent upon the activity in the urban area (as well as the emissions factor). In Shanghai and Beijing, 30 percent and 71 percent of total electricity, respectively, were imported across their boundaries in 2006 (Dhakal 2009). The same argument also applies to some heating systems. Greater Prague, for example, has a district energy system that provides 17 percent of the heat used in the urban region; the GHG emissions attributable to Prague include those from a coal-fired power plant at Melnik, 60 kilometers away, which generates steam for the heat pipes (Kennedy and others 2009).

Determining GHG emission from mobile sources poses different challenges than with stationary consumption. For road transportation, questions are asked as to whether travel outside of the urban region, that is, by commuters, should be included. This is a moot issue for metropolitan regions, but significant when determining emissions from central cities. In the city of Paris, for example, internal automobile trips generate emissions of 3,670 kilotons of carbon dioxide equivalent (CO_2e), and trips with origins or destinations outside of the city contribute a further 2,862 kilotons of CO_2e (Mairie de Paris 2009); these are life-cycle emissions discussed further below. Nevertheless, for all the urban regions considered in table 2.2, tailpipe emissions within the urban region were what was quantified, so consensus is seen here. A further issue, however, is the means by which travel activity data are determined— an important issue to address given that GHGs from road transportation can account for more than 30 percent (50 percent in Sacramento) of emissions in some North American urban regions.

The IPCC guidelines on mobile combustion recognize two approaches for quantifying emissions for road transportation: (1) based on quantity of fuel sold and (2) from vehicle kilometers traveled (VKT). Approach 1 is preferred for CO_2 emissions, because it is far more accurate. Indeed, for reasons of data availability, consistency, and the typically small size of cross-border traffic, the use of fuel sales to calculate CO_2 emissions prevails over the strict application of the national territory (IPCC 2006, vol. 2, section 1.28). Emissions of CH_4 and N_2O from road transportation are, however, dependent on the age and technology of vehicles, as well as the number of cold starts; hence, approach 2 is preferred for CH_4 and N_2O.

To quantify GHG emissions from road transportation in urban areas, both of the approaches have been used (for the three GHGs associated with energy: CO_2, CH_4, and N_2O) and a third approach involving scaling of fuel use from wider regions, such as states or provinces (table 2.2). Several potential pitfalls are seen here. Fuel sales data are not always available for urban areas—and even if one can find such data, an implicit assumption is that the fuel purchased within the region is representative of activity within the region. This approach may be considered compatible with the IPCC guidelines, which suggest the use of fuel sales (although this may be more appropriate on a national basis). Meanwhile means of determining VKT may be inconsistent between cities because of differences in computer modeling, surveying, or vehicle-counting techniques. Nevertheless, by using multiple approaches for Bangkok, New York City, and Greater Toronto, differences between the three approaches have been shown to be less than 5 percent (Kennedy and others 2010).

Moving to emissions from air transportation, three distinct alternatives have been used for urban areas:

1. *Exclude airplane emissions:* In several of the studies in table 2.2, no emissions from combustion of airplane fuels have been counted (or in the case of Tokyo, just operations within the area). Other than through fuel consumption on take-off and landing, airplane emissions occur outside urban regions and so are not counted in Scope 1. It might also be argued that emissions from air travel are outside the control of local government, and so it is appropriate to exclude them.

2. *Include emissions from domestic aviation but include only take-off and landings for international aviation:* This approach has primarily been used in the 18 GRIP studies (Carney and others 2009). It is consistent with the GRIP philosophy in that aviation emissions from all regions could be added to give the same national total as reported under IPCC guidelines. Emissions from cruising on international flights are excluded in accordance with the UNFCCC.

3. *Include all emission from domestic and international aviation:* Both London (Mayor of London 2007) and New York City (2007) report GHG emissions based on all fuels loaded at airports within their boundaries. This approach was adopted in the study of 10 cities by Kennedy and others (2009), with modification for Denver to account for transfers, following Ramaswami and others (2008). This approach is consistent with the notion of world cities as the headquarters, financial centers, and key gateways between national/regional economies and the global economy, or as global service centers (Friedman 1986; Sassen 1991; Taylor 2004).

Three different approaches have also been used for emissions from marine transportation, where these apply. In some cases, marine travel is excluded. For the GRIP studies, only emissions on inland water or within 12 miles of shore are included, whereas the studies of Cape Town, Los Angeles, and New York City included international marine emissions based on fuels loaded onto ships at these cities' ports.

It is worth noting that no international methodology has been agreed to for allocating emissions from international aviation and marine activities. In national emissions inventories, the fuel sales and associated emissions are reported but are not included in the total. On an urban scale, this is further complicated by the fact that their airports may be located outside their jurisdiction. Also, passengers may be using the airport to transfer to another region, or the airport or port may handle much freight destined for other areas. All these issues make the allocation of emissions to the urban scale a rather difficult task.

Nevertheless, Wood, Bows, and Anderson (2010) suggest a method by which to allocate these emissions. The emissions associated with the landing and take-off cycle are allocated to the area in which the airport is based (this is the same approach as is adopted in air quality emissions), and the emissions associated with the cruise phase are allocated to the region in which the passenger resides. More complicated issues concerning tourists, transferring passengers, and freight are also discussed next.

Waste

The determination of GHG emissions associated with waste is where the greatest discrepancies in methodology are apparent. In particular, emissions from the land filling of solid waste have been calculated using at least three different techniques (table 2.2): (1) scaling from national inventories, (2) a total yields gas approach, and (3) the U.S. Environmental Protection Agency's (EPA's) Waste Reduction Model (WARM). Two further techniques could also have been used: (4) measurement from waste in place and (5) local application of IPCC's first-order decay approach.

The divergence of approaches for determining emissions from waste is perhaps partly due to the complexity of emissions from landfills. The biodegradation of solid waste to form methane and other landfill gases occurs over time scales extending beyond a single year. Hence, researchers find it challenging to assign GHG emissions from waste to a particular year.

The IPCC's recommended approach (5) involves calculation of emissions in the inventory year, based on historical waste deposited over previous years. An alternative (4) would be to actually monitor and measure emissions in the inventory year, but this requires considerable monitoring and may be challenging for commercial and industrial waste streams if they are managed by the private sector.

Scaling solid waste emissions from national inventories (1) should give results that approximate those from approaches 4 and 5. Such scaling has been used in the GRIP studies (using its aforementioned level 2 and 3 methods; Carney and others 2009).

The total yields gas approach (2) was formerly recommended by the IPCC (1997). Essentially it takes the total amount of waste produced by an urban area in a given year and then determines the total emissions released from this waste, regardless of how many years transpire before the full release occurs. This approach has been used by Dubeux and La Rovere (2007) and Kennedy and others (2009, 2010).

The EPA's WARM model (3) uses a life-cycle accounting approach, which is ideal in some respects but not in others. The model recognizes, for example, that the recycling of waste reduces emissions from the harvesting of raw materials; hence a credit can be applied. The problem is that emissions associated with material flows of paper and plastics into cities are not currently counted in the GHG emissions for most urban areas. So use of the WARM model is not consistent with current means of determining urban GHG emissions, although the life-cycle methodology is indicative of the direction cities should be headed as consumption-based inventory procedures develop (this is discussed later).

A few other inconsistencies in reporting emissions from waste can be made with reference to table 2.2. First, waste emissions were not determined for the Chinese city-provinces. Second, the GRIP studies and those of Barcelona, Geneva, Prague, and Toronto include emissions from waste incineration within the waste category, although where such incineration includes energy recovery the IPCC recommends that the emissions be included under stationary combustion. Finally, emissions from waste water/sewerage were omitted in many studies, although these are relatively minor.

Industrial Processes and Product Use

GHG emissions from industrial processes and product use include only emissions that are not primarily for energy use purposes (IPCC 2006). A wide range of industrial processes and products emit GHGs that are not the result of intended combustion. The three broad categories of nonenergy use are feedstocks, reducing agents, and nonenergy products, such as lubricants, greases, waxes, bitumen, and solvents. Emissions from these types of uses can be assigned to various industrial sectors:

- Mineral industry (including cement, lime, glass, and other)
- Chemical industry
- Metal industry
- Nonenergy products from fuels and solvent use
- Electronics industry
- Product uses as substitutes for ozone-depleting substances
- Other product manufacture and use
- Others (including pulp and paper, food and beverage).

Given the diversity of these nonenergy industrial processes and products, reporting of emissions is recognized to be challenging (IPCC 2006).

The reporting of industrial process emissions for urban areas is somewhat mixed. Other than the GRIP studies, which have carefully recorded these emissions, other studies have been less consistent. For many of the urban areas in table 2.2, no emissions are recorded. This could be because there are no industrial process emissions or the emissions are unknown. The GRIP studies perhaps record more industrial process emissions because they are regional studies, including industrial areas on the edges of central cities (although emissions are often reported as zero to indicate no activity takes place). Again, it is clear that industrial process emissions are missing from some urban areas in table 2.2. Also, the emissions associated with "refilling" air conditioning units may require more attention than many studies currently adopt.

The magnitude of industrial process emissions is usually small, but these emissions are quite city specific. For most of the European regions reported by Carney and others (2009), the industrial process emissions are typically 1 to 2 percent of total emissions. Exceptions are found, however: Athens (11 percent), Turin (11 percent), Frankfurt (10 percent), Hamburg (7 percent), Naples (7 percent), Venice (7 percent), Paris (6 percent), and Madrid (5 percent). In absolute terms, Frankfurt has the largest industrial process emissions with 4,987 kilotons of CO_2e. Among the other urban areas studied, Toronto has 3,185 kilotons of CO_2e of emissions from just two cement plants and a lubricant facility. Given that some of these emissions are quite substantial, better reporting of industrial process emissions is generally required for urban areas.

Agriculture, Forestry, and Other Land Use

GHG emissions and removals in the agriculture, forestry, and other land use (AFOLU) category are typically small, often negligible, for most urban regions. These emissions become significant only if the regional boundary is large, including substantial rural area in addition to the urban core, or where agricultural activities are particularly intense; this applies to a few cases in the GRIP studies (Carney and others 2009).

For many of the urban areas in table 2.2, AFOLU emissions have not been quantified because they have been taken to be negligible. This may be a reasonable assumption for many urban regions. In the study of Calgary, for example, urban forestry sequesters 13 kilotons of CO_2e, but this is less than 0.1 percent of total emissions (reported as 16,370 kilotons of CO_2e).

Even for cities in the developing world with relatively low total emissions, the contribution of AFOLU is small. Sharma, Dasgupta, and Mitra (2002) determined the methane emissions from rice cultivation and livestock (dairy cattle, nondairy cattle, and buffaloes) for Kolkata and Delhi. The emissions from 300,000 hectares of paddy fields in Kolkata, in 1997–98, were 0.45 kilotons of CO_2e. This is negligible compared to Kolkata's CO_2 emissions for the energy sector, which in 2000 were reported to be 17,270 kilotons (Mitra, Sharma, and Ajero 2003). Delhi's methane emissions from paddy fields were even smaller than those for Kolkata, but it had substantially more livestock, which emitted 15.16 kilotons of CO_2e in 1992 (Sharma, Dasgupta, and Mitra 2002). Here again, though, these methane emissions from livestock are negligible compared with Delhi's 19,800 kilotons of CO_2 emissions in the energy sector (Mitra, Sharma, and Ajero 2003). Agricultural emissions of 13 kilotons of CO_2e for Rio de Janeiro were also considered negligible, although emissions of 256 kilotons of CO_2e for land-use change were reported (Dubeux and La Rovere 2007). This represents 2 percent of Rio de Janeiro's emissions, which is small but still large enough to be counted.

Among the 18 European regions in the GRIP study, several of the larger regions do have substantial emissions for the AFOLU sector (Carney and others 2009). In the Hamburg Metropolitan Region, the agricultural emissions of 4,463 kilotons of CO_2e also represent 11 percent of the regions total emissions. Over half of these emissions were from agricultural soils; Hamburg is situated in the largest fruit-growing region of Europe. For other urban areas in the GRIP study, emissions from agriculture were found to be negligible, such as for Brussels, Helsinki, and Oslo. So although AFOLU emissions are usually small or negligible for many urban areas, exceptions are found, and this category needs to be carefully considered.

Inclusion of Scope 3 "Cross-Boundary" GHG Emissions Relevant to Cities

Having discussed Scope 1 and Scope 2 emissions, some consideration of the inclusion of Scope 3 emissions is necessary.

Why Include Scope 3 Items?

This section discusses methods for including the GHG impact of activities that occur within urban areas that spur production (and associated GHG emissions) elsewhere, often outside the geographical boundaries of the city of interest. Before we discuss which Scope 3 items to include, it is useful to articulate why Scope 3 items should be included in the first place. There is fairly wide acceptance that end use of electricity in urban areas should be systematically tracked back to GHG emissions occurring at power plants located outside city boundaries, such that these emissions are explicitly counted as Scope 2 emissions for that urban area. The same logic could apply, for example, to transport fuels such as diesel and gasoline used for transport in cities—the GHG emissions associated with refining these fuels should also be included just as is the impact of generating electricity. The GHG emissions associated with fuel refining (termed wells-to-pump [WTP]) emissions are 20 to 25 percent of the emissions associated with the combustion of the refined products in vehicles (termed pump-to-wheel [PTW] emissions) and thus are a significant contributor to global GHG emissions. Likewise, agriculture and food production contribute 20 to 25 percent of global and national GHG inventories yet are usually negligible in city-scale Scope 1–2 GHG accounting because much of the food production occurs outside the geographic boundaries of cities; at the same time, life in cities would not be possible without food consumption.

Which Scope 3 Items to Include?

This discussion suggests two criteria for inclusion of cross-boundary GHG emission motivated by activities occurring within urban areas. First, these activities should be critical for the functionality of cities, and, second, the resulting GHG emission should be significant contributors at larger spatial scales, such that their *exclusion* at the city scale creates a discontinuity in GHG accounting across spatial scales. We suggest that Scope 1–2–3 emissions accounting not be used in place of Scope 1–2 accounting, which may be preferable for carbon trading schemes but be used to augment Scope 1–2 reporting.

Several urban areas have included various cross-boundary emissions on an ad hoc basis; for example, GHG emissions associated with food consumption in cities have been included for Paris (Mairie de Paris 2009), Delhi, and Kolkata (Sharma, Dasgupta, and Mitra 2002), with Delhi and Kolkata focusing on nonenergy emission from rice and milk production only. Embodied emissions from producing various construction materials such as cement, steel, and asphalt have been included in inventories for Kolkata, Delhi, Denver, Paris, and Seattle. In pioneering a holistic emissions inventory for Denver, Ramaswami and others (2008) articulated a small set of Scope 3 inclusions critical for functionality of cities; these included the following:

- Energy associated with transport of good and people outside city boundaries, essential for trade and commuter travel to and from cities, allocated equally to origin-destination locations.
- Embodied energy and associated GHG emissions associated with production of key urban materials critical for life in cities, such as the following:
  - Food
  - Transport fuels (other fuels already being accounted for)
  - Water and waste water (if such production occurs outside city boundaries)
  - Materials for shelter—chiefly cement because it is the single second-largest CO_2 emitter following fossil fuel combustion.

The de minimus rule (CCAR 2007) can be applied, yielding a stopping rule: that is, no further Scope 3 activities need be included unless they show more than a 1 percent increase in the GHG accounting of a city. (Note that cities may also export CO_2 embodied in goods and services that needs to be accounted too; the "net" is of interest.) Thus, applying a full Scope 1–2–3 accounting can be made practical with the small and relevant list of Scope 3 activities just listed. Indeed, a small list of relevant Scope 3 items is the recommendation of WRI and the U.S. EPA Climate Leaders Program. The Scope 3 items listed focus on critical service provisions required for life in cities that often occur outside city boundaries; other material flows are assumed to be balanced out in the trade and exchange of goods and services between cities (Ramaswami and others 2008).

Measurement Impact

Inclusion of additional Scope 3 items has been shown to increase the GHG's attributed to cities. Incorporating primarily the impacts of fuel refining was shown to increase GHG emissions associated with eight global cities by as much as 24 percent (Kennedy and others 2009). Incorporating all five Scope 3 items increases the GHG accounting by an average of 45 percent for eight U.S. cities studied by Hillman and Ramaswami (2010). Further, incorporating all five Scope 3 activities (Ramaswami and others 2008) created consistency both in inclusions and in the numeric per capita GHG emission computed at the city scale for Denver versus the larger national scale, both of which converged to about 25 tons of CO_2e per capita (table 2.4).

A similar analysis repeated for eight U.S. cities showed remarkable consistency between per capita city-scale Scope 1–2–3 emissions and national per capita emissions in the United States (Hillman and Ramaswami 2010), which suggests that inclusion of the specific list of five Scope 3 items proposed by

TABLE 2.4
Denver's Average per Capita GHG Emissions Compared with the National Average, State of Colorado Average, and Other Colorado Cities

Inclusions	Denver's per capita GHG emissions (million tons CO_2e per capita)	National, state, or other city per capita GHG emissions (CO_2e per capita)
Scope 1 + 2 and waste plus airline travel and key urban materials	25.3	National: 24.5 Colorado: 25.2
Scope 1 + 2 and waste (no airline travel or embodied energy of key urban materials)	18	Other Colorado cities: 17.8–18.4

Source: Adapted from Ramaswami and others 2008.

Note: CO_2e = carbon dioxide equivalent; GHG = greenhouse gas.

Ramaswami and others (2008) may help cities develop a more holistic GHG emissions footprint that shows the overall impact of a city's activities on global GHG emissions.

Policy Impact

Incorporating a full Scope 1–2–3 accounting provides city residents with a measure that helps connect their everyday activities with GHG emissions. Important activities such as food consumption and airline travel that appear in personal GHG calculators and in national accounts also now appear in city-scale GHG accounts. This facilitates public understanding of GHG emissions and can also spur the development of win-win strategies for GHG mitigation that link demand for materials and energy in cities with their production. For example, accounting for embodied emissions associated with cement in Denver resulted in the city's adopting green concrete policies that require 15 percent fly ash inclusion in concrete to reduce cement consumption at the city scale (Greenprint 2007). Inclusion of airline emissions resulted in proposals to offer air travel off-set programs directly at Denver International Airport.

Furthermore, a Scope 1–2–3 emissions assessment can avoid unintended credit being given to policies that may merely shift emissions "out of boundary." For example, large-scale use of hydrogen-powered cars within city boundaries may result in zero PTW Scope 1 emissions, but significant WTP GHG emissions can occur outside city boundaries (Scope 3) if the hydrogen is produced from coal or natural gas. Conversely, many cross-sector strategies may be used to reduce a city's overall Scope 1–2–3 footprint. For example, information and communication technologies such as teleconferencing and telepresencing may increase energy use in buildings while displacing airline travel. Once again, a full Scope 1–2–3 GHG accounting protocol would support such innovative cross-sector, cross-boundary GHG reduction policies and strategies in a manner that boundary limited (Scope 1–2) accounting does not.

Methodology, Challenges, and a Proposed Framework for Scope 3 Inclusions

In the few studies that have included out-of-boundary impacts, the methodology has varied. In estimating GHG emission for Delhi and Kolkata, we estimate that Sharma, Dasgupta, and Mitra (2002) used national average consumption data for some of the urban materials studied and coupled these with nonenergy GHG emission factors for these materials as specified by the IPCC. Thus a city-specific material flow analysis was not conducted, and only partial emissions (nonenergy) associated with these products (rice, milk, cement, steel) were incorporated. For Paris, the city's Bilan Carbone (Mairie de Paris 2009) reported that national data from the food industry were used to determine average per capita consumption; however, methods used for estimating cement and steel consumption were not fully detailed nor were data sources for the requisite emission factors. In Paris, detailed analysis of resident airline travel and freight transport was conducted; both incoming and outgoing trips were counted and fully allocated to Paris. In contrast, Ramaswami and others (2008) applied a 50 percent allocation to destination and origin locations for allocating both airline and surface transport in Denver; such an origin-destination allocation procedure ensures that the same trip is not double counted at both ends of a trip.

For key urban materials in U.S. cities, Ramaswami and others (2008) used tools from industrial ecology—material flow analysis (MFA) and life cycle assessment (LCA). MFA for Scope 3 material flows in cities often using monetary consumption data available at the metropolitan spatial scale. These flows are calibrated with national material consumption data to ensure no methodological double counting for materials occurs. Emission factors for the various materials considered for Denver—food, cement, and transport fuels (gasoline and diesel)—were obtained from nationally calibrated LCA tools such as Carnegie Mellon University's Economic Input Output-LCA (Green Design Institute 2006), the U.S. National Renewable Energy Laboratory's Life Cycle Inventory database (NREL 2009), and the U.S. Argonne National Laboratory's GREET model (ANL 2009) for transportation fuels. With the exception of food—which is a complex supply chain—embodied energy and GHG emissions from industrial production of materials such as cement, steel, and petroleum fuels could be readily computed for the United States. The IPCC provides specific guidance on these parameters for international applications, particularly for nonenergy-related industrial emissions from cement production and the like (IPCC 1997, 2006).

The review indicates that methods that avoid double counting exist and have been applied to assess upstream impacts of key Scope 3 consumption activities in cities. International GHG emissions data for most of these materials exist or can be researched (for example, IPCC nonenergy emissions), with the exception of food (see also the work of Birch, Barrett, and Wiedmann 2004 in the United Kingdom). When food production activities or cement factories occur within city boundaries, case studies in Delhi and Kolkata (Sharma, Dasgupta, and Mitra 2002) demonstrate that the emissions from these in-boundary activities can be allocated to avoid double counting between in-boundary and out-of-boundary activities.

Thus, careful Scope 1-2-3 accounting of GHGs at the city scale is indeed possible. To be consistent with other GHG accounting protocols (WRI, ICLEI, CCAR), we propose that all cities and metropolitan regions be encouraged to report Scope 1 and Scope 2 emissions in their baselines (as well as Scope 3 waste emissions, where applicable). In addition, it is highly recommended that cities also report on the five specific Scope 3 items listed earlier (transport fuel production, food production, cement-steel production, water production, and origin-destination–allocated external transport emissions), yielding a Scope 1-2-3 emissions footprint.

The city-scale emissions (Scope 1-2) and a broader emissions footprint (Scope 1-2-3) can be used together with application of two logic rules, as described in Hillman and Ramaswami (2010, 1908):

- "Credit GHG reduction strategies that reduce a city's Scope 1+2 GHG inventory only if they also reduce the city's broader Scope 1+2+3 GHG emissions footprint; credit is recommended for the smaller of the two reductions. This prevents unintended incentives to shift GHG emissions across city boundaries.
- Incorporate flexibility to award cities credit for innovative strategies that demonstrate *additionality*[3] and can quantifiably reduce their Scope 1+2+3 GHG footprint, even if the Scope 1+2 emissions inventory does not show reductions. For example, GHG mitigation credit could be distributed between fly ash suppliers and a city, if the latter's green concrete policy explicitly demonstrates additional fly ash use to displace cement in concrete, when compared to business-as-usual."

With these rules, Scope 3 accounting can be used in conjunction with existing protocols for Scope 1-2 accounting to develop more holistic and policy-relevant GHG management at the city scale.

Baseline Emissions

GHG emissions for 44 urban areas can now be presented using a methodology that is consistent other than differences in industrial processes, waste, AFOLU, and aviation/marine emissions, discussed elsewhere in this chapter. For these sectors where there are differences in approach, it is necessary to refer to table 2.2.

The baselines presented in tables 2.5 and 2.6 are for the same set of urban areas shown in table 2.2, other than the following changes:

- Baselines for Beijing, Shanghai, and Tianjin have been revised, including new calculations for emissions from aviation and marine activities and waste.
- For Delhi and Kolkata, the AFOLU and waste emissions in 2000 have been calculated using per capita emissions taken from the study by Sharma, Dasgupta, and Mitra (2002).
- Paris I (City of Paris) is excluded because of its unique life-cycle approach, but Paris II (Île-de-France) is included.

TABLE 2.5
Greenhouse Gas Emissions for Cities and Metropolitan Regions

million tons of CO$_2$e

City or metropolitan region[a]	Year	Energy (excluding aviation and marine)	Aviation	Marine	Energy (including aviation and marine)	Industrial processes	AFOLU	Waste	Total (excluding aviation and marine)	Total
Europe										
Athens	2005				35.72	4.38	0.45	1.02		41.57
Barcelona	2006	3.68	2.67		6.35	0.07	0.72	0.39	4.07	6.74
Bologna	2005				8.93	0.14	0.02	0.25		9.97
Brussels	2005				7.34			0.04		7.55
Frankfurt	2005				44.40	4.99	1.61	0.61		51.61
Geneva	2005	2.45	0.74	0.00	3.19	0.25	0.72	0.16	2.61	3.35
Glasgow	2004				13.77	0.25	0.72	0.56		15.30
Hamburg	2005				33.96	2.82	4.46	0.28		41.52
Helsinki	2005				6.70	0.17	0.03	0.04		6.94
Ljubljana	2005				4.31	0.07	0.19	0.20		4.77
London	2003	46.31	23.00	0.00	69.31	0.00	0.00	1.53	47.84	70.84
Madrid	2005				36.25	2.23	0.36	2.15		40.98
Naples	2005				10.66	0.87	0.49	0.46		12.49
Oslo	2005				3.35	0.11	0.06	0.11		3.63
Paris II	2005				47.01	3.53	6.91	2.20		59.64
Porto	2005				11.14	0.07	0.38	0.56		12.14

	Year									
Prague	2005	9.33	1.06	0.00	10.39	0.51	0.00	0.13	9.97	11.03
Rotterdam	2005				17.08	0.15	0.13	0.28		17.64
Stockholm	2005				6.35	0.17	0.24	0.12		6.88
Stuttgart	2005				40.89	0.36	0.87	0.43		42.57
Turin	2005				17.60	2.51	1.47	0.28		21.86
Veneto	2005				39.55	3.29	3.28	1.18		47.29
North America										
Austin	2005	10.37	b		10.37			0.11	10.48	b
Calgary	2003	15.94					−0.01	0.44	16.37	
Denver	2005	10.11	0.86		10.97			0.11	10.22	11.08
Los Angeles	2000	83.36	17.83	16.10	117.29	2.10		4.65	90.11	124.04
Minneapolis	2005	7.00			7.00			0.03	7.03	
New York City	2005	62.65	14.19	6.20	83.04			2.83	65.48	85.87
Portland	2005	8.37	b		8.37			0.10	8.47	b
Seattle	2005	7.75	b		7.75			0.07	7.82	b
Toronto	2005	54.60	4.62		59.22	3.19		1.81	59.60	64.22
Washington, DC	2000	10.31		0.00	10.31	0.01	−0.02	0.74		11.04
Latin America										
Mexico City	2000	31.68		0.00				3.59	35.27	
Rio de Janeiro	1998	5.78	0.86		6.64	0.24	0.27	4.96	11.25	12.11
São Paulo	2000	9.57	0.94		10.51	0.01	0.00	3.70	13.28	14.22

continued

TABLE 2.5, *continued*

City or metropolitan region[a]	Year	Energy (excluding aviation and marine)	Aviation	Marine	Energy (including aviation and marine)	Industrial processes	AFOLU	Waste	Total (excluding aviation and marine)	Total
Asia										
Bangkok	2005	42.61	10.85		53.46			6.98	49.59	60.44
Beijing	2006	146.93	7.15	0.00	154.09			4.92	151.85	159.00
Delhi	2000	17.31						3.34	20.65	
Kolkata	2000	13.83						3.97	17.80	
Seoul	1998	42.03							42.03	
Shanghai	2006	197.07	8.55	5.00	210.62			1.36	198.43	211.98
Tianjin	2006	116.43	0.41	1.23	118.08			1.17	117.60	119.25
Tokyo	2006	55.88			60.04	1.42		0.56	57.86	62.02
Africa										
Cape Town	2006	17.81	1.14	3.34	22.29			3.04	20.85	26.57

Source: Studies as cited in table 2.2.

Note: AFOLU = agriculture, forestry, and other land use.

a. See table 2.1 for definitions.
b. Airline data for these cities pending review (Hillman and Ramaswami 2010).

TABLE 2.6 Per Capita Greenhouse Gas Emissions for Cities and Metropolitan Regions
tons of CO_2e

City or metropolitan region[a]	Year	Energy (excluding aviation and marine)	Aviation	Marine	Energy (including aviation and marine)	Industrial processes	AFOLU	Waste	Total (excluding aviation and marine)	Total
Europe										
Athens	2005				9.0	1.1	0.1	0.3		10.4
Barcelona	2006	2.3	1.7		4.0	0.0	0.0	0.2	2.5	4.2
Bologna	2005				9.9	0.1	0.8	0.3		11.1
Brussels	2005			0.0	7.3	0.1	0.0	0.0		7.5
Frankfurt	2005				11.8	1.3	0.4	0.2		13.7
Geneva	2005	5.7	1.7	0.0	7.4	0.0	0.0	0.4	6.0	7.8
Glasgow	2004				7.9	0.1	0.4	0.3		8.8
Hamburg	2005			0.0	8.0	0.7	1.0	0.1		9.7
Helsinki	2005				6.8	0.2	0.0	0.0		7.0
Ljubljana	2005			0.0	8.6	0.1	0.4	0.4		9.5
London	2003	6.3	3.1	0.0	9.4	0.0	0.0	0.2	6.5	9.6
Madrid	2005				6.1	0.4	0.1	0.4		6.9
Naples	2005				3.5	0.3	0.2	0.1		4.0
Oslo	2005				3.2	0.1	0.1	0.1		3.5
Paris II	2005			0.0	4.1	0.3	0.6	0.2		5.2
Porto	2005				6.7	0.0	0.2	0.3		7.3
Prague	2005	7.9	0.9	0.0	8.8	0.4	0.0	0.1	8.4	9.3

continued

TABLE 2.6, *continued*

City or metropolitan region[a]	Year	Energy (excluding aviation and marine)	Aviation	Marine	Energy (including aviation and marine)	Industrial processes	AFOLU	Waste	Total (excluding aviation and marine)	Total
Rotterdam	2005				28.8	0.2	0.2	0.5		29.8
Stockholm	2005				3.4	0.1	0.1	0.1		3.6
Stuttgart	2005			0.0	15.3	0.1	0.3	0.2		16.0
Turin	2005				7.8	1.1	0.7	0.1		9.7
Veneto	2005				8.3	0.7	0.7	0.2		10.0
North America										
Austin	2005	15.4	b	15.4				0.17	15.57	b
Calgary	2003	17.3		0.0		0.0	0.0	0.5	17.7	b
Denver	2005	17.69	1.5	19.19		0.0		0.19	17.88	19.38
Los Angeles	2000	8.8	1.9	1.7	12.3	0.2	0.0	0.5	9.5	13.0
Minneapolis	2005	18.28	b					0.06	18.34	b
New York City	2005	7.7	1.7	0.8	10.2	0.0	0.0	0.3	8.0	10.5
Portland	2005	12.26	b	12.26				0.15	12.41	b
Seattle	2005	13.5	b	13.57				13.68	13.68	b
Toronto	2005	9.8	0.8	0.0	10.7	0.6	0.0	0.3	10.7	11.6
Washington, DC	2000	18.0		0.0		0.0	0.0	1.3	19.3	
Latin America										
Mexico City	2000	3.7		0.0		0.0	0.0	0.4	4.1	
Rio de Janeiro	1998	1.0	0.2		1.2	0.0	0.0	0.9	2.0	2.1
São Paulo	2000	0.9	0.1		1.0	0.0	0.0	0.4	1.3	1.4

City	Year							
Asia								
Bangkok	2005	7.5	1.9	9.4		1.2	8.8	10.7
Beijing	2006	9.3	0.5	9.7		0.3	9.6	10.1
Delhi	2000	1.3	0.0	0.0		0.3	1.6	
Kolkata	2000	0.9				0.3	1.1	
Seoul	1998	4.1					4.1	
Shanghai	2006	10.9	0.5	11.6		0.1	10.9	11.7
Tianjin	2006	10.8	0.0	11.0		0.1	10.9	11.1
Tokyo	2006	4.4	0.0	4.7	0.1	0.0	4.6	4.9
Africa								
Cape Town	2006	5.1	0.3	6.4		0.9	6.0	7.6

Source: Studies as cited in table 2.2.

Note: AFOLU = agriculture, forestry, and other land use.

a. See table 2.1 for definitions.

b. Airline data for these cities pending review (Hillman and Ramaswami 2010).

Note that the baselines reported are largely for 2005 or 2006. Only in the cases of Calgary, Delhi, Glasgow, Kolkata, London, Los Angeles, Mexico City, Rio de Janeiro, São Paulo, Seoul, and Washington, DC, are emissions given for earlier years. Because 2005 is the reporting year for most of the studies, it could become a standard baseline year for reporting emissions for further urban areas.

A precautionary note on the accuracy of baselines should be made. The results for total emissions are reported to an accuracy of 10 kilotons in table 2.5, but this accuracy is only to facilitate the calculation of per capita emissions in table 2.6. Baselines reported in both tables are accurate at best to two significant figures.

Conclusion

For urban areas to become more effective at tackling climate change through GHG reductions, two key requirements are found. First, an open, global protocol for quantifying GHG emissions attributable to urban areas must be established. Second, comparable baseline measures of GHG emissions for urban areas are needed.

The primary contribution of this chapter has been to present GHG emissions for more than 40 urban areas (cities and metropolitan regions) from five continents. This has been achieved by assembling and assessing previous studies of urban GHG emissions and adding further analysis where necessary and where data permit. Discrepancies have been found between previous studies in the methodology for determining emissions from waste and in the reporting of emissions for aviation, marine, agricultural, and industrial processes. Our results have been presented (in tables 2.5 and 2.6) so that these differences can be recognized (through reference to table 2.2).

Despite these often minor differences, this work has shown that the potential clearly exists to establish an open, global protocol for quantifying GHG emissions attributable to urban areas. Such a protocol must be sufficiently robust and compatible with the UNFCCC, that is, the IPCC, guidelines. Such compatibility should include sectoral methodologies and emissions factors, but not necessarily a boundary limited scope.

The IPCC guidelines provide help with resolving some of the conflicting issues. Emissions from waste, for example, could be determined using the IPCC (2006) guidelines; this has primarily been hindered by the significant data requirements. Agricultural and industrial process emissions, though small for many urban areas, need to be more carefully accounted for; again, the IPCC guidelines can be followed. Whether emissions from aviation and marine are excluded or included primarily depends on whether the baseline GHG measures are only to inform local government policy or are to be a wider reflection of the carbon dependence of urban economies. If aviation and marine emissions are included, then they should reflect the global connections that exist between cities—and thus include all emissions from international transportation. (Data to support such calculations are already collected at national levels but not reported in national totals as per the UNFCCC.) The methodology of Ramaswami and others (2008) addresses issues with assigning emissions when passengers transfer between flights and incorporates most relevant cross-boundary energy flows critical for functioning of cities. Overall, resolution of these differences seems tractable.

The emissions attributable to urban areas may be considered from different perspectives. Emissions can be strictly based on spatially limited geographic boundaries of an urban area or on a broader consideration that also includes significant cross-boundary embodied energy flows occurring in cities. Emission attribution can also be made based on "producer" and "consumer" approaches or a combination of both or hybrid approach (Ramaswami and others 2008). Care must be taken in applying a hybrid approach to avoid double counting.

It is important that an emissions baseline is produced to meet its purpose. It may be of interest to local government, urban policy makers, or both. It may, if it is for policy purposes, need to provide data that enable a region to help deliver national and international commitments on emissions reduction. It may be used for public communication about GHG emissions, which often is also an implicit goal in developing baselines.

The baseline emissions include those for cities and some wider metropolitan regions. Merits exist for developing baseline emissions for both. Cities have a single administrative authority (albeit subject to national, provincial, and state governments), enabling them to have potentially greater control over emissions reductions. Metropolitan regions sometimes have more fragmented political authority, yet these regions typically have higher per capita emissions than cities because of low-density suburbs (Glaeser and Kahn 2008; VandeWeghe and Kennedy 2007), airports, and often higher concentrations of industry. A strong point of the methodology reviewed in this chapter is that it applies equally well to cities and to metropolitan regions.

Aside from the discussed differences with emissions from, for example, waste and airline and marine activities, the greatest uncertainty in urban GHG baselines lies with emissions from road transportation. In table 2.2, we distinguished between three techniques for estimating gasoline consumption in urban areas (sales, models and surveys, and scaling). Differences between these techniques may be less than 5 percent (Kennedy and others 2010). This uncertainty might be reduced further, however, if new urban transportation models and surveys were developed specifically for determining GHG emissions rather than urban transportation planning in general. For example, fuels sales data could explicitly be used in model calibration. Such improvements in quantifying urban GHG emissions would also likely support calculations made for national inventories.

Further assessment of the uncertainty in quantifying urban GHG emissions is warranted. Other than the color-coded scheme used in the GRIP studies (Carney and others 2009), little formal analysis has been done of uncertainty in urban emissions, such as using Monte Carlo simulation. Volume 1 of the IPCC (2006) guidelines provides recommended approaches for uncertainty assessment and quality assurance.

Improvements in the reporting of urban GHG emissions might also be made. Under ISO Standard 14064, emissions should be reported for six individual GHGs. This has not been common for cities (hence, we have not done so here). Perhaps more important for quality assurance purposes, urban areas should always report the activity data and emissions factors used to determine emissions.

A further recommendation of this work is the continued development of consumption-based measures of GHG emissions for urban areas. By including Scope 2 and 3 emissions, as per the WRI/WBCSD, the overall methodology of this work recognizes that emissions should be assigned to urban areas based on end-use activities. There are further consumption-based emissions that can also be attributed to urban areas, beyond those presented in our results. These include those embodied in food and materials consumed in cities and upstream emissions associated with the mining and refining of the fuels combusted in cities. Some of these emissions have been quantified in a few studies (table 2.2) but not in enough to be consistently applied to all cities at this point. Methodologies for determining further consumption-based emissions have been developed (Hillman and Ramaswami 2010; Mairie de Paris 2009; Ramaswami and others 2008), though perhaps they need to be compared. The main barrier is lack of data on material flows into urban areas. Standard approaches for applying principles of industrial ecology to urban areas need to be developed.

Notes

We are grateful to the Global Environment Facility for supporting this work. We also wish to thank Lorraine Sugar, David Bristow, and Abel Chavez for their help in compiling the results tables.

1. This is one of the main emissions sectors in UNFCCC inventories. This sector refers to emissions at industrial sites from noncombustion activities. The majority of emis-

sions from industry come from energy combustion, which is considered under energy in international reporting.
2. For example, stationary combustion in Bangkok, including industry, comprises the following fuels: 21 percent bagasse, 20 percent fuel oil, 14 percent lignite, 13 percent coal/coke, 10 percent natural gas, 8 percent liquefied petroleum gas, 5 percent rice husks, 5 percent wood, and 4 percent diesel (Kennedy and others 2009; Phdungsilp 2006). For CO_2 emissions from biofuel combustion, care has to be taken to distinguish between biological and fossil carbon (IPCC 2006).
3. Demonstrating additionality means to show that these reductions would not have occurred on their own in the absence of the specific policy or program.

References

ANL (Argonne National Laboratory). 2009. "Argonne GREET Model." Argonne Transportation Technology R&D Center. http://www.transportation.anl.gov/modeling_simulation/GREET/index.html.

Baldasano, J. M., C. Soriano, and L. Boada. 1999. "Emission Inventory for Greenhouse Gases in the City of Barcelona, 1987–1996." *Atmospheric Environment* 33: 3765–75.

Birch, R., J. Barrett, and T. Wiedmann. 2004. "Exploring the Consumption and Related Environmental Impacts of Socio-economic Groups within the UK." International Workshop on Sustainable Consumption. http://homepages.see.leeds.ac.uk/~leckh/leeds04/5.4%20leeds%20conference%20paper.pdf.

BEA (Bureau of Economic Analysis). 2009. "Gross Domestic Product by Metropolitan Area, Regional Economic Accounts." http://www.bea.gov/regional/gdpmetro/. For global measures, also see http://www.citymayors.com/statistics/richest-cities-2005.html.

Carney, S., N. Green, R. Wood, and R. Read. 2009. "Greenhouse Gas Emissions Inventories for Eighteen European Regions, EU CO_2 80/50 Project Stage 1: Inventory Formation." Greenhouse Gas Regional Inventory Protocol (GRIP), University of Manchester.

CCAR (California Climate Action Registry). 2007. *General Reporting Protocol.* Los Angeles, CA: CCAR. http://www.climateregistry.org/tools/protocols/general-reporting-protocol.html.

City of Calgary. 2003. "Calgary Community Greenhouse Gas Emissions Inventory." http://www.calgary.ca/docgallery/bu/environmental_management/2003_community_emissions_report.pdf.

DC Dept. of Health (District of Columbia, Department of Health). 2005. "District of Columbia Greenhouse Gas Emissions Inventories and Preliminary Projections." Air Quality Division, Bureau of Environmental Quality, Environmental Health Administration, Washington, DC.

Dhakal, S. 2004. *Urban Energy Use and Greenhouse Gas Emissions in Asian Mega-cities: Policies for a Sustainable Future.* Hayama, Japan: Institute for Global Environmental Strategies.

———. 2009. "Urban Energy Use and Carbon Emissions from Cities in China and Policy Implications." *Energy Policy* 37 (11): 4208–19.

Dodman, D. 2009. "Blaming Cities for Climate Change? An Analysis of Urban Greenhouse Gas Emission Inventories." *Environment and Urbanization* 21 (1): 185–201.

Dubeux, C. B. S., and E. L. La Rovere. 2007. "Local Perspectives in the Control of Greenhouse Gas Emissions—The Case of Rio de Janeiro." *Cities* 24 (5): 353–64.

Duffy, Hazel. 1995. *Competitive Cities: Succeeding in the Global Economy*. London: E & FN Spon.

Friedmann, J. 1986. "The World City Hypothesis." *Development and Change* 17: 69–83.

Glaeser, E. L., and M. E. Khan. 2008. "The Greenness of Cities: Carbon Dioxide Emissions and Urban Development." NBER Working Paper 14238, National Bureau of Economic Research, Cambridge, MA.

Green Design Institute. 2006. "EIO-LCA (Economic Input-Output Life Cycle Assessment)." Carnegie Mellon University, Pittsburgh, PA. http://www.eiolca.net.

Greenprint. 2007. "City of Denver Climate Action Plan: Recommendations to Mayor Hickenlooper." Mayor's Greenprint Denver Advisory Council, Denver, CO.

Harvey, L. D. D. 1993. "Tackling Urban CO_2 Emissions in Toronto." *Environment* 35 (7): 16–20, 33–44.

Hillman, T., and A. Ramaswami. 2010. "Greenhouse Gas Emission Footprints and Energy Use Metrics for Eight US Cities." *Environmental Science & Technology* 44 (6): 1902–10.

ICLEI. 2006. "International Progress Report, Cities for Climate Protection." ICLEI, Oakland, CA. http://www.iclei.org/documents/USA/documents/CCP/ICLEI-CCP_International_Report-2006.pdf.

———. 2009. "International Local Government GHG Emissions Analysis Protocol." Draft Release Version 1.0. http://www.iclei.org/fileadmin/user_upload/documents/Global/Progams/GHG/LGGHGEmissionsProtocol.pdf.

IGES/APN. 2002. *Policy Integration & Industrial Transformation towards Sustainable Urban Energy Use for Cities in Asia*. Proceedings of the IGES/ASPN Mega-city Project Workshop and the International Symposium on Sustainable Urban Development in Asia, Kitakyushu, Japan, January 23–25, Institute for Global Environmental Strategies (IGES), Japan and Asia-Pacific Network for Global Change Research (APN). http://enviroscope.iges.or.jp/contents/13/index.html.

IPCC (Intergovernmental Panel on Climate Change). 1997. "Revised 1996 IPCC Guidelines for National Greenhouse Gas Inventories." http://www.ipcc.ch/publications_and_data/publications_and_data_reports.shtml#4.

———. 2006. "2006 IPCC Guidelines for National Greenhouse Gas Inventories." Volumes 1 to 5. http://www.ipcc-nggip.iges.or.jp/public/2006gl/index.html.

Kates, R. W., M. W. Mayfield, R. D. Torrie, and B. Witcher. 1998. "Methods for Estimating Greenhouse Gases from Local Places." *Local Environment* 3 (3): 279–97.

Kennedy, C. A., J. Cuddihy, and J. Engel Yan. 2007. "The Changing Metabolism of Cities." *Journal of Industrial Ecology* 11 (2): 43–59.

Kennedy, C., J. Steinberger, B. Gasson, T. Hillman, M. Havránek, D. Pataki, A. Phdungsilp, A. Ramaswami, and G. Villalba Mendez. 2009. "Greenhouse Gas Emissions from Global Cities." *Environmental Science & Technology* 43 (19): 7297–7302.

———. 2010. "Methodology for Inventorying Greenhouse Gas Emissions from Global Cities." *Energy Policy* 38 (9): 4828–37.

Llewelyn-Davies, D. Banister, and P. Hall. 2004. "Transport and City Competitiveness: Literature Review." Department of Transport and Office of the Deputy Prime Minister, London.

Mairie de Paris. 2007. *Le Bilan Carbone de Paris: Bilan des émissions de gaz à effet de serre.* Paris: Mairie de Paris. http://www.paris.fr/portail/viewmultimediadocument? multimediadocument-id=94991.

Mayor of London. 2007. "Action Today to Protect Tomorrow—The Mayor's Climate Change Action Plan." Mayor of London. http://static.london.gov.uk/mayor/.../ climate-change/docs/ccap_summaryreport.pdf.

Mitra, A. P., C. Sharma, and M. A. Y. Ajero. 2003. "Energy and Emissions in South Asian Mega-cities: Study on Kolkata, Delhi and Manila." In *Proceedings of International Workshop on Policy Integration towards Sustainable Urban Energy Use for Cities in Asia,* East-West Center, Honolulu, Hawaii, Kanagawa, Japan, IGES, February 4–5. http:// www.iges.or.jp/en/ue/pdf/megacity03/HTML/pdf/1.2%20APMitra%20paper.pdf.

Nagoya University/NIES (National Institute for Environmental Studies, Japan)/GCP (Global Carbon Project). 2009. International Symposium: Realizing Low Carbon Cities—Bridging Science and Policy; and International Workshop: Towards Low Carbon Cities—Understanding and Analyzing Urban Energy and Carbon, Nagoya Japan, February 16–18.

NREL (National Renewable Energy Laboratory. 2009. "U.S. Life-Cycle Inventory Database." http://www.nrel.gov/lci/.

New York City. 2007. "Inventory of New York City Greenhouse Gas Emissions." Office of Long-Term Planning and Sustainability, New York.

Phdungsilp, A. 2006. "Energy Analysis for Sustainable Megacities." Licentiate of Engineering Thesis, Department of Energy Technology, Royal Institute of Technology, Stockholm.

Ramaswami, A., T. Hillman, B. Janson, M. Reiner, and G. Thomas. 2008. "A Demand-Centered, Hybrid Life Cycle Methodology for City-Scale Greenhouse Gas Inventories." *Environmental Science & Technology* 42 (17): 6455–61.

Rosenzweig, C., S. Mehrotra, C. E. Natenzon, A. Omojola, R. Folorunsho, and J. Gilbride. 2009. "Creating Risk-Based Climate Change Information for Urban Areas." Paper presented at the 5th Urban Research Symposium Cities and Climate Change: Responding to an Urgent Agenda, Marseille, France, June 28–30.

Sassen, S. 1991. *The Global City.* Princeton, NJ: Princeton University Press.

Satterthwaite, D. 2008. "Cities' Contribution to Global Warming: Notes on the Allocation of Greenhouse Gas Emissions." *Environment and Urbanization* 20 (2): 539–49.

Sharma, C., A. Dasgupta, and A. P. Mitra. 2002. "Inventory of GHGs and Other Urban Pollutants from Agriculture and Waste Sectors in Delhi and Calcutta." In *Proceedings of IGES/APN Mega-city Project,* Kitakyushu, Japan, January 23–25. Institute for Global Environmental Strategies (IGES), Japan, and Asia-Pacific Network for Global Change Research (APN). http://enviroscope.iges.or.jp/contents/13/data/iges_m. html.

SMA-GDF (Secretaría del Medio Ambiente, Gobierno del Distrito Federal). 2000. *Estrategia Local de Acción Climática de la Ciudad de México* [Local Climate Action Strategy Mexico City]. Gobierno del Distrito Federal, México.

SVMA (Secretaria Municipal do Verde e do Meio Ambiente de São Paulo). 2005. "Inventário de Emissões de Efeito Estufa do Município de São Paulo." Centro de Estudos Integradossobre Meio Ambiente e Mudanças Climáticas (Centro Clima) da Coordenação dos Programas de Pós-graduação de Engenharia (COPPE), Universidade Federal do Rio de Janeiro (UFRJ), Rio de Janeiro.

Taylor, P. J. 2004. *World City Network: A Global Urban Analysis.* New York: Routledge.

Tokyo Metropolitan Government. 2006. Environmental White Paper. http://www2
.kankyo.metro.tokyo.jp/kouhou/env/eng_2006/index.html.

VandeWeghe, J., and C. A. Kennedy. 2007. "A Spatial Analysis of Residential Greenhouse
Gas Emissions in the Toronto Census Metropolitan Area." *Journal of Industrial Ecology* 11 (2): 133–44.

Wood, F. R., A. Bows, and K. Anderson. 2010. "Apportioning Aviation CO_2 Emissions
to Regional Administrations for Monitoring and Target Setting." *Transport Policy* 17: 206–15.

WRI/WBCSD (World Resources Institute/World Business Council for Sustainable
Development). 2009. "The Greenhouse Gas Protocol: A Corporate Accounting
and Reporting Standard: Revised Edition." http://www.ghgprotocol.org/standards/
corporate-standard.

3

Comparing Mitigation Policies in Five Large Cities: London, New York City, Milan, Mexico City, and Bangkok

Edoardo Croci, Sabrina Melandri, and Tania Molteni

Urban areas contribute significantly to global greenhouse gas (GHG) emissions, in particular carbon dioxide (CO_2), with some estimates suggesting this contribution may be as high as 80 percent (UNEP and UN-HABITAT 2005). This reflects the concentration of people and economic activities in urban agglomerations and the high levels of energy consumption associated with residential, production, and mobility needs. The negative externalities associated with congestion and pollution tend to increase with urbanization. Nevertheless, in most cases, major cities have lower per capita CO_2-equivalent emissions (CO_2e) than at the corresponding national level (Dodman 2009).

As cities assume a higher profile in the area of climate change, many are recognizing the potential to reduce emissions and are committing to voluntary reduction targets. This can happen both individually and as part of collective commitments (such as the U.S. Conference of Mayors Climate Protection Agreement and the European Covenant of Mayors).[1] International associations and city networks (such as ICLEI and the C40 Climate Leadership Group) play a major role in sharing best practices on mitigation. In the past 20 years, many cities in industrialized countries have developed climate change plans. More recently, cities in developing countries have followed suit, as in the cases of Mexico City and Bangkok.

The objective of this chapter is to identify the main drivers of emissions and the most relevant mitigation measures planned or adopted by five global cities: London, New York City, Milan, Mexico City, and Bangkok.[2] The selection was based on the availability of data, the existence of a mitigation strategy, and the desire to have a representative sample of both developing and industrialized countries.

Although best efforts were employed to ensure comparability of the data, the results presented includes some biases because of (1) differences in territorial units referenced by the data: definitions of urban areas differ among countries, city administrative boundaries do not always coincide with the limits of the urban agglomeration,[3] and not all global cities have a metropolitan body managing the wider urban area and (2) differences in methodologies to estimate local emissions at the local level: There is as yet no single accepted international standard for city emissions inventories across sectors and sources.

The analysis is structured in four main sections: the first compares inventories across cities according to criteria applied to collect and organize data, the second analyzes the emissions context of each city through a set of indicators, the third compares the main components and measures of each city's mitigation plan, and the last draws some conclusions with regard to the coherence, effectiveness, and efficiency of city mitigation plans.

Comparative Analysis of Local Emission Inventories

In this section, we compare city-level emissions inventories with specific reference to five global cities: London, New York City, Milan, Mexico City, and Bangkok.

City Emissions Measurement

In recent years, the use of city emissions inventories has increased as more cities become engaged with climate change issues. In the absence of an agreed-upon international standard providing methodological guidance for cities' inventories, many cities use the Intergovernmental Panel on Climate Change (IPCC) methodology (IPCC 2006), which was developed for national emissions inventories. The main challenge cities face in compiling urban emission inventories is to identify and define the precise area and activities that should be included, as well as the decision on whether to include direct and indirect emissions. Direct emissions are associated with emission sources (point, linear, diffused) located inside city boundaries. Indirect emissions are emissions from sources that are neither controlled by a city government nor located within its jurisdiction, but that occur wholly or in part as a result of the city's activities (for example, purchased electricity or emissions embedded in the consumption of goods and services).[4] ICLEI's protocol (ICLEI 2008) suggests three scopes for classifying emissions at the community level:

1. Direct emissions, from sources located within the city boundary.

2. Indirect emissions, from sources located outside the city boundary, but that result from activities occurring within the boundary.

3. Other indirect or embodied emissions, which can be included when more comprehensive accounting is desired.

These scopes should enable emissions to be categorized while avoiding double counting.

GHG Accounting Methods

There are two main approaches for estimating emissions: "top-down" and "bottom-up." The top-down approach uses estimates derived from national or regional data and scales them to the area being analyzed (Hutchinson 2002) according to such variables as population, energy consumption, and mobility. The bottom-up approach uses local data, from single sources whenever possible. This is naturally the preferred method and is used in this chapter. For the five city cases, table 3.1 summarizes the types of GHGs, activities, and indirect emissions included.

TABLE 3.1
Comparison of Emission Inventories

Quantified by the inventory	London	New York City	Milan	Mexico City	Bangkok
Gases					
CO_2	✓	✓	✓	✓	✓
CH_4		✓	Q*	✓	✓
N_2O		✓	Q*	✓	
HFC		✓	Q*		
PFC		✓	Q*		
SF_6		✓	Q*		
Direct emissions					
Domestic heating	✓	✓	✓	n.a.	n.a.
Commercial/tertiary heating	✓	✓	✓	n.a.	n.a.
[Road transport]	✓	✓	✓	✓	✓
Public transport	✓	✓	✓	✓	n.s.
Private transport	✓	✓	✓	✓	n.s.
Aviation	Q	Q			

continued

TABLE 3.1, *continued*

Quantified by the inventory	London	New York City	Milan	Mexico City	Bangkok
Shipping	Q	Q	n.a.	n.a.	
Waste management	✓		Q*	✓	✓
Wastewater management		✓			✓
[Industry]	✓	✓	✓	✓	
Energy use in industrial buildings	✓	✓	✓	✓	
Energy use for industrial processes (combustion)	✓		✓	✓	
Emissions from industrial processes (non-combustion)				✓	
Agriculture			Q*	✓	✓
Sinks				✓	✓
Energy supply plants within the city boundaries	✓	✓	✓	✓	n.s.
Indirect emissions					
[Purchased electricity]	✓	✓	✓	✓	✓
Domestic (electricity)	✓	✓		✓	
Commercial/tertiary (electricity)	✓	✓		✓	
Transport (electricity)	✓			n.s.	
Industrial (electricity)	✓	✓		✓	

Source: Authors for different source data: AMA 2007; BMA 2008; BMA, Greenleaf Foundation, and UNEP 2009; City of New York 2007b, 2008b; IEFE 2009; SMA-GDF 2008; Mayor of London 2006b; Pardo and Martínez 2006.

Note: Inventories were available for the following base years: 1990–2000, *2003*, 2004–05 (London); *2005*, 2006, 2007 (New York City); *2005* (Milan); 2000, *2004* (Mexico City); *2005* (Bangkok). The inventory considered in the checklist is highlighted in italics. For Greater London, the checklist was filled with reference to the 2003 inventory (called the London Energy and CO_2 Emissions Inventory), which focuses on CO_2 emissions. The 2004–05 inventory (called the London Energy and GHG Inventory) also comprises estimates of CH_4, N_2O, HFC, PFC, and SF_6. Estimates for Greater London Authority's operations and buildings are included in the Climate Change Action Plan.

HFC = hydrofluorocarbon; PFC = perfluorocarbon; Q = quantified but not included in the emission values of the plan base year; Q* = non-CO_2 gases had been quantified in a previous inventory (AMA 2007), but these emissions have not been included in the Climate Plan of Milan because they added a negligible quantity to total emissions; n.a. = not applicable; n.s. = not specified.

All inventories report at least emissions of carbon dioxide. Recent guidelines recognize that collecting detailed local data on all Kyoto GHGs may be quite onerous and thus suggest focusing on carbon dioxide and methane, the two most relevant gases at the city level.

In terms of sectors, heating sector emissions are considered in all cities' inventories, except Bangkok and Mexico City, because of their relatively warm climates. Emissions from industry have been reported in all inventories, except for Bangkok, in relation to energy use within industrial processes and to the operations of industrial buildings. Emissions from power plants within city boundaries are generally quantified by all cities.

For road transport, there are two main approaches: Bangkok estimates emissions from fuels consumed within city boundaries, whereas Mexico City, London, New York City, and Milan use kilometers traveled by different categories of public and private vehicles. New York and London consider kilometers traveled within city boundaries, whereas Milan also includes kilometers traveled by vehicles crossing city borders. Furthermore, London estimates emissions from taxiing aircraft and during take-off and landing, including these in ground-based transport emissions. Only New York City and London quantify emissions from aviation and shipping, using different methodologies while excluding these from their emissions targets.

All cities consider GHG emissions from waste except London, which in its climate plan considers only CO_2 emissions sources. New York City quantifies methane emissions from previously disposed solid waste in in-city landfills each year over the life of the gas. Mexico City and Bangkok quantify methane emissions from landfills but the latter does not specify the location of these landfills. Milan quantifies emissions from waste only in relation to combustion in waste-to-energy. Methane from wastewater plants is quantified only in the inventories of New York City and Bangkok.

Agriculture has no relevance in the urban contexts of Greater London and New York City and has limited relevance in the other cities. CO_2 and methane have been estimated in relation to fuel consumption and emissions from agricultural operations in the inventories of Mexico City and Bangkok. Both inventories also evaluate the offsetting potential of sinks—urban forestry and green areas within administrative boundaries.

As for indirect emissions, all inventories include emissions related to imported electricity but exclude emissions embedded in goods and services consumed within the city. Only New York City, London, and Mexico City detail electricity consumption for each end-use sector.

Inventories are based on international references. New York City uses ICLEI's protocol for the inventory structure and software to convert all data on energy use, transportation patterns, waste disposal, and other inputs into GHG emissions. London and Milan use the CORINAIR[5] methodology for the choice of main sector-based sources and emissions factors (even if both refer, in some cases, to their own emissions factors). Mexico City refers to the IPCC methodology for calculation methods and emissions factors.

Emissions by Source

The collected data and emissions inventories show that energy consumption is the most important determinant for city GHG emissions. Direct emission sources such as industrial processes, power stations, and agricultural activities are usually located outside city boundaries or in periurban areas. Because "urban" power supply covers a limited part of local consumption, cities generally rely on end uses to estimate emissions: That is, if the energy was consumed in the city (regardless where it was produced), then its estimated emission impact is attributed to the city. All inventories analyzed in this research assign emissions due to energy uses. Emissions per capita in the selected cities are thus strictly related to local energy demand and consumption.

Table 3.2 suggests some interesting relationships. First, per capita emissions are clearly related to per capita gross domestic product (GDP), with the exception of Bangkok, which has higher emissions than would be expected for a city at its level of per capita GDP because of higher energy intensity of GDP. Second, energy consumption follows a similar pattern in relation to per capita GDP. New York City and Bangkok have the highest per capita emissions (7.7 and 7.1 tons of CO_2 per capita, respectively) but with substantial differences in energy consumption (24.6 and 20.0 megawatt-hour [MWh] per capita, respectively) and in electricity consumption (6.7 and 4.8 MWh per capita, respectively). Milan and London have similar per capita emissions, energy, and electricity consumption. Mexico City produces the least emissions per capita (3.9 tons of CO_2 per capita) and shows the lowest energy (10.9 MWh per capita) and electricity consumption per capita (1.7 MWh per capita).[6]

These differences in per capita emissions are due to differences in carbon intensity of energy consumption, energy intensity of production, and GDP per capita (the Kaya identity).[7] Carbon intensity is determined by emission factors of fuel consumption, energy intensity depends on morphological and territorial features as well as on socioeconomic and behavioral characteristics of the city's population, and GDP per capita is an indicator of economic activity.

The carbon intensity of energy consumption depends on the share of electricity in energy consumption and on the carbon intensity of the fuels used to generate this electricity. In terms of energy consumption patterns, Milan has a higher share of electricity consumption than London (table 3.3), and this may explain the difference in average carbon intensity of energy between the two cities. Bangkok and Mexico City show different energy consumption values but a similar fuel consumption pattern and similar carbon intensities. Bangkok's lower carbon intensity may be explained by a lower emission factor used to estimate emissions from electricity for this city.[8]

TABLE 3.2
Emission Values and Main Emission Indicators

	London	New York City	Milan	Mexico City	Bangkok
Base year of emission values	2006	2005	2005	2000	2005
Total emissions (million tons CO_2e)[a]	44.2	63.1	7.0	33.5	42.8
Emissions per capita (tons CO_2e per capita)[a]	5.9	7.7	5.4	3.9	7.1
Emissions from the transport sector per capita (tons CO_2e per capita)[a]	1.28	1.69	1.10	1.68	3.53
Emissions from the building sector per capita (tons CO_2e per capita)[a]	4.19	5.94	4.22	0.93	2.48
Energy consumption per capita (MWh per capita)[b]	20.7	24.6	21.7	10.9	20.0
Electricity consumption per capita (MWh per capita)[c]	5.2	6.7	5.3	1.7	4.8
Carbon intensity of energy consumption (tons CO_2e per GWh)[d]	284	310	250	317	300
Energy intensity of GDP (kWh/$)[b,e]	0.45	0.47	0.61	0.76	2.55
GDP per ppp ($ per capita)[e]	46,200	52,800	35,600	14,300	7,845

Source: Authors for different source data:

a. BMA 2008; City of New York 2008b; IEFE 2009; Mayor of London 2007a; Pardo and Martínez 2006. For London and Milan, emission values refer to CO_2 only.

b. AMA 2007; BMA 2008; Kennedy and others 2010; Mayor of London 2007b; Pardo and Martínez 2006. For Bangkok, the energy consumption value refers only to sectors for which GHG emissions were calculated.

c. BMA 2008; City of New York 2008a; IEFE 2009; Mayor of London 2007b; Pardo and Martínez 2006.

d. BMA 2008; IEFE 2009; Kennedy and others 2010; Mayor of London 2007a, 2007b; Pardo and Martínez 2006.

e. OECD 2006, except for Bangkok (Yusuf and Nabeshima 2006).

Note: Organisation for Economic Co-operation and Development indicators do not refer to the administrative boundaries of the cities, but to comparable areas that have been defined as follows: New York City as an area including New York county, nine other counties of New York state, and 12 counties of New Jersey; Milan as the province of Milan and seven adjacent provinces; Mexico City as the federal district of Mexico City and 53 adjacent districts; and London as Greater London and 10 adjacent counties.

Bangkok seems to have an energy consumption index comparable to those of European cities, but this value may be affected by a significant error according with an underestimation of Bangkok's population. The National Institute of Development Administration estimated that Bangkok's unregistered population could be around 3.2 million, compared with a total registered population of 5.6 million (NIDA 2000, in BMA and UNEP 2002).

Per capita values have been calculated by authors. Sources for population values: BMA 2009; Comune di Milano 2007; GLA 2008b; U.S. Census Bureau. GDP = gross domestic product; GWh = gigawatt-hour; kWh = kilowatt-hour; MWh = megawatt-hour; ppp = parity purchasing power.

TABLE 3.3
Energy Consumption by Fuels
percent

Fuel	London	New York City	Milan	Mexico City	Bangkok
Natural gas	53	36	25	7	
Oils (transportation)	19	23	16	62	76
Oils (nontransportation)	2	16	10	15	
Electricity	25	25	45	15	24
Waste (used as fuel)			3		
Biomass: wood				0.3	
Coal and similar substances	<0.1				
Other	0.2		1		

Source: Authors on different source data: AMA 2007; BMA 2008; Kennedy and others 2010; Mayor of London 2007b; Pardo and Martínez 2006. Oils for transportation include gasoline and diesel; nontransportation oils include fuel oils, liquefied petroleum gas, and kerosene.

TABLE 3.4
Emissions by Sectors
percent

	New York City (CO_2e)	London (CO_2)	Mexico City (CO_2e)	Milan (CO_2)	Bangkok (CO_2e)
	2005	2006	2000	2005	2005
Energy use in buildings	77	71	24	78	35
Transportation	22	22	43	20	50
Industrial		7	22	2	
Waste (landfill emissions)	0.4		11		3
Agriculture			1		13
Other	0.3				

Source: Authors on different source data: BMA 2008; City of New York 2008b; IEFE 2009; Mayor of London 2007a; Pardo and Martínez 2006.

As for sectors, buildings and transportation are the most emissive sources (see table 3.4). In industrialized cities (London, New York City, Milan), emissions from energy use in buildings (residential, commercial, tertiary, and public) amount to approximately 70 percent of the total. In developing cities, emissions from buildings are the second most relevant source and amount to 24 percent of emissions in Mexico City and 35 percent in Bangkok. Transportation is a relevant emission source in all selected cities, representing almost half of total emissions in Mexico City and Bangkok, but much less in New York City, London, and Milan. The industrial sector shows a limited contribution to total emissions, reflecting the sector's relatively small contribution to the economies of the selected cities, with the exception of Mexico City. Solid waste stored in landfills scarcely contributes to urban emissions, except for Mexico City, whose landfill emissions account for 11 percent of the total. For Bangkok, agriculture accounts for 13 percent of emissions, but this sector also contains unspecified emissions.

As expected, there is a strong correlation between emissions and energy consumption, as well as between emissions and economic activity, measured by GDP. Because these indicators are influenced by local conditions and lifestyles, the following section takes account of urban features that may characterize each local context and discusses differences in the emission levels of those cities.

Comparative Analysis of Local Emissions Contexts

We now turn to a comparison of the local context in which each city is found, identifying a number of key factors that influence emissions.

Drivers for the Characterization of Local Emissions Contexts

Almost all anthropogenic GHG emissions come from the consumption of material goods and energy and the production of waste, which depend on living standards and behaviors. As cities concentrate population, high living standards, and economic activities, they are responsible for consuming large amounts of goods, services, and, indirectly, energy (Dhakal 2004). Energy use, in particular, is strongly influenced by specific urban features, namely, the spatial structure of the city, its infrastructure, and the characteristics of urban population and activities. These factors have been identified as follows (Dhakal 2004):

- Compactness of the urban settlement
- Urban zoning and functions
- Nature of the transportation system
- Income level and lifestyle
- Energy efficiency of key technologies
- Nature of economic activities
- Building technologies and building floor space use
- Waste management
- Climate factors

Analyses of energy consumption and GHG emissions have been developed mainly at the national level. Studies at the city scale are limited because of difficulties in obtaining data at urban level and in linking decisions on energy issues (usually taken at the national level) to urban contexts (Dhakal 2004).

This section focuses on a set of city indicators that characterize the populations' living standards and can be understood as drivers of energy consumption, energy intensity, production, and consequently emissions at urban level. The indicators are classified as socioeconomic features, urban territorial features, local climate, urban transportation, and waste production and management (table 3.5).

Socioeconomic Features

Cities from industrialized countries show similar socioeconomic features in terms of population, age structure, and labor force, as described by the elderly-young ratio and the activity rate.[9] Milan stands out for its old-age population structure and Bangkok for the highest activity rate. Cities from developing countries show a relatively younger population.

Urban Territorial Features

Density and compactness of a city may influence energy demand for transportation and heating/cooling. High levels of both population and dwelling density characterize all five cities. New York City and Milan show the highest densities, Bangkok, the lowest.[10] Higher emission levels seem related with higher population and dwelling density, but emissions vary significantly among cities whose densities are similar (such as London and Mexico City).

As far as green spaces are concerned, cities from industrialized countries have high availability of green public spaces per capita, whereas cities from developing countries show a low availability of green spaces. However, low emissions are not necessarily associated with a high supply of green urban spaces. This urban feature may be better interpreted as an indicator of local environmental quality, resulting from territorial policies implemented by the city government.

Local Climate

Local climate conditions affect energy consumption for heating and cooling and thus emissions associated with buildings. Table 3.6 shows average temperature for the selected cities. The local climate in London, New York City, and Milan is more variable throughout the year compared with Mexico City and Bangkok. In particular, Bangkok has a tropical monsoon climate with a yearly average temperature significantly higher than the other cities, which leads to greater electricity demand for air conditioning.

TABLE 3.5
Drivers That Characterize the Local Emission Context

Socioeconomic features	London	New York City	Milan	Mexico City	Bangkok
Elderly/young ratio[a]	65.5	64.0	190.0	31.0	30.55
Activity rate (%)[b]	48.5	46.7	48.0	39.2	77.4
Territorial features					
Population density (residents per square kilometer)[c]	4,780	10,470	6,990	5,810	3,610
Dwelling density (dwellings per square kilometer)[d]	1,990	4,080	3,250	1,420	1,330
Public green space per capita (square meter per capita)[e]	25.5	16.6	15.9	5.4	1.8
Monthly average temperature (°C)			See table 3.6		
Urban transportation					
Car ownership rate[f]	310.8	228.1	623.5	164.0	271.0
Waste production and management					
Amount of solid waste collected (tons per capita per year)[g]	0.59	0.81	0.57	0.55	0.54
% waste collected for recycling[h]	18.1	37.8	30.6	n.a.	8.04

Source: Authors for different source data:

a. Comune di Milano 2009; GLA 2008c; SEDECO 2009; UNESCAP 2009; U.S. Census Bureau.

b. OECD 2006, except for Bangkok (UNESCAP 2009).

c. BMA 2009; DF 2007; EUROSTAT Urban Audit 2010; GLA 2008a; U.S. Census Bureau.

d. BMA 2009; GLA 2007; IEFE 2009; Pardo and Martínez 2006; U.S. Census Bureau.

e. Comune di Milano 2007; DF 2010; GLA 2008b; Thaiutsa and others 2008.

f. EUROSTAT Urban Audit 2010; NYS 2006; APERC (Asia Pacific Energy Research Centre) in Shrestha 2008.

g. DF 2006; EUROSTAT Urban Audit 2010; NYC Department of Sanitation 2004, 2007; Phdungsilp 2006. All data refer to domestic and commercial solid waste. For Mexico City index, data are not specified.

h. BMA and UNEP 2002; HDR 2004; NYC Department of Sanitation 2004; Mayor of London 2007b; Pitea 2008. All data refer to domestic and commercial waste.

Note: Other sources (INEGI 2005) estimate availability of green spaces per capita in Mexico City as 15.1 square meters; this value includes private green spaces, ecological reserves, and other areas with limited accessibility. Trucks, motorcycle, and commercial vehicles are not included for New York City car ownership rate. Data on selective collection of waste for Mexico City are not comparable with the other values.

TABLE 3.6
Average Temperature
degrees Celsius

	Annual	Jan.	Feb.	Mar.	Apr.	May	Jun.	Jul.	Aug.	Sep.	Oct.	Nov.	Dec.
London	10	3	3	6	7	11	14	16	16	13	10	6	5
New York City	12	—	1	6	11	17	22	25	24	20	14	8	2
Milan	11	1	3	7	10	15	19	22	21	18	12	6	2
Mexico City	15	12	14	16	18	18	17	17	17	16	15	14	12
Bangkok	28	26	28	29	30	30	29	29	28	28	28	27	26

Source: Weatherbase.

Urban Transportation

The car ownership rate (the number of registered cars per thousand inhabitants) shows no relevant differences among the case studies, except for Milan, which is characterized by the highest rate. The cities chosen from developing countries have reached a car ownership rate that is similar to cities in industrialized countries. To define a picture of local transportation that includes urban trips, data on the modal share of total daily trips within the city have been considered. Table 3.7 shows that public transport covers at least 35 to 45 percent of daily trips in all cities. For Mexico City, the share of public transport amounts to 80 percent of total trips.

Despite the high modal share of public transport, the contribution of transportation to total emissions in Mexico City is considerable, and its per capita emissions due to transportation are similar to cities with a lower share of public transport (table 3.2). This comparison suggests that the efficiency of the operating public transport, the motor vehicle stock, and kilometers traveled by circulating vehicles are determinants in characterizing emissions in this sector.

TABLE 3.7
Modal Share on Daily Trips
percent

Modes of transport	London	New York City	Milan	Mexico City	Bangkok
Private auto/motorcycle	51	50	61	17	54
Taxi	1	5	—	5	—
Public transport	46	46	36	78	46
Bicycle	2	—	3	—	—

Source: Authors for different source data: City of New York 2007c; IEFE 2009; SMA-GDF 2008; TfL 2007; World Bank 2007.

Waste Production and Management

Indicators on waste show a similar amount per capita, except for New York City, which has the highest production of solid waste per capita. Still, the percentages of solid waste collected for recycling show quite different patterns: Bangkok has the lowest recycling rate, whereas cities from industrialized countries (such as New York City and Milan) have significant recycling rates. Within the latter group, London has the lowest recycling rate. London's and Milan's emission values do not account for emissions from landfill waste. For these cities, it would be misleading to consider waste production and management as an emission driver.

Links between Drivers and Emissions

The small size of our sample limits our ability to draw general conclusions on which drivers have the most profound effect on emissions. Nonetheless, a few preliminary observations can be made:

- First, emission levels appear to be related with key features of industrialized countries, namely, the age structure of the population (elderly-young ratio) and GDP per capita.
- Second, no direct relationship was found between spatial features, in particular, population density and per capita emissions levels. This is probably because of the sample of cities from countries with differing lifestyles and income levels. Yet recent studies suggest that densely populated regions have lower CO_2 emissions per capita, compared with other urban and rural areas in the same country.[11] This is an area in which further research is urgently needed.
- Third, mobility patterns, in particular transit use, are more relevant than private vehicle ownership in determining levels of GHGs from urban transport. Recent data from the International Association of Public Transport (Allen 2009) show that cities with a high share of transit and nonmotorized modes (overall higher than 55 percent) are able to limit CO_2 emissions from transport below one ton of CO_2 per capita. Furthermore, the characteristics of the motor vehicle stock—size and age—as well as behavioral factors, such as driving and maintenance habits, and the efficiency of the transport network, also significantly affect emissions.
- Fourth, it is not possible to compare values for emissions from waste because they are measured by different criteria. Nonetheless, waste management appears as a policy area that may be targeted effectively by mitigation measures, as in the case of Mexico City.

Comparative Analysis of City Plans

This section compares the plans of the cities to reduce emissions in order to mitigate climate change.

Main Components of the Local Climate Plans

According to ICLEI, building a local emissions inventory is the first step for local governments wishing to implement a mitigation strategy. The inventory provides a basis that is necessary to identify mitigation options and actions. Besides, it provides a basis to elaborate a business-as-usual (BAU) projection of future GHG levels, against which reduction targets may be set and the effectiveness of mitigation measures assessed.

Mitigation strategies in the five cities are compared by reviewing the contents of each plan and taking into account the following:

- The local BAU scenario: Which assumptions and drivers have been considered in projecting future local emissions?
- The choice of the base year and of reduction targets: Which criteria has the local government followed in choosing and defining its reduction commitment?
- Mitigation measures: How relevant is each measure, and which roles does the local government play in each sector?
- Implementation and monitoring: Does the plan identify who will be responsible for the plan's implementation and the monitoring system?
- Financing: Does the plan address the funding of measures?

Comparison of Plan Components

We now compare the elements within the cities' plans, with specific reference to baselines, targets, reduction measures, and financing.

Business as Usual Scenarios

BAU scenarios estimate future GHG emissions if no additional measures, other than those that would naturally occur or already conceived, were implemented (Dubeux and La Rovere 2007). They provide a basis to assess the results of new climate mitigation actions. According to the IPCC, the main driving forces of future GHG trajectories are demographic trends, socioeconomic developments, and the rate and direction of technological change (Nakicenovic and Swart 2000).

BAU emission projections are available in all plans of the selected cities. In London, New York City, Milan, and Mexico City, BAU emissions projections are based on estimates of future energy consumption, namely, heating for buildings, electricity use, and fuel consumption for transportation. London also includes emissions from the industrial sector, whereas Mexico City and New York City include emissions generated from solid waste. Forecasts of the main drivers are based on the expected evolution of socioeconomic conditions (London, Mexico City, and Milan) or from historical emissions growth rates (New York City), assuming steady city growth.

Population and economic activities are projected to grow in all scenarios, leading to growing demand for energy, transport, and housing. The underlying assumption is that these global cities will continue to attract people, because of job and study opportunities (London, New York City, and Mexico City) or because of specific local policies aimed at increasing density (Milan). The projections were made before the 2008–09 global financial crisis and do not account for the restraining effect that the crisis may have on energy demand and emissions.

Base Year and Reduction Targets

Guidelines on local GHG accounting suggest choosing the base year according to the completeness of data in the local emission inventory. Data for the Kyoto reference year (1990) are usually difficult to obtain at the local level. The European Union (EU) Covenant of Mayors suggests—for local authorities that have not yet developed an emissions inventory—2005 as a base year, to maintain homogeneity with the EU energy and climate targets. In most of the case studies, inventories are available for a unique year. For New York City, inventories were also available for 1995 and 2000, but 2005 was chosen to be consistent with the climate change mitigation strategy and the wider sustainability framework of PlaNYC (City of New York 2007b). London chose 1990 to align with national and international targets.

As for reduction targets, London adopted a long-term reduction target with intermediate steps, whereas New York City and Milan chose a medium-term target. Milan, in particular, refers to 2020 for coherence with the time frame of EU energy and climate policies. Bangkok and Mexico City adopt a shorter-term target (2012). Table 3.8 shows the average yearly emission reduction that needs to be achieved in each city to comply with its planned target. Interestingly, the required annual reductions in each city, as a percentage of the respective baseline, are similar, although some cities have chosen longer-term horizons than others.

TABLE 3.8
Reduction Targets, Base Years, and Target Years in the Case Studies

	London	New York City	Milan	Mexico City	Bangkok
Targeted GHGs	CO_2	CO_2, CH_4, N_2O	CO_2	CO_2, CH_4, N_2O	CO_2, CH_4
Reduction target and target year	−20% (2016), −60% (2025)	−30% (2030)	−20% (2020)	7 million tons CO_2e to be reduced in the period 2008–12	−15% (2012)
Base year GHG level	1990: 45.1 million tons CO_2	2005: 63.1 million tons CO_2e	2005: 7.05 million tons CO_2	2000: 33.5 million tons CO_2e; 2006: 36.2 million tons CO_2e	2005: 42.65 million tons CO_2e
Estimated GHG level for target year (BAU scenario)	2025 BAU: 51 million tons CO_2 (+15%)	2030 BAU: 80.1 million tons CO_2e (+27%)	2020 BAU: 8.03 million tons CO_2 (+8%)	2012 BAU: 35–49 million tons CO_2e (+11% low, +25% medium, +35% high)	2012 BAU: 48.69 million tons CO_2e (~+14%)
Emission reductions to be achieved, calculated for the target year	33 million tons CO_2	36 million tons CO_2e	2.4 million tons CO_2	7 million tons CO_2e to be reduced in the period 2008–12	7 million tons CO_2e
Annual reductions over the plan time frame (% of base year)	2.1	2.3	2.3	4.1	2.13

Source: Authors on different source data: BMA 2008; City of New York 2007a; IEFE 2009; Lapeyre and others 2008; Mayor of London 2007a.

Note: 2005 is the base year for the emissions inventory for Bangkok. Bangkok Metropolitan Administration fixes a reduction target of −15 percent below 2012 BAU emission levels. Net emissions: Parks and trees absorb 0.1 million tons CO_2e every year. BAU = business as usual.

In each city, mitigation potential is influenced by roles the local government can play to regulate or control each emissive sector, emissions, or both. This varies according to the specific national context and administrative structures.

National, state, and regional policies on climate and energy may affect city policies, legislation, and instruments and may overlap with local mitigation strategies. This is the case in the climate plan of London, which assesses the achievable reductions, highlighting the roles of the national government and the EU level in the following sectors:

- Energy supply: Because the city imports most of the consumed electricity from the national grid, national policies on energy supply directly influence carbon emissions associated with citizens' consumption. Furthermore, national legislation can directly enable or discourage the use of decentralized or renewable supply systems (such as in London, statutory barriers prevent combined cooling, heat, and power plants from being installed).
- Energy efficiency and savings in the building sector: The national government defines standards for new buildings; is responsible for the implementation of directives on energy efficiency in appliances and buildings (such as EU Performance of Buildings Directive, EU Energy End Use and Efficiency Directive); and may provide grants, incentives, or advice to support the realization of energy efficiency measures.
- Transport sector: In addition to funds for transport infrastructure, the national level may influence circulating vehicles with taxes and incentives.

BOX 3.1

City Governments' Roles and Climate Change

A city government can act as one or more of the following:

- Consumer, intervening directly on municipal energy and transport consumption
- Planner and regulator, orientating urban development and using authoritative powers to set mandatory conditions related to energy efficiency
- Provider and supplier, investing in infrastructure in the transport, waste, and energy supply sectors, either directly or by owning companies providing such public services
- Enabler and adviser, influencing other actors through information campaigns on sustainable behaviors or supporting them directly with incentives and counseling aimed at enhancing measures that can contribute to climate change mitigation.

Source: Adapted from Alber and Kern 2008.

Alber and Kern (2008) classify the governing mode that each role implies:

- Self-governing is the capacity of the local authority to govern its activities through reorganization, institutional innovation, and investments. It is associated with the role of the local government as consumer.
- Governing by authority refers to regulations and sanctions the city government can set. It is based on the authoritative powers of the local government.
- Governing by provision consists in delivering resources and services, and it is thus connected with the "provider and supplier" role.
- Governing by enabling refers to the capacities of the local government to coordinate actors and encourage community engagement, as in the adviser and enabler role.

Mitigation Measures

With governing modes as a basis, emission reduction measures included in the climate plans are categorized for the sectors of energy, transport, waste, and urban planning. To weigh mitigation measures in each local strategy, the expected impacts of measures included in plans are analyzed.[12] The weight of each measure is expressed as a percentage of the total emission reductions that should derive from the implementation of the plan. Emission reductions that are achievable through each measure are usually expressed in the plans as annual reductions.

Table 3.9 shows that New York City, London, and Milan assign great relevance to policies concerning energy supply, energy efficiency, and savings throughout all governing modes. Policies combine advice and counseling to citizens with incentives to support both energy efficiency measures in existing buildings and installation of renewable energy microplants. More than half of expected emissions reductions for London and Milan come from measures in these fields. These cities assign a relevant role for mitigation to their main energy supplier, whom they are able to influence. For London, influence on carbon intensity is limited because it is related to the national government policies on lower carbon intensity in the national grid and national targets within European directives on renewable sources (Mayor of London 2007a). Milan has more power in influencing strategic investments of its main energy supplier, A2A, because the municipality is a majority shareholder in the company. New York City authorities schedule a set of energy measures, with the collaboration of its main energy supplier, to secure a cleaner energy supply to the city.[13]

In the plans of Mexico City and Bangkok, the highest local mitigation potential is in the transport sector, enhanced by investments in infrastructure for sustainable use of public transport: This sector contributes nearly half of expected emissions reductions. Transport reductions also contribute significantly to

TABLE 3.9
Mitigation Measures of the Plans Classified in Sectors and Governing Modes

Governing modes	Mitigation measures	London	New York City	Milan	Mexico City	Bangkok
Energy						
Self-governing	Energy efficiency schemes and use of CHP within municipal buildings	<1		1	2	<1
	Procurement of energy-efficient appliances					
	Purchasing of green energy					
	Eco-house and renewable energy demonstration projects				<1	
Enabling	Campaigns for energy efficiency	37		9	7	28
	Advice on energy efficiency to businesses and citizens					
	Promotion of the use of renewable energy					
Provision	Minor carbon intensity in the main energy supplier	17		22	<1	
	Decentralized energy supply (CHP, waste-to-energy)	19		7		
	Network upgrading to improve energy savings				<1	
	Energy service companies					
	Provision of incentives and grants for energy efficiency measures			11	<1	
	Provision of incentives and grants for renewable energy in private buildings			1		
Authority	Strategic energy planning to enhance energy conservation					
	Mandatory use of renewable energy in the new build sector	4		6	<1	
	Energy efficiency standards in the new building sector					
	Subtotal: Energy	78		57	14	29

continued

TABLE 3.9, *continued*

Governing modes	Mitigation measures	London	New York City	Milan	Mexico City	Bangkok
Transport						
Self-governing	Mobility management for employees	<1				
	Green fleet				2	
Enabling	Education campaigns	6				
	Green travel plans			6		
	Quality partnerships with public transport providers	11				
Provision	Public transport service provision	4			37	39
	Provision of infrastructure for alternative forms of transport			5	<1	17
	Upgrading of road network to increase traffic efficiency					
	Logistic centers for goods transport and freight management			4	2	
	Incentives to purchase low-emission cars			25		
Authority	Transport planning to limit car use and provide walking and cycling infrastructure			2		
	Workplace levies and road-user charging					Study
	Subtotal: Transport sector	22		42	42	56
Waste						
Self-governing	Waste prevention, recycling, and reuse within the local authority					
	Procurement of recycled goods					
Enabling	Campaigns for reducing, reusing, and recycling waste					3
	Promotion of the use of recycled products					

Provision	Waste service/waste water treatment provision	9	<1
	Installations for recycling, composting, and waste-to-energy facilities	4	Study
	Recycling, composting, and reuse schemes	1	
	Methane capturing from landfills (energy production)	31	
Authority	Regulations on methane combustion from landfill sites		
	Subtotal: Waste sector (if applicable)	44	5

Urban planning and land use

Self-governing	High energy-efficiency standards and use of CHP in new public buildings		
	Demonstration projects: house or neighborhood scale		
Enabling	Guidance for architects and developers on energy efficiency and renewables		
	Promotion of tree planting		3
Authority	Strategic land-use planning to enhance energy efficiency and renewables		
	Planning of sites for renewable installations		
	Strategic land-use planning to enhance public transport		
	Urban forestation	<1	7
	Subtotal: Urban forestry and land use sector (if applicable)	1	10

Source: Authors for different sources, based on Alber and Kern 2008; BMA 2008; City of New York 2007a; IEFE 2009; SMA-GDF 2008; Mayor of London 2007a.

Note: Numbers refer to the weight of specific measures on annual total emission reductions expected from the implementation of the plan. CHP = combined heat and power. Shaded cells mean that these measures are included in the respective city's plan; no shading and no number means that the measure does not have a quantitative target to go with it in the plan.

the plans of London and Milan. For Milan, relevant reductions are expected from local policies aimed at reducing the use of private cars and lowering the average carbon emissions factor in circulating vehicles, including a pollution charge. These policies are complemented by incentives to consumers for the purchase of low-emissions vehicles provided by regional and national authorities.

Measures on urban planning are difficult to associate with quantified emissions reductions. Planning policies usually set a framework that indirectly influences the building and transport sector. Within land use, only Milan and Bangkok evaluate a potential increase in urban forestry and assign a role to tree planting in the comprehensive mitigation strategy (1 and 10 percent of all expected reductions. respectively). In the waste sector, Mexico City identifies mitigation potential in a project for energy production from landfill methane (31 percent of expected reductions). London, New York City, and Milan address issues related to solid waste in specific plans and do not include measures in this sector in their local climate strategies.

Weights assigned to mitigation measures reveal that climate plans in these cities are coherent with emissions contexts defined in the local inventories. This aspect is verified by comparing the contribution of the two most relevant sectors (buildings, transportation) to emissions, expressed as a percentage of total emissions, with the weights of measures belonging to these sectors within each plan (figure 3.1). The plans of London, Milan, Mexico City, and Bangkok identify a reduction potential for emissions from energy use in buildings and transportation that is very similar to the sectors' shares of total emissions. Milan's plan shows a gap in defining measures targeting energy consumptions in buildings. Mexico City's plan assigns a significant weight to measures on waste (44 percent), despite a more limited contribution of this sector to total emissions (11 percent). The plan does not include measures for the industrial sector, which contributes considerably to total emissions (22 percent). This aspect may be due to difficulties in identifying local measures to target the industrial sector. Conclusions regarding the efficiency of these plans are not possible, because marginal costs of emissions abatement are not available for specific measures. In fact, efficient plans would require the equalization of marginal abatement costs among included measures.

Implementation and Monitoring

Two alternative approaches are used to implement urban mitigation plans: (1) a unit in charge of climate policy is created in each relevant department or (2) a group with climate change competencies (climate steering group, coordination office, overarching unit) is established in the local government (Alber and Kern 2008). The second approach seems more promising if the climate

Figure 3.1 Coherence among Emission Sectors (Inventories) and Reduction Measures (Local Mitigation Plans)

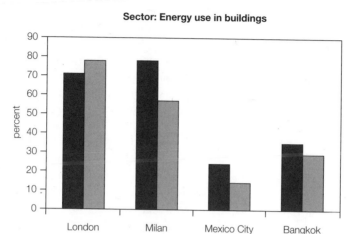

Sector: Energy use in buildings

Sector: Transportation

■ % for total base year emissions   ▨ % measures for total reductions

Source: Authors for different sources: Mayor of London 2007a (London), IEFE 2009 (Milan), Ministry of Environment, Mexico City 2008 (Mexico City), and BMA 2008 (Bangkok).

group can act within a general framework (strategic plans with sector-based targets, policies, and measures) and if a project-based approach is adopted, because it prevents departmental segregation. Competencies for climate change policy are often concentrated in environmental departments, and this feature may lead to coordination and integration problems if such skills are not complemented by competencies to implement comprehensive concepts (Alber and Kern 2008).

London and New York City have chosen the second approach. New York City has created the Mayor's Office of Long-Term Planning and Sustainability, an office charged with coordination and implementation of the sustainability vision of the city, including climate change issues. This office cooperates with city agencies and the Mayor's Advisory Board. A specific agency, the NYC Energy Planning Board, will be created to coordinate all energy supply-and-demand initiatives of the city.

London has assigned to a preexisting institution, the London Climate Change Agency (LCCA), the task of implementing all measures in the city's climate action plan related to advice and counseling, such as giving support to citizens and businesses in investing in energy efficiency and renovation of buildings (that is, activities categorized under "enabling" in table 3.9, energy sector). Furthermore, as the public half of the London Energy Service Company formed with EDF Energy Ltd, LCCA directly manages CO_2 reduction and energy efficiency projects.

Mexico City has assigned coordination of measures to the environmental secretariat (Secretaría del Medio Ambiente). For each measure, the internal sectors and external actors that are responsible and jointly responsible for implementation are identified. Bangkok and Milan have not yet defined issues concerning implementation. Milan's plan has been developed by the environmental department, with the support of a municipal agency with competencies on mobility, environment, and territorial issues (Agency for Mobility, Environment, and Territory). The effectiveness of the coordination role of specific units or environmental units within city climate change strategies should be investigated in future research.

Inventory updating is identified as a key tool to assess progress toward targets (London, New York City, and Milan). Monitoring reports are assigned to units charged with plan implementation (New York City) or to an ad hoc monitoring and evaluating committee (Mexico City). London, besides periodic reporting by the mayor, includes CO_2 reduction reporting in assessments provided by agencies and departments linked to climate-relevant sectors. This feature may be considered as a sign of a high degree of integration of climate strategy in the local government and its institutionalization therein.

Financing

Financial aspects of mitigation are addressed in various ways: estimating the costs for each measure (Mexico City) or foreseeing a budget allocation (London and New York City). For Mexico City, Clean Development Mechanism

(CDM) credits and revenues from the Kyoto market will be essential for financing mitigation measures. These resources will be included in the Public Environmental Fund of the Federal District. The use of Kyoto credits as a means to offset emissions can be found only in the plan of Milan, which considers the possibility of relying upon CDM projects to compensate for indirect emissions from purchased electricity.

Conclusions and Future Research

The analysis of emissions inventories shows that local emissions strongly depend on energy uses, particularly in buildings and transportation. Considering the main indicators of emissions, GDP is a major factor explaining emissions levels of the selected cities, except for Bangkok, whose emissions are more characterized by energy intensity of production.

The sector-based urban drivers analyzed are not sufficient to explain cities' GHG emissions. This suggests that further analysis of more specific determinants, such as the characteristics of the building stock, dwelling density, motor vehicle stock, and transport network, is needed. Even among cities with similar emissions levels, the sources of emissions may vary: This is the case with New York City and Bangkok, where the contributions of the transport and buildings sectors to total emissions are very different.

Comparing emissions values and mitigation strategies reveals that cities from industrialized countries, namely, London, New York City, and Milan, share similar emissive contexts and mitigation strategies. For these cities, the highest contribution to urban emissions is related to energy consumption in buildings (residential, commercial, and institutional). Their climate plans point to the energy sector as having the greatest potential, and their policies share the following essential features:

- Stimulating energy efficiency and savings from individual actions, of both citizens and businesses (that is, direct incentives or tax breaks and technical counseling)
- Promoting high-energy efficiency and renewable energy in the newly built sector, mainly through standards, regulation, and incentives
- Supporting decentralized supply and combined heat and power systems
- Relying on lower carbon intensity in the energy supply of the main provider (London and Milan).

This last point will depend mainly on the kind of relationship that exists between each city government and its major energy supplier. Where the energy supplier is a public utility owned by the local government, the municipality may engage it in programs that affect the energy mix of electricity production. Otherwise, agreements between the city government and energy providers may promote investments that contribute to the local GHG reduction objective (see the cases of Calgary and Heidelberg in Kamal-Chaoui and Robert 2009).

The transport sector is the second-highest contributor to urban emissions for London, New York City, and Milan and is targeted by policies aimed at enhancing the existing public transport infrastructure and its use. Daily modal share of public transport is already high in these three cities, but private motorized travel shows potential for further reductions. Investments planned by the municipality of Milan to extend the underground network, combined with incentives to support the renewal of cars in use, are highly coherent with the markedly high car ownership that is typical of this city. Bangkok and Mexico City share an emissive context and mitigation strategies strongly influenced by transportation. Their climate strategies identify the most relevant mitigation potential within the transport sector and strongly rely on public transport provision.

All cities considered in the chapter have defined a strategy that is coherent with their local emission contexts because they focus mitigation measures on sectors identified as most relevant in determining their urban emissions.

As local mitigation policies and city planning instruments for climate change are developed worldwide, a wider range of case studies will become available. Further research may also benefit from a greater availability of comparable city-level data on energy, GHG emissions, and territorial features. Emissions values in particular can be standardized through the establishment of a common methodology for local GHG emissions inventories. Research is urgently needed on the costs of local mitigation measures and, more broadly, the costs of implementing local climate plans.

As cities publish data and progress reports on their climate strategies, the effectiveness and efficiency of each mitigation strategy may be assessed and compared to identify the most cost-effective measures, instruments, and governing modes in pursuing reduction targets. Mitigation strategies should be reviewed in relation to other city plans to explore synergies, cobenefits, and links. Finally, the integration of mitigation and adaptation strategies should be further explored.

Notes

1. The U.S. Conference of Mayors Climate Protection Agreement sets the American Kyoto target at the city level and is currently endorsed by more than 1,000 municipalities (http://www.usmayors.org/climateprotection/agreement.htm); the European

Covenant of Mayors already involves more than 2,200 municipalities and commits them to adopt a sustainable energy action plan, with a target going beyond the 20 percent reduction of GHG emissions by 2020 (http://www.eumayors.eu/).

2. See the definition of global cities in Sassen (2001).

3. Several boundaries can be identified within large cities: the core city, the contiguous built-up area, the metropolitan area, and an extended planning region (Satterthwaite 2008).

4. The definition has been adapted from Hakes (1999). Other classifications are possible (Dodman 2009).

5. The European Monitoring and Evaluation Programme/European Environment Agency (EEA) air pollutant emission inventory guidebook (CORINAIR) provides guidance on estimating emissions from both anthropogenic and natural emission sources. See the website of the EEA, http://www.eea.europa.eu/publications/emep-eea-emission-inventory-guidebook-2009.

6. Although London, Mexico City, Milan, and New York City have lower emissions per capita than their respective countries, Bangkok produces much higher emissions per capita than the rest of Thailand. Per capita emissions in 2002 were the following: 9.7 tons, Italy (UNFCCC 2003); 9.8 tons, Mexico; 3.2 tons, Thailand; 4.2 tons, United Kingdom; 20 tons, United States (UNEP/GRID 2005).

7. The Kaya identity expresses global GHG emission levels as the product of the following inputs: CO_2 emissions per capita = Carbon content of energy × Energy intensity of economy × GDP per capita (Kaya 1990, in Nakicenovic and Swart 2000).

8. Carbon intensity of electricity consumption shows the following values: Bangkok, 509 grams of CO_2/KWh (BMA 2008); London (supplied from the National Grid), 520 grams of CO_2/KWh; Mexico City, 683 grams of CO_2/KWh (Pardo and Martínez 2006); Milan, 311 grams of CO_2/KWh (IEFE 2009).

9. This elderly-young ratio is the ratio of the number of inhabitants aged over 60 to the number of inhabitants aged under 19. The activity rate is the percentage of the total population aged from 15 to 65 years in the labor force.

10. If we consider the estimate of Bangkok's registered and unregistered population of 8.8 million inhabitants, the density of Bangkok would be 5,612 inhabitants/km², similar to the other selected cities.

11. A study by the Greater London Authority compares the environmental performance of London with other regions of England that are on average 14 times less dense than London. London turns out to be the region with the lowest domestic CO_2 emissions per capita and the lowest CO_2 emissions per billion pounds gross value added, whereas the transport sector has low CO_2 emissions per passenger bus and the highest CO_2 emissions per vehicle kilometer traveled, mainly because of traffic congestion (GLA 2008b).

12. New York's plan does not include estimates on emission reductions that should derive from each measure.

13. The New York City plan foresees (1) facilitating repowering and construction of cleaner power plants and dedicated transmission lines, (2) expanding Clean Distributed Generation connected to the city grid, (3) fostering the market for renewable energy, and (4) supporting expansion of the city's natural gas infrastructure (City of New York 2007a).

References

Alber, G., and K. Kern. 2008. "Governing Climate Change in Cities: Modes of Urban Climate Governance in Multi-level Systems." http://www.oecd.org/dataoecd/22/7/41449602.pdf.

Allen, H. 2009. "Co-benefits and GHG Reductions with Public Transport." UITP, Brussels.

AMA (Agenzia Mobilità e Ambiente). 2007. "Rapporto qualità dell'aria, energia e agenti fisici. Relazione sullo stato dell'ambiente del Comune di Milano." Comune di Milano, Italy.

BMA (Bangkok Metropolitan Administration). 2008. "Action Plan on Global Warming Mitigation 2007—2012. Executive Summary." http://www.baq2008.org/system/files/BMA+Plan.pdf.

———. 2009. Data Center Website. http://203.155.220.230/stat_search/stat_06/stat06_01.html.

BMA, Green Leaf Foundation (GLF), and UNEP (United Nations Environment Programme). 2009. "Bangkok Assessment Report on Climate Change 2009." BMA, GLF, and UNEP, Bangkok. http://www.unep.org/Dewa/pdf/BKK_assessment_report2009.pdf.

BMA and UNEP (United Nations Environment Programme). 2002. "Bangkok State of the Environment 2001." http://rrcap.unep.org/pub/soe/bangkoksoe01.cfm.

City of New York. 2007a. "PLANYC. A Greener, Greater New York." http://www.nyc.gov/html/planyc2030/html/downloads/the-plan.shtml.

———. 2007b. "Inventory of New York City Greenhouse Gas Emissions." April. http://www.nyc.gov/html/planyc2030/downloads/pdf/emissions_inventory.pdf.

———. 2007c. "PlaNYC. New York City: Mobility Needs Assessment 2007–2030." http://www.nyc.gov/html/planyc2030/downloads/pdf/tech_report_transportation.pdf.

———. 2008a. "PlaNYC Progress Report. Energy." http://www.nyc.gov/html/planyc2030/downloads/pdf/progress_2008_energy.pdf.

———. 2008b. "Inventory of New York City Greenhouse Gas Emissions." http://www.nyc.gov/html/planyc2030/downloads/pdf/inventory_nyc_ghg_emissions_2008_-_feb09update_web.pdf. Updated February 24, 2009.

Comune di Milano. 2007. "MilanParks. Un piano del verde ... verso l'Expo 2015." Milan, Italy.

———. 2009. "Pubblicazioni: Milano statistica." Milan, Italy.

DF (Distrito Federal, Ciudad de México). 2006. "Inventario de Residuos Sólidos del Distrito Federal." http://www.sma.df.gob.mx/rsolidos/inventario_residuos_solidos.pdf.

———. 2007. "Primer Informe de Gobierno 2007." http://www.df.gob.mx/work/sites/gdf/resources/LocalContent/189/5/3_aspectos_demograficos.pdf .

———. 2010. Estrategía Institucíonal del Plan Verde de la Secretaria del Medio Ambiente." http://www.sma.df.gob.mx/planverde/.

Dhakal, S. 2004. "Urban Energy Use and Greenhouse Gas Emissions from Asian Megacities: Policies for a Sustainable Future." Urban Environmental Management Project, Institute for Global Environmental Strategies, Kanagawa, Japan. http://www.gcp-urcm.org/Resources/R200711290036.

Dodman, D. 2009. "Blaming Cities for Climate Change? An Analysis of Urban Greenhouse Gas Emissions Inventories." *Environment & Urbanization* 21 (1): 185–201.

Dubeux, C., and E. La Rovere. 2007. "Local Perspectives in the Control of Greenhouse Gas Emissions—The Case of Rio de Janeiro." *Cities* 24 (5): 353–64.

EIU (Economist Intelligence Unit). 2008. "Sustainable Urban Infrastructure. London Edition—A View to 2025." Siemens AG, Munich, Germany. https://www.cee.siemens .com/web/at/de/corporate/portal/Nachhaltigkeit/Documents/SustainableUrban Infrastructure-StudyLondon.pdf.

EUROSTAT Urban Audit. 2010. Urban Audit home page. http://www.urbanaudit.org/.

GLA (Greater London Authority). 2007. "National Statistics. Focus on London." http:// www.statistics.gov.uk/focuson/london/.

———. 2008a. "Information London." GLA, London.

———. 2008b. "London's Environmental Effectiveness—An Update: Comparing London with Other English Regions." GLA Economics. http://www.london.gov.uk/ publication/londons-environmental-effectiveness.

———. 2008c. "Demography Update." http://www.london.gov.uk/who-runs-london/ mayor/publications/society/facts-and-figures/population.

Hakes, J. 1999. "Testimony of Jay Hakes, Administrator, Energy Information Administration, U.S. Department of Energy before the House Government Reform Committee. National Economic Growth, Natural Resources, and Regulatory Affairs Subcommittee on the Voluntary Reporting of Greenhouse Gases Program, July 15, 1999." http://www.eia.doe.gov/neic/speeches/htest715/testmony.htm.

HDR (Henningson, Durham, and Richardson). 2004. "Commercial Waste Management Study. Volume II. Commercial Waste Generation and Projections. Prepared for New York City Department of Sanitation for submission to New York City Council." http://home2.nyc.gov/html/dsny/downloads/pdf/swmp/swmp/cwms/cwms-ces/ v2-cwgp.pdf.

Hutchinson, D. 2002. "Emission Inventories." In *Handbook of Atmospheric Science: Principles and Applications,* ed. C. N. Hewitt and A. Jackson, 473–502. Malden, Oxford, and Carlton: Blackwell.

ICLEI (International Council for Local Environmental Initiatives). 2008. "International Local Government GHG Emissions Analysis Protocol." Release Version 1.0. http:// www.iclei.org/index.php?id=8154.

IEFE (Centre for Research on Energy and Environmental Economics and Policy, Universita Bocconi). 2009. "Piano d'Azione per l'Energia Sostenibile ed il Clima del Comune di Milano. Rapporto finale." Milan, Italy.

INEGI (Instituto Nacional de Estadística, Geografía e Informática). 2005. "Estadísticas del Medio Ambiente del Distrito Federal y Zona Metropolitana 2002." http://www .sma.df.gob.mx/sma/index.php?opcion=26&id=313.

IPCC (Intergovernmental Panel on Climate Change). 2006. "2006 IPCC Guidelines for National GHG Inventories." Institute for Global Environmental Strategies, Kanagawa, Japan. http://www.ipcc-nggip.iges.or.jp/public/2006gl/index.html.

Kamal-Chaoui, L., and A. Robert. 2009. "Competitive Cities and Climate Change." OECD Regional Development Working Papers No. 2, Organisation for Economic Co-operation and Development, Paris.

Kennedy, C., J. Steinberger, B. Gasson, T. Hillman, M. Havránek, D. Pataki, A. Phdungsilp, A. Ramaswami, and G. Villalba Mendez. 2010. "Methodology for Inventorying Greenhouse Gas Emissions from Global Cities." *Energy Policy* 38 (9): 4828–37.

Kosayodhin, A. 2008. "Defining the Issues for Green ASEAN Cities." In *Proceedings of The Greening of ASEAN Cities*, ASEAN + 6 Cities Forum on Climate Change, Bangkok, Thailand, June 25–27.

Mayor of London. 2006a. "Draft Further Alterations to the London Plan (Spatial Development Strategy for Greater London)." GLA, London.

———. 2006b. "London Energy and CO_2 Emissions Inventory 2003 Methodology Manual." GLA, London.

———. 2007a. "Action Today to Protect Tomorrow—The Mayor's Climate Change Action Plan." http://static.london.gov.uk/mayor/.../climate-change/docs/ccap_summaryreport.pdf..

———. 2007b. "Greener London. The Mayor's State of the Environment Report for London." GLA, London. http://legacy.london.gov.uk/gla/publications/environment/soereport/soe_summary.pdf.

Nakicenovic, N., and R. Swart, eds. 2000. *IPCC Special Report: Emissions Scenarios.* Cambridge: Cambridge University Press.

NYC (New York City) Department of Sanitation. 2004. "Commercial Waste Management Study." http://www.nyc.gov/html/dsny/html/swmp/cwms-ces.shtml.

———. 2007. "Performance Report." http://www.nyc.gov/html/ops/downloads/pdf/_mmr/dsny.pdf.

NYS (New York State). 2006. "Department of Motor Vehicles: Archives of Statistical Summaries." http://www.nydmv.state.ny.us/stats-arc.htm.

OECD (Organisation for Economic Co-operation and Development). 2006. "Competitive Cities in the Global Economy." OECD Territorial Reviews. Paris.

Pardo, C., and O. Martínez. 2006. "Estrategia Local de Acción Climática del Distrito Federal." Secretaría del Medio Ambiente del Distrito Federal. http://www.sma.df.gob.mx/sma/index.php?opcion=26&id=399.

Phdungsilp, A. 2006. "Energy Analysis for Sustainable Mega-Cities." Licentiate Thesis, School of Industrial Engineering and Management, Department of Energy Technology, Royal Institute of Technology. http://www.gcp-urcm.org/Resources/R200711290112.

Pitea, D. 2008. "Ciclo integrato di gestione dei rifiuti." In *Milano sostenibile: Rapporti di ricerca*, ed. A. Balducci, 153–200. Milan: Fondazione Cariplo, Camera di Commercio di Milano.

Sassen, S. 2001. *The Global City.* Princeton, NJ: Princeton University Press.

Satterthwaite, D. 2008. "Cities' Contributions to Global Warming: Notes on the Allocation of Greenhouse Gas Emissions." *Environment & Urbanization* 20 (2): 539–49.

SEDECO (Sistema de Información Económica, Geográfica y Estadística). 2009. Sistema de Información Económica, Geográfica y Estadística. Government of the Federal District of Mexico City, Mexico City. http://www.siege.df.gob.mx/.

Shrestha, R. M. 2008. "Energy Solutions and Climate Change: Is There a Choice for Developing Countries?" http://www.jgsee.kmutt.ac.th/seminar_programme/DAY%201/Ram_Shrestha_Presentation.pdf.

SMA-GDF (Secretaría del Medio Ambiente, Gobierno del Distrito Federal). 2008. *Programa de Acción Climática de la Ciudad de México 2008–2012.* http://www.sma.df.gob.mx/sma/links/download/archivos/paccm_documento.pdf.

TfL (Transport for London). 2007. "London Travel Report 2007." http://www.tfl.gov.uk/assets/downloads/corporate/London-travel-report-2007-final.pdf.

Thaiutsa, B., L. Puangchit, R. Kjelgren, and W. Arunpraparut. 2008. "Urban Green Space, Street Tree and Heritage Large Tree Assessment in Bangkok, Thailand." *Urban Forestry & Urban Greening* 7 (3): 219–29.

UNEP/GRID (United Nations Environment Programme/Global Resource Information Database). 2005. "National Carbon Dioxide (CO_2) Emissions per Capita." http:// maps.grida.no/go/graphic/national_carbon_dioxide_co2_emissions_per_capita.

UNEP (United Nations Environment Programme) and UN-HABITAT (United Nations Human Settlements Programme). 2005. "Climate Change: The Role of Cities." http:// www.unhabitat.org/downloads/docs/2226_alt.pdf.

UNESCAP (United Nations Economic and Social Commission for Asia and the Pacific). 2009. "Key Statistics of Population and Households of Bangkok." http://www .unescap.org/esid/psis/population/database/thailanddata/central/bangkok.htm.

UNFCCC (United Nations Framework Convention on Climate Change). 2003. "Italy: Greenhouse Gas Emissions per Capita." Data for 1990–2003 submitted to the United Nations Framework Convention on Climate Change, UNFCCC greenhouse gas inventory. http://globalis.gvu.unu.edu/indicator_detail.cfm? IndicatorID=199&Country=IT.

Weatherbase [database]. http://www.weatherbase.com.

World Bank. 2007. "Strategic Urban Transport Policy Directions for Bangkok." Urban Transport Development Partnership report, June. http://siteresources.worldbank .org/INTTHAILAND/Resources/333200–1177475763598/2007june_bkk-urban- transport-directions.pdf.

Yusuf, S., and K. Nabeshima. 2006. *Postindustrial East Asian Cities: Innovations for Growth.* Washington, DC, and Stanford, CA: World Bank and Stanford University Press.

4

GHG Emissions, Urban Mobility, and Morphology: A Hypothesis

Alain Bertaud, Benoit Lefèvre, and Belinda Yuen

Introduction

This chapter explores the link between greenhouse gas (GHG) emissions, transport mode, and city shape. Urban productivity is dependent on people's mobility within a metropolitan area. GHG emissions, however, are only weakly linked to the number of kilometers traveled per person because of large variations between the emissions per passenger kilometer of different transport modes and differences in the carbon content of the various energy sources used for transport. Thus, to reduce urban GHG emissions due to transport, it is important to look at all the parameters that contribute to emissions. In this chapter, three concurrent strategies that could contribute to reducing GHG emissions due to urban transport are reviewed: technological improvements within mode, mode shift, and land-use strategy allowing spatial concentration of jobs. In particular, the chapter explores options for improving travel in urban areas by investigating the links between GHG emissions and transport modes, with consideration of associated travel costs and city shape. However, it is our contention that none of these strategies are likely to succeed if not supported by an energy pricing policy directly linking energy price to carbon content.

The central hypothesis is that carbon-based energy pricing could trigger a demand shift toward transit in dominantly monocentric cities, providing adequate zoning changes were made. More specifically, this chapter seeks to develop and determine the following:

Hypothesis 1: Price signals, including energy prices and carbon market–based incentives, road tolls, and transit fares, are the main drivers of technological change, transport modal shift, and land-use regulatory changes.

Hypothesis 2: Price signals could shift transport mode from individual cars to public transit for trips from the periphery to the central business district (CBD) only in cities that are densely populated (more than 50 people/hectare (ha) in built-up areas) and already dominantly monocentric.

GHG Emissions and Urban Transport

Urban GHG emissions per person in large cities are a fraction of the national average (figure 4.1). This difference appears as a paradox because cities have a higher gross domestic product (GDP) per person than the national average, and it is usually assumed that higher GDP means higher GHG emissions. In fact, modern cities with a large proportion of service jobs consume less energy per capita than smaller towns and rural areas. However, because GHGs are emitted in urban areas by a very large number of small sources—cars, appli-

Figure 4.1 CO_2 Emissions in Cities Compared with Countries

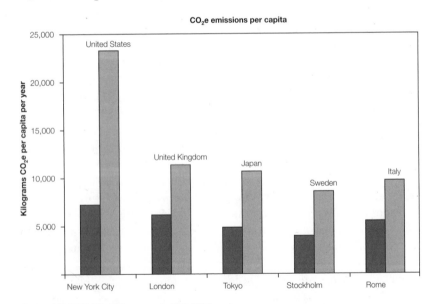

Source: EIU 2008; World Resources Institute 2009.

Note: CO_2e = carbon dioxide equivalent.

ances, individual buildings—as opposed to concentrated sources such as power plants or factories, it is difficult to develop an emission reduction strategy that would work for all emitters.

Reliable data on emissions in cities are difficult to collect because of ambiguity in determining which sources to include as urban. Should urban GHG emissions be limited to sources located within metropolitan boundaries? Or should emissions be counted on the basis of urban residents' consumption in urban areas? The data for cities shown in figure 4.1 correspond to the first definition, although emissions from electricity are accounted for on the basis of consumption and not on emissions at the location of the power plant.

Some analyses solve the problem posed by emission location versus location of consumption by including life-cycle emissions (Button 1993; McKinsey and Co. 2007; Schipper, Unander, and Marie-Lilliu 1999). For instance, the emissions of a car are not limited to the fuel consumed but include also the energy used to manufacture it, to maintain it, and to scrap it after its useful life. Although this type of definition is reasonable, the resulting numbers are difficult to calculate, and the method implies a number of assumptions, in particular, concerning the number of years and the number of kilometers traveled during the useful life of a vehicle. It is important to be aware of the limitations of the data set available when comparing cities' performance in GHG emissions. Some apparent inconsistencies in the data presented below can be attributed to slightly different assumptions in the data collected about emissions attributions.

The sample of five large cities[1] in high-income countries shown in figure 4.1 gives a range of emissions from 4 to 7 tons per person per year in 2005 (EIU 2008). It is likely that GHG emissions in cities in low- and middle- income countries, for which no reliable data are available, are even higher than the Organisation for Economic Co-operation and Development (OECD) cities shown in figure 4.1. The use of older cars and buses, and the prevalence of two-stroke engines for motorcycles and three-wheelers, might contribute to higher GHG emissions per capita. The three main sources of GHG emissions in cities are buildings, transport, and industries. In the sample of five high-income cities included in figure 4.1, the proportion of GHG emissions due to transport varies from 25 percent of total emissions in New York City to 38 percent in Rome (figure 4.2).

This chapter will be limited to identifying the best strategies to reduce GHG emissions due to transport in a context of increasing urban productivity. The conclusions of this study would be particularly relevant to cities that have more than 1 million inhabitants. According to United Nations data and projections, cities with populations above 1 million accounted for about 1.2 billion, or 18 percent of the world population, in 2005. By 2025, it is expected that this will increase to 1.85 billion and will then represent 23 percent of the world population.

Figure 4.2 CO_2 Emissions in Five High-Income Cities

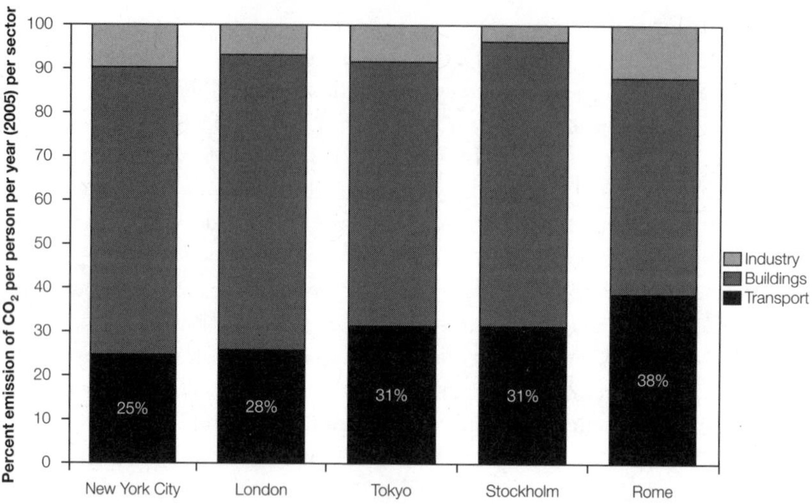

Source: EIU 2008.

Transport is a key driver of the economy and is highly dependent (98 percent) on fossil oil. Although already a significant sector of GHG emissions, it is also the fastest growing sector globally. Between 1990 and 2003, emissions from the transport sector grew 1,412 million metric tons (31 percent) worldwide. The sector's share of carbon dioxide (CO_2) emissions is also increasing. In 2005, the transport sector contributed 23 percent of CO_2 emissions from fossil fuel combustion. It is also the sector where the least progress has been made in addressing cost-effective GHG reductions (Sperling and Cannon 2006). As mentioned earlier, the fragmentation of emissions sources and the complexity of demand and supply issues in urban transport explain the lack of progress. Making transport activity more sustainable must be a top priority policy if climate change is to be addressed.

In most cities, numerous urban problems are transport related, such as congestion on urban roads, poor air quality, fragmented labor markets, and social fractioning due to poor access to economic and social activity and the like (Ng and Schipper 2005; World Bank 2009). Road transport accounts for, by far, the largest proportion of CO_2 emissions from the transport sector, principally from automobile transport. Against the projected increase in car ownership worldwide (expected to triple between 2000 and 2050), road transport will continue to account for a significant share of CO_2 emissions in the coming decades. Within cities, modal share and measures facilitating less GHG-intensive modes such as public transport require closer examination. Modal shift policies are generally inadequately assessed in CO_2 policy (OECD 2007). Because GHG emissions caused by urban transport have to be reduced while urban productivity has to increase, it is important to establish the links between urban transport, labor mobility, and city productivity.

Mobility and Cities' Economies

Economic literature, both theoretical and empirical, linking the wealth of cities to spatial concentration is quite abundant and no longer controversial in academic circles (Annez and Buckley 2009; Brueckner 2001; Brueckner, Thisse, and Zenou 1999). The World Bank's World Development Report (2009), "Reshaping Economic Geography," and the Commission on Growth and Development report "Urbanization and Growth" (Annez and Buckley 2009) exhaustively summarize and document the theoretical and empirical arguments justifying the economic advantage provided by the spatial concentration of economic activities in large cities. The necessity to manage urban growth rather than to try to slow it down is eventually reaching mayors, city managers, and urban planners. The size of cities is not critical; what matters is the connectivity insured by urban transport networks[2] between workers and firms and between providers of goods and services and consumers, whether these consumers are other firms or individuals. This connectivity is difficult to achieve in large cities. It requires coordination between land uses and investments in transport networks; difficult pricing decisions for road use, parking, and transit fares; and finally, local taxes and user fees that makes the maintenance and development of the transport network financially sustainable (Staley and Moore 2008).

Traffic congestion in slowing down mobility represents a management failure on the part of city managers. Congestion has a double negative effect: It acts as a tax on productivity by tying down people and goods, and it often increases GHG emissions even for vehicles that would otherwise be performing satisfactorily. It is conceivable that mismanaged large cities may reach a level of congestion that negatively offsets the economic advantage of spatial concentration. In this case, these cities would stop growing. However, the positive economic effect of agglomeration must be very powerful to offset the chronic congestion of cities such as Bangkok and Jakarta that are still the economic engine of their region in spite of their chronic congestion.

Poor migrants moving to large cities often have difficulties in participating in the urban economy, either because their housing is located too far from the urban transport networks or because they cannot afford the cost of transit or motorized transport. It has been observed that some slums appear to be self-sufficient and that many slum dwellers are able just to walk to work. Some have argued that slum dwellers' lack of motorized mobility and inclination toward walking would constitute an advantage in terms of GHG emissions and should be emulated by higher-income groups. This argument is a cruel joke on the poor because their lack of mobility condemns them to live in large cities with all its costs but none of its benefits. The lack of mobility in many slums and in some badly located government housing projects constitutes a poverty trap rather than an advantage to be emulated in the future (Gauteng in South Africa being a case in point).

Although walking and cycling do constitute an indispensable transport mode in large cities, people using these modes should do it by choice, not because they are forced to do so by lack of access or affordability of other means of transport. Because mobility is a necessity for economic survival in large cities, a reduction of GHGs should not be made by reducing mobility and certainly not by preventing an increase in mobility for the poor. The reduction of the number of passenger kilometers traveled (PKmT) should not be targeted for reduction to reduce GHG emissions. To the contrary, because of the lack of mobility of a large number of poor people living in large cities, PKmT should increase in the future. Various alternative solutions to decrease GHG emissions while increasing PKmT are discussed.

Identifying Key Parameters in Urban Transport GHG Emission Sources

GHG emissions from transport are produced by trips that can be divided into three broad categories:

1. Commuting trips

2. Noncommuting trips

3. Freight

Commuting trips are the trips taken to go from residence to work and back. In most low-income cities, commuting trips constitute the majority of trips using a motorized vehicle (with exceptions in some East Asian cities where nonmotorized trips still constitute a large number of commuting trips). Noncommuting trips are trips whose purpose is other than going to work, for instance, trips to schools, to shops, or to visit family or other personal reasons.

In high-income countries, commuting trips constitute only a fraction of total trips. For instance, in the United States, commuting trips represented 40 percent of all motorized trips in 1956; in 2005, they represented only slightly less than 20 percent of all motorized trips (Pisarski 2006). In low-income cities, most of these trips involve short distances and are using nonmotorized transport. When noncommuting trips become more numerous and longer they tend to be made via individual cars or motorcycles because destinations are not spatially concentrated and transit networks cannot easily accommodate them. For instance, in New York City in 2005, transit was used for 30.8 percent of all commuting trips but only for 9.6 percent of all commuting and noncommuting trips (O'Toole 2008).

Freight trips, including public vehicle travel and urban goods and services travel, constitute a sizable portion of all trips but vary significantly between cities. Because freight trips within urban areas are always done by individual vehicle and cannot use transit, these trips are adversely affected by road congestion, which results in significant costs to the economy of cities.

Will the trends observed in the United States anticipate what will happen in other parts of the world when these cities reach a level of income comparable to that of the United States today? This appears unlikely because of differences in city density between the United States and other parts of the world. Most cities outside the United States have a density far higher than U.S. cities, often by two orders of magnitude. Although densities of large cities tend to decrease over time, the decrease is slow and is unlikely to ever reach the low density of U.S. cities. It is probable that in high-density cities noncommuting trips will largely use nonmotorized transportation, taxis, or transit, as is the case in high-density Manhattan today.

Analysis in this research will therefore concentrate on emissions from commuting trips because these trips are the most common type in low- and middle-income cities. In addition, commuting trips require the most capital investment because of the transport capacity required during peak hours. Commuting trips often define a transport network whereas the other types of trips, including freight, piggy-back onto the transport investments made initially for commuting trips.

In East Asia, commuting trips, using walking or bicycles, constituted the majority of commuting trips in the 1980s and 1990s. During the past 20 years, because of the physical expansion of cities and increase in floor space consumption due to rising incomes, the share of nonmotorized transport has unfortunately been shrinking. In 2006, for instance, the share of nonmotorized commuting trips has been reduced to about 20 percent in Shanghai from about 75 percent in the early 1980s.

Disaggregating Commuting Trips by Mode

Commuting trips can be disaggregated into three modes: nonmotorized mode (walking and cycling, and increasingly included in this category, people working at home and telecommuting); motorized self-operated vehicles (SOVs), including motorcycles and private cars (car pools included); and transit mode (minibuses, buses, bus rapid transit [BRT], light rail, subways, and suburban rail). The types of vehicles used in the last two modes vary enormously in emission performance. In addition, within each mode—SOV and transit— each city has a fleet of vehicles, which have a wide range of GHG emissions performance. Comparisons between vehicles often differ by orders of magnitude depending on technology, maintenance, age of vehicle, energy source, and load (the average number of passengers per vehicle). To see more clearly the impact of different transport strategies on the reduction of GHG emissions, we have built a simple model linking the various vehicle fleet parameters to GHG emissions per commuter. The model is limited to analyzing CO_2 emissions from commuting trips, which are still the most common motorized trips in low- and middle-income cities. For each mode, the inputs of the model are the following:

1. The percentage of commuters using the mode

2. The average commuting distance (in kilometers)

3. The CO_2 equivalent (CO_2e) emission per vehicle kilometer traveled (VKmT), calculated for full life cycle when data available

4. The load factor per type of vehicle

Numerous publications provide GHG emissions expressed in grams of CO_2 per PKmT (table 4.1). However, the data assume a passenger load to calculate the CO_2 per PKmT. Because the load is a crucial parameter in the model, it has been necessary to calculate the CO_2 emissions per VKmT. However, fuel consumption may vary for the same vehicle, depending on the load; therefore, load and fuel consumption are not completely independent variables. We have therefore slightly adjusted the energy consumption values by VKmT to reflect this. A more sophisticated model would establish more accurately the relationship between load and fuel consumption for each type of vehicle. For demonstration purposes of the proposed methodology, results were found to be robust enough to allow this simplification. The equation used in the model showing the daily GHG emissions as a function of the number of passengers using different modes, with different average commuting distances, load factor, and engine fuel performance, is presented in the annex.

Based on the equation given in the annex, it can be shown that trying to reduce the average commuting distance per day (variable D)—de facto reducing labor mobility—would not provide much effect on Q (GHG emissions per day) compared with a change in vehicle fleet performance (variable E), a mode shift (variable P), or an increase in the load factor (variable L). As seen in table 4.1, the possible values taken by E vary by a factor of four between a hybrid diesel

TABLE 4.1
GHG Emissions for Various Vehicles with
Various Passenger Load Assumptions

Vehicle type	Grams of CO_2 per passenger mile	Grams of CO_2 per passenger kilometer
SUV	416	258
Average U.S. car	366	227
Motor buses	221	137
Light rail	179	111
Commuter rail	149	93
Hybrid gas	147	91
Toyota Prius	118	73
Hybrid diesel	101	63
Metro	94	58
New York MTA	73	45
New York subway	58	36

Source: Demographia 2005; EIU 2008; O'Toole 2008.

Note: MTA = Metropolitan Transportation Authority.

and an SUV, and by a factor of two between the New York City subway and a Toyota Prius! By contrast, land-use changes might, at best, reduce average commuting distance *D* by 5 to 10 percent within a minimum period of 20 years. This model, which could be used as a rough policy tool, was tested for parameters for New York City and Mexico City. The inputs and outputs of the model using New York City parameters in 2000 are shown in table 4.2.

The model shows the difference of performance in terms of GHG emissions between transit and cars in New York City: Emissions per car passenger per year are nearly six times more than the emissions per transit passengers. The model allows testing of the impact of alternative strategies; for instance, what would be the impact of an increase of hybrid cars over the total number of cars, everything else staying constant? Or what would be the impact of an increase in transit passengers, or in the load factor of buses, and so on? Table 4.3 shows the impact of two alternatives in reducing GHG emissions.

Table 4.3 demonstrates the potential impact in New York City of a change in the composition of the car fleet and, alternatively, a mode shift from cars to transit. The changes concern only the value of variable *P* in the model's equation. The current situation in 2005 is shown in column A. In column B, an increase from 0.5 to 19 percent in the number of commuters using hybrid cars, representing about one out of five cars used by commuters, bring a 28 percent reduction in GHG emissions. In column C, a mode shift from car to transit, raising the share of transit from 36 percent of commuters to 46 percent, decreases GHG

TABLE 4.2
Input and Output of GHG Emissions for New York City

Mode / Symbol	Average distance per passenger per commuting trip	Number of commuters per mode	Percent of commuters per mode	Grams of CO_2e per VKmT	Load factor of vehicle	Load factor as % of total vehicle capacity	Grams of CO_2e per PKmT	Total tons of CO_2 emitted by commuters per day
Units	Km	people	%	gr CO_2e	people	%	gr CO_2e	T CO_2e
	D	Pn	P	E	L	L/Ca %	gr CO_2e	Qi
Walk	2.5	470,000	5	—	1	100	—	—
Cycle	5.0	94,000	1	—	1	50	—	—
Car (gasoline)	19.0	4,324,000	46.0	375	1.63	33	230	37,802
Car (diesel)	19.0	47,000	0.5	256	1.63	33	157	281
Car (hybrid)	19.0	47,000	0.5	105	1.63	33	64	115
Car (electric)	19.0	—	0	163	1.63	33	100	—
Motorcycle 2-stroke	8.0	94,000	1	119	1.1	55	108	163
Minibus gasoline	20.0	—	0	720	7	58	103	—
Minibus diesel	20.0	—	0	600	7	58	86	—
Bus diesel	20.0	564,000	6	1,000	30	50	33	752
Bus natural gas	20.0	1,128,000	12	1,200	30	50	40	1,805
Rail transit	20.0	2,632,000	28	3,950	110	73	36	3,781
		9,400,000	100				Tons per day	Q = 44,698

Total transit   46

Number of people in New York City MSA	*14,687,500*	Kg/per year per commuter	1,240
E/P ratio (%)	64	Kg/year by transit passenger	38
Number of commuting days per year	*261*	Kg/year by Car passenger	2,217

Source: Authors' analysis.

Note: Total number of commuters (*T*) = 9,400,000. Figures in italics are input of the model, other figures are output. MSA = metropolitan statistical area; PKmT = passenger kilometer traveled; VKmT = vehicle kilometer traveled.

Table 4.3
Potential Impact of Vehicle Shift and Mode Shift on GHG Emissions in New York City Metropolitan Area

i	Mode / Symbol	(A) P	(B) P	(B) Change in CO_2e emissions	(C) P	(C) Change in CO_2e emissions
1	Walk	5%	5%		5%	
2	Cycle	1%	1%		1%	
3	Car (gasoline)	56%	37.5%	–33%	46%	–18%
4	Car (diesel)	0.5%	0.5%		0.5%	
5	Car (hybrid)	0.5%	19.0%	n.a.	0.5%	
6	Car (electric)	0%	0%		0%	
7	Motorcycle 2-stroke	1%	1%		1%	
8	Minibus gasoline	0%	0%		0%	
9	Minibus diesel	0%	0%		0%	
10	Bus diesel	5%	5%		6%	20%
11	Bus natural gas	10%	10%		12%	20%
12	Rail transit	21%	21%		28%	33%
	Tons per day	51,545	36,918		44,698	–13%
	Kilograms per year per commuter	1,418	1,024	–28%	1,240	–13%

Source: Authors' analysis.

Note: n.a. = not available.

emissions by 13 percent. Further reductions could be achieved by introducing hybrid buses or increasing loads of both cars and transit.

The use of the model allows a back-of-the-envelope calculation of the impact of potential changes in technology and transport mode on GHG emissions. The model does not have anything to say about the feasibility or the probability of such a change to occur. Although the rough calculations shown imply that the combined impacts of technology change and mode shift could be large, how to achieve these changes remains the main problem to be solved. Most of the vehicle technology, such as hybrid engines, that reduces fuel consumption has been around for at least 10 years. Rail transit using electricity has been common in large cities for more than 100 years. The fact that in many cities the use of transit represents a minority mode raises important questions about consumer preferences for urban transport. The transport mode split for New York City in 2005 shown in table 4.2 represents a state of equilibrium. It is important to know what factors could change this equilibrium to a new state that would be more favorable for GHG reductions.

Consumers' Demand for Transport

The loss of transit share over the past few decades in most of the world's major cities has to be acknowledged. Even in Singapore transit mode share declined from 55 percent of commuters in 1990 to 52.4 percent in 2000[3] (Singapore Department of Statistics 2000). This decrease is striking because Singapore has had the most consistent transport policy over two decades favoring transit, including strict limits on car ownership, and has been a world pioneer for congestion pricing using advanced technology. In addition, Singapore has always had excellent coordination between land use and transport investments. Although the preceding section has shown that there is an overwhelming case for increasing transit mode to reduce GHG emissions, consumer choice seems to follow the opposite trends. It is therefore important to understand why transit is losing ground in so many cities and what alternative strategies exist and in which type of cities the trend could possibly be reversed.

Consumers' decisions to use one mode of transport over others depend on three main factors:

1. Cost

2. Speed

3. Convenience, as determined by frequency and reliability of service and comfort

For low-income commuters, the cost of transport is the major consideration. For very low-income commuters, walking is often the only affordable option, which significantly lowers their ability to take advantage of the large labor market offered by large cities. In Mumbai, for instance, about 4 million people walk to work every day (about 45 percent of the active population). Middle- and low-income users above extreme poverty are the prime customers for transit, as buying and maintaining a car is beyond the means of most of these, although subsidized fares frequently exist to make transit more affordable. However, in numerous middle- and high-income countries, some cities retain a significant number of transit users who are middle or high income—for instance, Hong Kong, London, New York City, Paris, and Singapore, among others. How these cities have managed to maintain a high use of transit among affluent households will be described in the next section.

In an increasing number of cities in low- or middle-income countries, the dispersion of employment makes it inconvenient to use transit, because no transit route goes directly to their location of employment. For those commuters who cannot afford to use individual cars or motorcycles, the most convenient options are collective taxis or minibuses. Commuting by microbuses at the expense of transit has become the dominant transport mode in Gauteng, Mexico City, and Tehran, for instance. As households' income increases, the speed of transport and convenience become more important factors than cost, or rather, higher-income commuters give a higher value to the time spent commuting than do lower-income ones. Speed of transport is limited in most transit system by frequent stops and the time required for transfers. In city structures where a car is a feasible alternative mode of transport, commuters who can afford the cost would normally switch to individual cars.

The exhaustive study conducted by Pisarski (2006) on commuting characteristics in U.S. cities gives an order of magnitude of the speed difference between transit and individual cars in those cities (figure 4.3). The average commuting distance is about the same between the different modes except for walking, cycling, and rail transport. One can see that in spite of the congestion prevalent in most U.S. cities, commuting time by transit requires about double the time required by individual cars. Travel time for car pooling when involving

Figure 4.3 Average Travel Time in U.S. Cities by Transport Mode

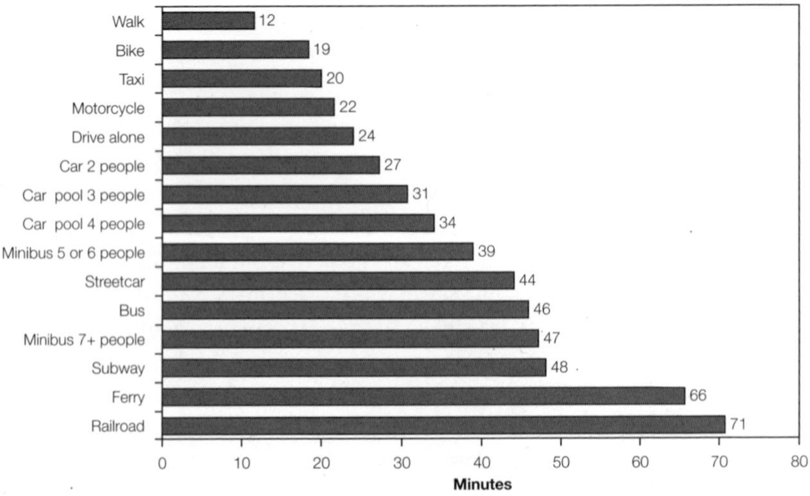

Source: Pisarski 2006.

more than four people becomes similar to transit. This explains in great part the loss of transit share in U.S. cities in the past two decades.

In Singapore, with one of the most efficient transit systems in the world, the ratio of transit travel time to car driving time is lower than in U.S. cities. However, the difference in travel time is significant enough (see table 4.4) to indicate that transit would not be a first-choice transport mode for people who can afford an alternative. The high speed of car commuting is, of course, part of the success of Singapore's transport strategy. Congestion pricing, constantly adjusted to facilitate fluid traffic, ensures high speed for all car commuters who can afford the high premium paid for car ownership and for congestion tolls.

The challenge is to propose urban transport strategies that would result in reducing GHG emissions while maintaining mobility as reflected by commuters' mode preference. These different strategies would have to be adapted to different spatial forms of urban growth—monocentric, polycentric, high and low densities—and to a context of increasing urban income and a decreasing cost of car acquisition. These strategies will have to rely on the three tools available to urban managers: pricing, regulations, and land-use policy.

Energy Pricing, GHG Emissions, and Market-Based Incentives

As discussed earlier, a significant reduction in GHG in urban transport could be achieved in two ways: technological change to reduce carbon content per VKmT and transport-mode shift from private car to transit. As alluded to earlier, the pricing of energy based on its carbon content is an indispensable policy instrument to trigger these changes to reduce GHGs in the long run. The pricing of energy based on carbon content could be achieved through a carbon tax or through "cap and trade." The merit of each approach is discussed next.

TABLE 4.4
Singapore: Travel Time by Transport Mode

Mode	Median travel time (minutes)	Distance (kilometers)	Speed (kilometers/hour)
Car	27	29.2	65
Metro	41	11.5	17
Metro + bus	51		
Bus alone	38		

Source: Singapore Department of Statistics 2000.

In each city the current use of low-carbon technology and the ratio between transit and car commuting is reflecting an equilibrium state between supply and demand. Any change in technology or transport-mode share will require a move to a new state of equilibrium in the economy of transport. Significantly higher gasoline prices, as experienced in 2008, temporarily modified this state of equilibrium. Demand for transit increased and VKmT decreased. However, as long as renewable energy sources were not available at a competitive price, the high price of oil made it cheaper to generate electricity from coal or shale oil. Electricity is used mostly as a source of energy for rail transit, but electrical cars that would recharge their batteries from the electricity grid will use it increasingly. Electricity produced by coal-burning power plants generates twice as much GHG per kilojoule than power plants using natural gas. Without a system of pricing energy based on its carbon content, higher oil and natural gas prices could increase GHG emissions rather than reducing them by shifting electricity generation to coal-fueled power plants.

However, carbon pricing cannot be decided at the local level and is dependent on national policy and increasingly on international agreements. It must be acknowledged that these policy instruments will have a limited impact in the absence of carbon pricing.

Various policy instruments are currently available to reduce GHG emissions due to urban transport. Their effectiveness is often limited by the quality of national and local governance, as well as a city's income distribution and spatial structure. Policy instruments can be divided among three principal categories:

1. Regulatory instruments, such as limitations on the number of vehicles on the road on a given day (for example, Beijing, Bogota, and Mexico City *pico y placa* (peak and [license] plate) and limitation on the number of cars registered in the city (for example, Singapore car quota system)

2. Pricing instruments modifying relative prices between private car and transit modes, such as road pricing: fixed tolls and congestion pricing (for example, London, Singapore, and Stockholm); a fuel tax, which needs to be compared with an increase in the price of a barrel of oil due to oil market evolution (for example, Bogota, Singapore, Chicago, and most other U.S. cities); transit fare subsidies (for example, Los Angeles and San Francisco); and pricing and taxing of parking (for example, Edinburgh, New York City, Peterborough, and Sheffield)

3. Investment in transport infrastructure in order to increase and improve the supply of transit modes (for example, Bogota, Jakarta, and Singapore)

Regulatory Instruments

Regulatory instruments aiming at mode shift from car to transit are generally not effective because the choice of a transport mode must be demand driven. Regulatory instruments aiming to limit or reduce car ownership and car usage could seriously limit mobility in the absence of adequate investments in transit to replace the decrease in car trips. The example of Singapore in fixing a quota for car growth is rather unique. It could have been very disruptive to the economy if the government had not simultaneously been able to finance and develop a very effective transit system consistent with its land-use policy. This important aspect will be developed later.

In countries with high economic inequality (such as Colombia or Mexico), policies such as *pico y placa*[4] create an incentive for higher-income households to buy a second car. This second car is often a secondhand car with worse engine performance than most recent models. As a result, the *pico y placa* policy has often resulted in worse pollution and higher GHG emissions than the status quo ante. The availability of a new type of low-cost car—the Tata Nano, for example—could make this policy even more ineffective.

Pricing Instruments

Pricing instruments are normally aimed at pricing transport at its real economic price (Button 1993; Goodwin, Dargay, and Hanly 2004). When this can be achieved, it removes the distortions that hidden subsidies introduce in resource allocation. Congestion pricing and parking pricing, for instance, aim at adjusting the price of using a highway or of a parking space to reflect its real economic value, including externalities due to congestion (Luk 1999). The aim of economic pricing is not to be punitive but to seek a more efficient allocation of resources. Pricing instruments also include subsidies, which have a different aim than economic pricing. Subsidies aim at being redistributive. For instance, most transit fares are heavily subsidized.[5] Transit-fare subsidies are aiming at increasing the mobility of low-income households, allowing them to fully participate in a unified metropolitan labor market.

It is tempting also to use transit-fare subsidies as a financial incentive to convince car commuters to switch to transit. This is not a very effective way to increase transit-mode share in the long run. The subvention for transit operation and maintenance often comes from local government budget allocation. The larger the number of users, the larger the subsidies required. This works as a reverse incentive for the transit operator to improve services. In the long run, the subsidies paid by the government to the transit authority usually fall short of the real cost of operation and maintenance, resulting in a deterioration of service. An example of this problem came to light during the latest financial crisis in the United States. Local governments, because of increasing deficits, were obliged to scale down transit services, including frequency, right at the moment when the high price of fuel and declining households' income were forcing some commuters to switch from car to transit commuting.

Transit-fare subsidies, when they exist, should be targeted to low-income households or to the unemployed. Transit-fare subsidies directed to the affluent are in fact a transfer payment made by government to commuters for not polluting instead of charging car commuters for the externalities they cause.

Pricing instruments reflecting real economic costs have a value in themselves because they contribute to better allocation of resources. However, they do not necessarily change consumer behavior. For instance, a toll charge on a highway may not reduce congestion if it is set too low. Congestion pricing, as practiced in Singapore, involves increasing tolls until the desired decrease in congestion is achieved. Congestion pricing consists of increasing or decreasing prices until equilibrium between supply and demand is reached. Congestion pricing does not aim at recovering the cost of a highway, but at limiting traffic volume to obtain a desired speed.

Pricing parking at the market price is equivalent to congestion pricing: The operator will increase the price of parking until all the parking spaces are filled. In New York City, the municipality taxes a private parking space at 18 percent of the daily rate paid (in addition to the property tax and business tax). In this way, the municipality recovers a share of the private market rate without having to set a municipal parking rate. The transaction cost of recovering the rate from consumers and adjusting it to the market price is paid by the private operator. Taxing privately operated parking garages might be a more effective way of recovering an area-wide congestion fee than the way it is currently recovered in London.

Congestion pricing is not always possible. It requires technology investment that may be expensive to install and operate, and the high transaction cost may greatly reduce the income of the operator. In some cases, congestion pricing is not politically acceptable. For instance, it would be difficult to increase or decrease the transit fare every hour depending on the number of commuters boarding at any given time.

In the case in which congestion pricing is not feasible, the effectiveness of increasing or decreasing prices (that is, changing prices to increase or decrease demand) depends on the price elasticity of demand. The price elasticity of demand depends on numerous factors and can be measured from empirical experience, but it cannot be calculated in advance without empirical data. Various factors affect how much a change in prices impacts travel demand for a given travel mode: type of price change, type of trip, type of traveler, quantity and price of alternative options, and time period (short term [one year] and long term [5–10 years]).

Nearly all studies assume that the effects of a reduction are equal and opposite to the effects of an increase or, in other words, that elasticity is "symmetrical" (Goodwin, Dargay, and Hanly 2004). Empirical evidence suggests that this assumption might not be true. However, because of the number of factors affecting elasticity, it is often difficult to extrapolate with certainty results from one city to another in the absence of an empirical local database. With this caveat, available data from the literature on the price elasticity of demand in urban transport are reviewed. The current literature on price elasticity in transports could be summarized as follows:

- Long-run elasticities are greater than short run ones, mostly by factors of 2 to 3 (Goodwin, Dargay, and Hanly 2004).
- Fuel consumption elasticities to fuel price are greater than traffic elasticities, mostly by factors of 1.5 to 2.0 (Goodwin, Dargay, and Hanly 2004).
- Motorists appear to be particularly sensitive to parking prices. Compared with other out-of-pocket expenses, parking fees are found to have a greater effect on vehicle trips, typically by a factor of 1.5 to 2.0 (Gordon, Lee, and Richardson 2004): A $1 per trip parking charge is likely to cause the same reduction in vehicle travel as a fuel price increase that averages $1.50 to $2.00 per trip.
- Shopping and leisure trips elasticities are greater than commuting trip elasticities. Although we can reduce or avoid travel or the need to travel for shopping, we are more likely to continue traveling to commute.
- Road pricing and tolls effects depend on the pricing mechanism design. Luk (1999) estimates that toll elasticities in Singapore are −0.19 to −0.58, with an average of −0.34. Singapore may be unique; the high cost of car ownership constitutes a very high sunk cost, which may tend to make travel less sensitive to price.
- Transit price effects are significant: Balcombe and others (2004) calculate that bus fare elasticities average around −0.4 in the short run, −0.56 in the medium run, and 1.0 over the long run, whereas metro rail fare elasticities are −0.3 in the short run and −0.6 in the long run. Bus fare elasticities are lower during peak (−0.24) than off-peak (−0.51).

Carbon-Based Investment in Transport Infrastructure

Carbon-based investments in transport infrastructure face three main barriers: financial, institutional, and political. Carbon markets have been positioned as an economically efficient market-based incentive for answering these three barriers.

Today, however, their usage for cities, and even more for urban transportation, is limited for several reasons:

- Cities' participation in carbon markets is limited to flexibility mechanisms such as offset, voluntary, or Clean Development Mechanism (CDM)/Joint Implementation projects.
- These markets have been rarely used for promoting a more energy- and carbon-efficient urban transportation pattern: To date, 1,224 CDM projects have been registered by the UN Framework Convention on Climate Change Executive Board, and only two have been transportation projects, representing less than 0.13 percent of total CDM projects (the Bogota BRT TransMilenio and the Delhi subway regenerative breaking system).
- Carbon markets favor low-hanging fruit projects, which do not have the greatest potential to reduce GHG emissions: The majority of the CDM transportation projects accepted or proposed claim their emission reductions through switching fuels used. Some entail improvements of vehicle efficiency through a different kind of motor or better vehicle utilization. Few projects deal with modal shift, and none involves a reduction of the total transportation activities.

Given these barriers, two questions must be addressed. The first is, How and why are carbon markets biased against projects targeting urban transportation? Several explanations can be explored:

1. CDM and transport projects differ widely in terms of challenges and opportunities. There is a scale gap between the two realities in which the main leaders of each project evolve:
   a. (Local) transport projects aim to change the city and make it economically attractive. Challenges include involving all stakeholders in the decision-making process.
   b. (International) challenges for CDM projects are technical (convincing CDM executive boards and international experts) and financial.

2. Diffuse emissions, such as in the transportation sector, are costly to aggregate, thus the CDM "act and gain money" incentive has rather limited effects.

3. Classic CDM challenges are particularly vexing for the transport sector:
   a. Defining project boundaries, because of complex up- and downstream leakages.
   b. Establishing a reliable baseline, when behavioral parameters are key.
   c. Implementing a reliable monitoring methodology, because data generation is costly.

The consequences of this bias are that transport and CDM projects are conducted in parallel; without interaction, cities outsource CDM projects to international experts and organizations without much involvement; and CDM project-based design is missing the main GHG reduction opportunities. Thus, within their existing framework, carbon markets can be used as a source of funding significant only at the local level to do the following:

- Subsidize (and reduce) transit fares.
- Finance intermodality infrastructures and thus facilitate modal shift.
- Finance well-bounded technology-oriented CDM projects, such as changes in fuels and technology, optimization of the balance between bus supply and demand, traffic-light systems, and more generally, new information technologies for vehicle or system operations. These well-bounded, technology-oriented CDM projects could be levered by bundling them through the newly existing programmatic CDM.

The second question asks: How could the design of carbon markets evolve to be more "urban transportation friendly"? In the perspective of the post-2012 transportation sector, a unanimous call is heard for changes in the carbon markets' design. Many important opportunities for transportation emission reductions would not easily fit into an individual CDM project. Various propositions are under discussion:

1. A sectoral policy-based approach crediting new green policy or enforcement of standards. A sectoral approach would not reduce methodological difficulties. Its advantages would rather be to scale activities up to a level that is equal to the scale of the challenges faced in redirecting transport into a more sustainable direction.

2. Cities' commitment to reduce GHG emissions and a "No Loose Target" approach.

3. Registries including National Appropriate Mitigation Actions for cities and the urban transportation sector.

4. Integrate Global Environment Fund and Official Development Assistance in CDM funding, notably to finance transaction costs, to fund capacity-building activities, and to generate data.

In brief, a broader and flexible approach, based on a bottom-up mechanism, would do the following:

- Foster cities to take the lead on GHG emissions reduction strategies (financial and electoral motivations)
- Give cities incentives to act for the short term (low-hanging fruits) as well as for the long term and, thus, change the urban development trajectory

- Leave intact their ability to create and implement solutions that are relevant and palatable with local specificities—for example, to implement land-use policies that increase the floor area ratio (FAR) in CBDs or transport policies that modify the relative prices of different transport modes

Urban Spatial Structures and Transport Mode

Price and speed are not the only determinant of consumers' choice for transport mode; urban spatial structures play a major role in determining the type of transport that is likely to be the most convenient. Urban structures are defined by the spatial distribution of population densities within a metropolitan area and by the pattern of daily trips. Depending on a city's spatial structure, commuters may be able to switch from car to transit, or their choices may be limited between individual cars, minibuses, and collective taxis. In high-density cities, sidewalks and cycle lanes could be designed in such a way as not to discourage walking and cycling. Although urban structures do evolve with time, their evolution is slow and can seldom be shaped by design. The larger the city, the less it is amenable to change its structure. However, it is important for urban managers to identify the opportunities present in their city and to take full advantage of them to reduce GHG emissions with transport strategies consistent with their spatial structures. Identified next are the most common types of spatial structures and the transport strategies that would have the most chances of success for each type of spatial structure.

Type of Urban Spatial Structures and Choice of Transport Modes

Urban economists have studied the spatial distribution of population densities intensively since the pioneering work of Alonso (1964), Mills (1970), and Muth (1969, 1985), which developed the classical monocentric urban density model. Empirical evidence shows that in most cities, whether they are polycentric or monocentric, the spatial distribution of densities follows the classical model predicted by Alonso, Muth, and Mills (Bertaud and Malpezzi 2003).

The density profile of most large cities shows that the traditional monocentric city model is still a good predictor of density patterns. It also demonstrates that markets remain the most important force in allocating land, in spite of many distortions to prices due to direct and indirect subsidies and ill-conceived land-use regulations. The profile of the population densities of 12 cities on four continents (figure 4.4) shows that in spite of their economic and cultural differences, markets play an important role in shaping the distribution of population around their centers. All the cities shown in figure 4.4 follow closely the

Figure 4.4 Distribution of Population Densities in 12 Cities

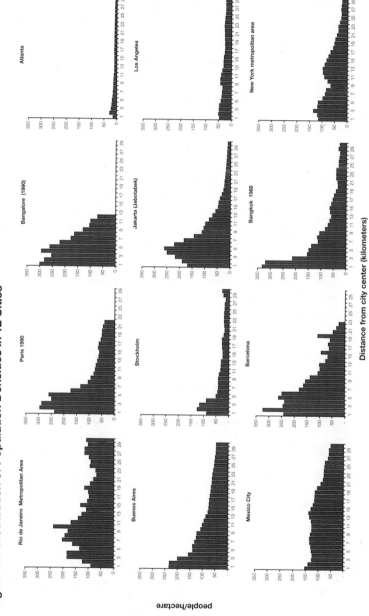

Source: Bertaud 2006.

negative sloped gradient predicted by the classical monocentric urban model, although several cities in the samples are definitely polycentric (Atlanta, Mexico City, Portland, and Rio de Janeiro). The density profile indicates that some parts of metropolitan areas are incompatible with transit. In areas where residential densities fall below 50 people per hectare, the operation of transit is ineffective.

Land use and the transport network determine the pattern of daily trips taken by workers to commute to work. As income increases, noncommuting trips—trips to shopping centers, to take children to school, to visit relatives, or to take leisure trips—become more important. The proportion of commuting trips in relation to other types of trips is constantly decreasing.

Figure 4.5 illustrates in a schematic manner the most usual trip patterns in metropolitan areas. In monocentric cities (figure 4.5A) where most jobs and amenities are concentrated in the CBD, transit is the most convenient transport mode because most commuters travel from the suburbs to the CBD. The origin of trips might be dispersed, but the CBD is the most common trip destination. Small collector buses can bring commuters to the radials, where BRT or an underground metro can bring them at high speed to the CBD. Monocentric cities are usually dense (density more than 100 people per hectare).

In polycentric cities (figure 4.5B), few jobs and amenities are located in the center, and most trips are from suburbs to suburbs. Although a very large

Figure 4.5 Urban Trip Patterns in Monocentric and Polycentric Cities

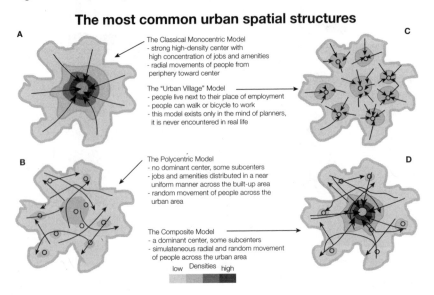

The most common urban spatial structures

A

The Classical Monocentric Model
- strong high-density center with high concentration of jobs and amenities
- radial movements of people from periphery toward center

The "Urban Village" Model
- people live next to their place of employment
- people can walk or bicycle to work
- this model exists only in the mind of planners, it is never encountered in real life

C

B

The Polycentric Model
- no dominant center, some subcenters
- jobs and amenities distributed in a near uniform manner across the built-up area
- random movement of people across the urban area

D

The Composite Model
- a dominant center, some subcenters
- simulateneous radial and random movement of people across the urban area

low Densities high

Source: Bertaud 2006.

number of travel routes are possible, most will have few passengers per route. The trips have dispersed origins and dispersed destinations. In this type of city structure, individual means of transportation or collective taxis are more convenient for users. Mass transit is difficult and expensive to operate because of the multiplicity of destinations and the few passengers per route. Polycentric cities usually have low densities because the use of individual cars does not allow or require much concentration in any specific location.

Figure 4.5C shows the so-called urban village model that is often shown in urban master plans but does not exist in the real world. In this model, there are many centers, but commuters travel only to the center that is the closest to their residence. This is a very attractive model for urban planners because it does not require much transportation or roads and it dramatically reduces VKmT and PKmT and, as a consequence, GHG emissions. According to this model, everybody could walk or bicycle to work even in a very large metropolis. The hypothesis behind this model is that urban planners are able to perfectly match work places and residences! This model does not exist in reality because it contradicts the economic justification of large cities. Employers do not select their employees on the basis of their place of residence, and specialized workers in large cities do not select jobs on the basis of their proximity from their residence (with the exception of the very poor who walk to work and are limited to work within a radius of about 5 kilometers from their home). The "urban village model" implies a systematic fragmentation of labor markets, which would be economically unsustainable in the real world.

The five satellite towns built around Seoul are an example of the urban village conceit. When the towns were built, the number of jobs in each town was carefully balanced with the number of inhabitants, with the assumptions that these satellite towns would be self-contained in terms of housing and employment. Subsequent surveys are showing that most people living in the new satellite towns commute to work to the main city, and most jobs in the satellite towns are taken by people living in the main city.

The "composite model" shown in figure 4.5D is the most common type of urban spatial structure. It contains a dominant center, but a large number of jobs are also located in the suburbs. In this type of city most trips from the suburbs to the CBD will be made by mass transit, whereas trips from suburb to suburb will use individual cars, motorcycles, collective taxis, or minibuses. The composite model is, in fact, an intermediary stage in the progressive transformation of a monocentric city into a polycentric one. As the city population grows and the built-up area expands, the city center becomes more congested and progressively loses its main attraction. The original raison d'être of the CBD was its easy accessibility by all the workers and easy communication within the center itself because of spatial concentration.

As a city grows, the progressive decay of the center because of congestion is not unavoidable. Good traffic management, timely transit investment, strict parking regulations and market price of off-street parking, investments in urban environment (pedestrian streets), and changes in land-use regulations allowing vertical expansion would contribute to reinforce the center, to make it attractive to new business, and to keep it as a major trip destination. These measures have been taken with success in New York City, Shanghai, and Singapore, for instance. However, the policy coordination between investments and regulations is often difficult to implement. This coordination has to be carried out consistently for a long period to have an impact on the viability of urban centers. Failure to expand the role of traditional city centers through infrastructure and amenities investments weakens transit systems in the long run because the number of jobs in the center becomes stagnant or even decreases while all additional jobs are created in suburban areas.

The comparison between the distributions of population in Jakarta (Jabotabek) and Gauteng (figure 4.6) explains why Jakarta is able to successfully

Figure 4.6 Spatial Distribution of Population in Jakarta and Gauteng Represented at the Same Scale

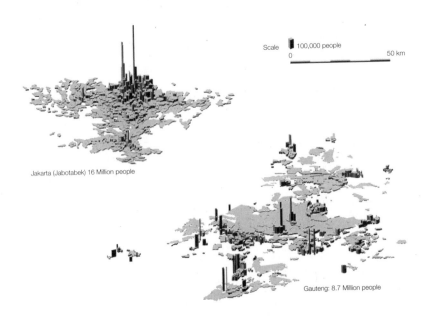

Scale ▊ 100,000 people
0   50 km

Jakarta (Jabotabek) 16 Million people

Gauteng: 8.7 Million people

Source: 2001 census.

implement a BRT network in addition to the existing suburban rail network, whereas in Gauteng suburban rail is carrying barely 8 percent of commuters, and the great majority of low-income commuters rely on microbuses. The dispersion of population in Gauteng is due in part to its history of apartheid. In the past 10 years, a very successful subsidized housing program has contributed to further disperse low-income people in distant suburbs while significantly attenuating the extreme poverty created by apartheid. The comparison as seen on the three-dimensional representation of population densities between the resulting city structure of Gauteng and that of Jakarta is striking. A BRT is being planned for the municipality of Johannesburg (one of the municipalities in the Gauteng metropolitan region), but the current urban structure will make it difficult to operate for a long time. In addition, the violent opposition of microbus operators is making the project politically difficult. A change in transit mode involves a new equilibrium of transit types, which creates losers as well as winners. This is not an easy process, even when the final long-range outcome seems desirable for all.

The structure of cities is path dependent. Once a city is dominantly polycentric, it is nearly impossible to return to a monocentric structure. Monocentric cities, by contrast, can become polycentric through the decay of their traditional center. The inability to adapt land-use regulations, to manage traffic, and to operate an efficient transit system are the three main factors that explain the decay of traditional CBDs.

Transport Strategies Need to Be Consistent with Cities' Spatial Structures

Findings concerning the relationship between urban spatial structures and transit can be summarized as follows:

- Transit is efficient when trips' origins are dispersed but destinations are concentrated.
- Individual transport and microbuses are more efficient when origin and destinations of trips are both dispersed and for linked trips if amenities are dispersed.
- Mode shift toward transit will happen only if price and speed are competitive with other modes.
- Trips toward dense downtown areas (more than 150 people/ha) should be prevalently made by transit. Failure to provide efficient transit service to the CBD and to regulate traffic and parking would result in a dispersion of jobs in suburban areas, making transit inefficient as a primary means of transport in the long term.

The question to be answered is then: Is it possible to have a land-use and traffic policy to reinforce commuting destination concentration and enabling transit to be competitive with car trips?

Two cities are maintaining a high ratio of transit trips: Singapore with 52.4 percent of total commuting trips (Singapore Department of Statistics 2000) and New York City with 36 percent. Their performance is particularly intriguing because these two cities have a high-income population, and higher-income households are less likely to use transit than lower-income ones. By contrast, Mexico City, with a density more than twice that of New York City, has only 24 percent of commuters using transit. It implies that both New York City and Singapore have long had successful policies to keep such a large number of commuters using transit. Are these examples replicable in lower-income cities with less performing governance?

New York City, Singapore, and the Counterexample of Mumbai

This section reviews the policies of New York City and Singapore, comparing these with the counterexample of Mumbai, where transit is the dominant commuting mode but where city managers try to disperse jobs and housing

New York City

The high ratio of transit trips in New York City is the result of a deliberate policy of spatial concentration and diversification of land use. The extremely high concentration of jobs is the most striking feature of the spatial structure of the New York City metropolitan area: 35 percent of the total number of jobs are concentrated in Manhattan, which represents only 0.9 percent of the total metropolitan area (53 square kilometers). Within Manhattan, four districts (19 square kilometers) have 27 percent of the jobs in the entire metropolitan area (population 15 million). This concentration did not happen by chance; it was the result of a deliberate regulatory policy, which was responding to the high market demand for floor space in Manhattan. The Midtown district reaches the astonishing density of 2,160 jobs per hectare! This extreme spatial concentration of people and jobs is extremely intellectually fertile, innovative, and productive, in spite of the management problems it poses for providing services in such a dense area.

The zoning regulations controlling FARs[6] is one of the main factors contributing to this concentration. The map of Manhattan regulatory FARs shows high FARs in the Midtown and Wall Street areas (FAR values ranging from 11 to

15). The pattern of high FARs shows that the regulations have been adjusted to demand as the two main business centers in Manhattan expanded over time. The zoning of Manhattan also allows a mix of zoning for office space, commerce, theaters, and housing. The mixed land use favors transit because it generates trips outside the traditional rush hours. Because of the theater districts, the subway and buses run late at night, making transit more convenient for workers who work different shifts. In a different setting of homogenous land use, those workers with schedules outside normal hours would have to commute with individual cars. The land use in Manhattan makes it possible for New York City transit to have a high passenger load, significantly reducing GHG emissions, as discussed earlier. The urban management initiatives taken in New York City that contribute to a high share of transit use and, as a consequence, to a lower GHG emission per capita include the following:

- High FAR responding to market demand
- Mixed land use in the CBD
- Encouraging amenities in or close to the CBD (museums, theaters, and universities)
- Providing the majority of parking off the street in privately operated parking areas charging market price, but also specially taxed by the municipality; a complementary strategy is progressive removal of most on-street parking except for loading and unloading
- Improving the transit system continually with a radial-concentric pattern of routes

Singapore

In Singapore, the transport sector was the second-largest contributor to CO_2 emissions in 2005. Efforts to mitigate GHG emissions have mainly concentrated on buildings, and the transport sector has received less attention. Unlike the United States and other OECD countries, where transport data are readily available, statistics on Singapore's transport sector and CO_2 emissions by mode are extremely difficult to locate.

Like New York City, Singapore is a highly dense, compact city. It has a land area of 700 square kilometers, accommodating a population of 5 million. The average density in the built-up area was about 110 people per hectare in 2000. Through comprehensive planning, Singapore has expanded its downtown and redistributed population throughout the city-state. Transport infrastructure is closely integrated with land use. Key infrastructure such as the airport, port, and network of expressways and mass rapid transit is planned and safeguarded in the city's long-term development plan to support a good living environment. The long-term planning frame gives the assurance that projected needs can be met within the city's limited land area. To keep Singapore economically vibrant, its transport planning is focused on access and mobility with emphasis on a transit-oriented and compact urban structure, vigorous restraint of private car ownership and usage, and strong commitment to public transport. Urban development has been increasingly planned in such a way as to reduce the need to travel and dependence on motorized vehicles.

At the neighborhood level, neighborhoods and their new towns are structured with a host of amenities and services that could be readily reached within a five-minute walk. Smart infrastructure design reduces the need for transportation. Public housing towns where 80 percent of the population lives are connected to one another and to the city by public transport, principally the mass rapid transit. At the city level, with the redistribution and growth of population in new towns in the suburbs, new growth centers have been planned in these regions in immediate proximity of the transit network to provide employment to the local population in concentrated areas, which are easily accessible by transit.

Decentralizing some economic activities to the dense regional centers helps bring numerous jobs closer to homes and facilitates linked trips using public transport. It also reduces the usual peak hour traffic congestion to and from the CBD. At the same time, these centers provide lower costs for businesses that do not require a central area address, supporting a competitive economy. Over the next 10 to 15 years, more regional centers will be developed.

To manage the usage of private cars, much focus is given to travel demand management, including a choice of transport mode and making public motorized transport more efficient. Singapore is one city that has actively promoted the use of public transport as a more sustainable way to travel. Strong policy measures have been implemented to discourage private car usage, including high vehicle and fuel taxation measures and parking management, vehicle quota systems, and congestion pricing. These deterrents are complemented by mode-shift strategies aimed at improving the public transport system and new solutions such as car sharing. Improvements to public transport involve the following:

- Expanding the system or service, such as extending the geographical coverage of the bus and rail networks, including an extensive rail network that has been planned to serve high-population areas
- Improving the operation of the system, such as mode transfer improvements, better coordination of schedules, through ticketing, and increased frequency
- Improving the service with increased vehicle comfort and bus shelter/rail station enhancements

The government continues to invest in the mass rapid transit network to improve its accessibility to the population as the city grows. It has announced an additional $14 billion investment to double the rail network from the present 138 to 278 kilometers by 2020, thus achieving a transit density of 51 kilometers per million people, comparable to that of New York City. To allow more rail usage, land use is intensified around the mass rapid transit stations, and mixed-use developments are encouraged.

One of the most crucial land-use decisions has been to develop a new downtown area adjacent to the existing CBD. To increase the accessibility of the new and current downtown, floor area ratios have been kept high (some lots have a FAR of 25, but the majority of FAR values are about 12). Once completed, this new downtown will reinforce the effectiveness of the radial-concentric metro system.

Mumbai

Mumbai, with a metropolitan population of 18 million people in 2001 and a density of about 390 people per hectare in the municipal built-up area, is both much denser and larger than Singapore or New York City. The transit mode share is evaluated at 71 percent of commuters using motorized travel (the number of people walking to work is estimated to be around 4 million). The main modes of transit are buses and two main lines of suburban train. Private cars, taxis, and rickshaws account for about 12 percent of commuting trips, and motorcycles 17 percent (Baker and others 2004).

Since 1964, Mumbai urban managers have tried to reduce congestion by reducing the number of people living in the city and by trying to disperse jobs and people in far-away suburbs or satellite towns such as Navi Mumbai. Strict control of the FAR, which was progressively reduced from an initial 4.5 in the CBD (Nariman Point) to the current 1.33, has been the main tool used to reach their dispersion objective. The objective was to promote a density reduction in the central areas of the city and a dispersion of jobs. In a certain way, Mumbai urban managers were trying to transform a dense monocentric Asian city into a "Los Angeles" model where jobs and population are dispersed randomly within the metropolitan area.

However, the suburban railway lines carrying 6.4 million commuters a day converge on the traditional CBD. The policy of reducing the FAR to promote dispersion did not succeed because it contradicted the pattern of accessibility established by the transit network. The highest demand for office space is still in Nariman Point, the traditional CBD. The price of office space in Nariman Point is about the same as the average in Manhattan. The number of passengers boarding and exiting at various suburban train stations shows that the two stations closest to Nariman Point handle most commuters. The map of maximum regulatory FARs completely contradicts demand as expressed by floor space price and the pattern of boarding and exiting railway stations. A FAR value of 1.33 imposed on the CBD of a dense city of 18 million people is completely unrealistic (as compared with 15, the value in New York City, and 25, the highest value in Singapore). The highest FAR values are 4 in the slum of Dharavi and in the new business center of Bandra-Kurla, which is not currently connected to the railway network, thus requiring a bus transfer to access it from the railway network. The railways are operating at full capacity with the existing tracks, and although new metro lines are being planned, it is without a clear spatial strategy for changing the current land-use regulations to adapt them to the new transport system and consumers' demand.

The very low FAR values in Mumbai have succeeded only in making land and floor space more expensive. Density has increased because location is everything in a large metropolis, but floor space consumption has decreased to one of the lowest in India (and probably in Asia).

The absence of a clear spatial strategy linking land use regulations, consumer demand, and the transport network has been the major failure of the urban management of Mumbai. The major lesson to be drawn from the Mumbai example is that designing cities through regulations without taking into account consumer demand does not achieve the desired results. If the strict low limit put on the FAR regulations had succeeded and jobs and population had dispersed, the impact on GHG emissions would have been disastrous. The current transit system, for all its flaws, would have been made less efficient because it would have not have been able to connect commuters to dispersed businesses. Motorcycles and minibuses would have become the most practical and efficient modes of transportation.

Summary of Measures in New York City and Singapore That Maintain a High Level of Transit Share

Singapore and New York City are succeeding in maintaining a high rate of transit use even among high-income populations. This strategy will contribute in the future in significantly lowering GHG emissions due to transport. It is useful to summarize the measures that have been taken by New York City and Singapore to maintain a high density of jobs and activities in their downtown areas:

- High FARs in the CBD (up to 15 in midtown Manhattan, up to 25 in Singapore)
- Physical expansion of the downtown area through land reclamation in both Singapore and New York City
- Prioritizing and improving connections to public transport, including a high level of transit services by buses and metro (in other cities, BRT might

prove more cost effective than underground metro for conveying commuters toward areas with high job concentrations)

- Charging relatively high prices for the use of cars in downtown areas, implemented through congestion pricing in Singapore, tolls to enter Manhattan from bridges and tunnels, and allowing parking prices to be set by the market in New York City and Singapore
- Ensuring a high level of amenities that make the downtown area attractive outside office hours, such as theater districts, museums, and the new Chelsea art gallery district in New York City, and cultural centers, auditoriums, rehabilitation of ethnic districts and waterfront with restaurants, leisure and entertainment, commerce, seaside promenade, pedestrian streets, and so on in Singapore
- As in Singapore, promoting large-scale but compact mixed-use development located at integrated bus-transit transport hubs such as Ang Mo Kio and Woodlands, new towns where shopping centers, amenities, offices, and civic functions in the bus/metro hub allow linked trips while using transit

Conclusions

Differential pricing of energy sources based on carbon content is often posited as the only way to promote better urban transport efficiency and to reduce GHG emissions due to urban transport in the long run for most cities. As demonstrated in this chapter, integrating transport and land-use planning, investing in public transport, improving pedestrian environment and links, and dynamically managing parking provision and traffic management are equally important for improving the effectiveness of the transport network serving the city. GHG emissions arising from suburb-to-suburb trips will be reduced not only through energy carbon pricing but also from better traffic management to reduce congestion and improvements in car technology.

GHG emissions in many dense and still monocentric cities could be reduced if the demand for suburbs to CBD trips increased. This would require coordinating carefully land use and transit networks. Large increases in the FAR in CBDs could trigger a transport mode shift toward transit if coordinated with new BRT networks and parking pricing policy.

An increase in the job concentration in CBDs could also increase urban productivity by increasing mobility without increasing VKmT or trip time. However, this does not mean that all economic activities should be concentrated in the CBD. To the contrary, flexibility in zoning should allow commerce and small enterprise to grow in the best location to operate their business, as has been the case in Singapore. Too often, zoning laws overestimate the negative externalities created by mixed use—preventing, for instance, small retail shops from locating in residential areas—while underestimating the positive externality of reducing trip length for shopping or even entertainment. Most current zoning laws should be carefully audited to remove the bias against mixed land use and against large concentrations of businesses in a few areas.

The coordination needed between transport investment and management, pricing of roads and parking, and land use to manage existing and future transport infrastructure and capacity is difficult to achieve in the real world. Urban problems cannot be solved sector by sector but spatially. This is why the autonomy of municipal authorities is so important. In some cities, urban transport is managed by national line agencies (this is the case in Mumbai). However, in very large cities the urban area covers several autonomous local governments, making it difficult to coordinate land use, transport networks, and pricing across the many boundaries of a typical metropolitan area.

The population of New York City includes less than half of the metropolitan area population, making coordination and policy consistency difficult. Most of Mumbai's regulatory decisions and infrastructure investment budget are decided by the legislature of the state of Maharashtra, not by the municipal corporation, which may explain the lack of spatial development concepts being applied to zoning regulations. Singapore, being a city-state, has the advantage of avoiding the contradictions and cross-purpose policies of a metropolitan area divided into many local authorities with diverging interests. This may explain in part the extraordinary consistency and continuity in urban development policies over a long period that has contributed to create such a successful city. The same could be said of Hong Kong, continuing the tradition of Italian renaissance city-states such as Venice and Florence.

Although good governance and policy consistency are important in reducing GHG emissions, in the long run only the pricing of energy based on carbon content will be able to make a difference in urban transport GHG emissions. Pricing transport as close as possible to the real economic cost of operation and maintenance is the only way to obtain a balance between transport modes that reflects consumer convenience and maintains mobility.

Annex

For each motorized transport mode:

$$Q = VKmT \times E,$$
$$VKmT = PKmT/L,$$
$$PKmT = 2D \times P,$$

where

Q is the total carbon equivalent emitted per day by passengers while commuting to work (does not include noncommuting trips) in metric tons per day

$VKmT$ is the total VKmT

E is the carbon equivalent emitted per vehicle kilometer traveled

$PKmT$ is the PKmT per day

L is the load factor

D is the average commuting distance per passenger

P is the number of passengers per day using the transport mode.

$$Q = T \times \sum_{i=1}^{N} \frac{2 \times D_i \times P_i \times P_i}{L_i \times 10^6}$$

where

Q is the total carbon equivalent emitted per day by passengers while commuting to work (does not include noncommuting trips) in metric tons per day

T is the total number of commuters per day

N is the number of commuting transport modes types numbered from 1 to N

D_i is the average commuting distance one way per passenger in kilometers per type i of commuting mode

P_i is the percentage of commuters using transport mode type i

E_i is the carbon emissions of vehicle used for mode i in grams of carbon equivalent (full life cycle) per VKmT

L_i is the load factor expressed in average number of passengers per vehicle of type i.

Notes

1. London, New York City, Rome, Stockholm, and Tokyo.
2. We define urban transport network as including all public or private spaces and systems devoted to circulation of good and people, from sidewalks, elevators, and cycle tracks to bus rapid transit networks and underground rail.
3. This figure from the 2000 census reflects resident working persons aged 15 years and above by mode of transport to work, which includes public bus, mass rapid transit, or taxi.
4. *Pico y placa* consists of limiting the number of vehicles on the road on a given day by allowing on alternative days only vehicles with a license plate ending with an odd or even number.
5. The Hong Kong metro is an exception: Neither capital cost nor operation and maintenance are subsidized.

6. The limits imposed on FAR is a common regulation linked with zoning. A FAR of 2, for instance, allows building an area of floor space equal to twice the area of the plot on which it is built. A FAR of 2, therefore, would allow 2,000 square meters of floor space to be built on a 1,000 square meters plot. If half of the land is built on, the building would have four floors to fully use the allowed FAR. A regulatory limit put on FAR is therefore not the equivalent of a limit on height or number of floors because most buildings have to leave some of their lot open for light ventilation or circulation or often to follow regulations on setbacks.

References

Alonso, W. 1964. *Location and Land Use.* Cambridge, MA: Harvard University Press.

Annez, P. C., and R. M. Buckley. 2009. "Urbanization and Growth: Setting the Context." In *Urbanization and Growth,* ed. M. Spence, P. C. Annez, and R. M. Buckley. Washington, DC: Commission on Growth and Development.

Balcombe, R., R. Mackett, N. Paulley, J. Preston, J. Shires, H. Titheridge, M. Wardman, and P. White. 2004. "The Demand for Public Transport: A Practical Guide." Report TRL 593, Transportation Research Laboratory, Crowthorne, U.K.

Baker, J., R. Basu, M. Cropper, S. Lall, and A. Takeuchi. 2004. *Urban Poverty and Transport: The Case of Mumbai.* Washington, DC: World Bank.

Bertaud, A. 2006. "Order without Design." http://alain-bertaud.com.

Bertaud, A., and S. Malpezzi. 2003. "The Spatial Distribution of Population in 48 World Cities: Implications for Economies in Transition." Center for Urban Land Economics Research, University of Wisconsin.

Brueckner, J. K. 2001. "Urban Sprawl: Lessons from Urban Economics." Papers on Urban Affairs 2001, Brookings Institution–Wharton School, Washington, DC, and Philadelphia.

Brueckner, J. K., J. Thisse, and Y. Zenou. 1999. "Why Is Central Paris Rich and Downtown Detroit Poor? An Amenity Based Theory." *European Economic Review* 43: 91–107.

Button, Kenneth. 1993. *Transport Economics.* Cheltenham, U.K.: Edward Elgar.

Demographia. 2005. "Greenhouse Gas Emissions per Passenger Mile: Public Transport & Personal Mobility: USA: 2005." http://www.demographia.com/db-ghg-carstr.pdf.

EIU (Economist Intelligence Unit). 2008. "Sustainable Urban Infrastructure. London Edition—A View to 2025." Siemens AG, Munich, Germany. https://www.cee.siemens .com/web/at/de/corporate/portal/Nachhaltigkeit/Documents/SustainableUrban Infrastructure-StudyLondon.pdf.

Goodwin, P., J. Dargay, and M. Hanly. 2004. "Elasticities of Road Traffic and Fuel Consumption with Respect to Price and Income: A Review." *Transport Reviews* 24 (3): 275–92.

Gordon, P., B. Lee, and H. W. Richardson. 2004. "Travel Trends in U.S. Cities: Explaining the 2000 Census Commuting Results." Lusk Center for Real Estate, University of Southern California, Los Angeles.

Luk, J. Y. K. 1999. "Electronic Road Pricing in Singapore." *Road and Transport Research* 8 (4): 28–30.

McKinsey and Co. 2007. *Reducing U.S. Greenhouse Gas Emissions: How Much at What Cost?* U.S. Greenhouse Gas Abatement Mapping Initiative Executive Report. http://www.mckinsey.com/clientservice/ccsi/pdf/us_ghg_final_report.

Mills, E. S. 1970. "Urban Density Functions." *Urban Studies* 7: 5–20.

Muth, R. F. 1969. *Cities and Housing.* Chicago: University of Chicago Press.

———. 1985. "Models of Land-Use, Housing, and Rent: An Evaluation." *Journal of Regional Science* 25: 593–606.

Ng, W. S., and L. Schipper. 2005. "China Motorization Trends: Policy Options in a World of Transport Challenges." World Resources Institute, Washington, DC.

OECD (Organisation for Economic Co-operation and Development). 2007. *Cutting Transport CO_2 Emissions: What Progress?* Paris: OECD.

O'Toole, R. 2008. "Does Rail Transit Save Energy or Reduce Greenhouse Emissions?" Policy Analysis Paper 615, Cato Institute, Washington, DC.

Pisarski, A. E. 2006. "Commuting in America: The Third National Report on Commuting Patterns and Trend." Transportation Research Board, Washington, DC.

Schipper, L., F. Unander, and C. Marie-Lilliu. 1999. "The IEA Energy Indicators Effort: Increasing the Understanding of the Energy/Emissions Link." IEA, Paris. http://www.iea.org/papers/2000/eneinl.pdf.

Singapore Department of Statistics. 2000. "Population Census." Department of Statistics, Singapore.

Sperling, D., and J. Cannon, eds. 2006. *Driving Climate Change: Cutting Carbon from Transportation.* New York: Academic Press.

Staley, S., and A. Moore. 2008. *Mobility First: A New Vision for Transportation in a Globally Competitive Twenty-First Century.* Lanham, MD: Rowman & Littlefield.

World Bank. 2009. "World Development Report: Reshaping Economic Geography." World Bank, Washington, DC.

World Resources Institute. 2009. "Climate Analysis Indicators Tool." http://cait.wri.org/.

5

The Role of Institutions, Governance, and Urban Planning for Mitigation and Adaptation

Harriet Bulkeley, Heike Schroeder, Katy Janda, Jimin Zhao,
Andrea Armstrong, Shu Yi Chu, and Shibani Ghosh

Introduction

Two major waves of activities may be discerned in municipal action on climate change since the 1990s. The first involves individual cities and transnational municipal networks, such as ICLEI's Cities for Climate Protection (CCP), Climate Alliance, and Energy Cities, which started to mobilize action for reducing greenhouse gas (GHG) emissions (Kern and Bulkeley 2009). For the most part, national governments and the emerging international regime for governing climate change showed little interest in these activities (Bulkeley and Betsill 2003; for an exception, see Sugiyama and Takeuchi 2008, 425). It was dominated by a few pioneer cities, predominantly in North America and Europe, and it focused on mitigation (Bulkeley and Betsill 2003; Bulkeley and Kern 2006; Alber and Kern 2008). The second wave is more recent, where transnational municipal networks have grown and multiplied and a more geographically diverse range has emerged. The emergence of the C40 Cities Climate Leadership Group and the Rockefeller Foundation Climate Change Initiative, together with the continued work of ICLEI, is leading to increasing involvement of global and megacities in the urban climate change agenda. At the same time, the predominant focus on mitigation is giving way to the emergence of municipal climate policy in which both mitigation and adaptation are considered significant.

The research and evidence base is lagging behind this new trend. The earliest work on local climate policy and governance was conducted in the mid-1990s (such as Collier 1997; DeAngelo and Harvey 1998; Harvey and Danny 1993; Lambright, Chagnon, and Harvey 1996), and a large body of research has now been accumulated (for a review see Betsill and Bulkeley 2007). However, this research has tended to focus on mitigation and individual case studies, predominantly in cities in Australia, Canada, Europe, and the United States (see Allman, Fleming, and Wallace 2004; Betsill 2001; Bulkeley 2000; Bulkeley and Betsill 2003; Bulkeley and Kern 2006; Davies 2005; Kousky and Schneider 2003; Lindseth 2004; Yarnal, O'Connor, and Shudak 2003), although important work has been conducted in Asia, Mexico, and South Africa (Bai 2007; Dhakal 2004, 2006; Holgate 2007; Romero-Lankao 2007) and work has begun on urban climate adaptation in the global South (see Alam and Rabbani 2007; Huq and others 2007; Satterthwaite and others 2008).

There has also been a tendency to focus on "leaders," those cities that have been first-movers on the issue of climate change, whatever their significance in political and climate terms. As a result, we know little about the particular challenges for global and megacities—which may be both the most significant in carbon terms and the most important in relation to the impacts of climate change—and how climate change is being addressed in "ordinary" cities across the world. This research agenda may be particularly challenging because, as Bai and Imura (2000, cited in Bai 2007, 22) found, environmental issues facing "today's developing cities are complex in nature, as poverty-related issues, industrial-pollution-related issues, and consumption- and lifestyle-related issues are manifesting themselves in a telescoped, compressed manner."

The Challenges of Urban Governance and Planning

Climate change presents a number of challenges for urban governance and planning, in terms of both mitigation and adaptation.

Mitigating Climate Change

Over the past two decades, the main focus of both urban policy and research with respect to climate change has been on the issue of climate change mitigation—that is, on the reduction of GHG emissions from urban activities. Cities represent concentrations of economic and social activity. The International Energy Agency recently estimated that cities may be the location for approximately 70 percent of energy-related carbon dioxide (CO_2) emissions (IEA 2008), and the Stern Review suggests that "by some estimates, cities account for 78% of carbon emissions from human activities" (Stern 2006, 457). Other researchers have critiqued these figures, particularly the implicit arguments that all cities are equally culpable and that it is cities—rather than those that live in them—that are responsible for GHG emissions (Satterthwaite 2008a). However, in an increasingly urbanizing world with emissions-producing activities concentrated in cities, the question of how municipal authorities and other actors might intervene to reduce their impact remains a significant one.

If urban GHG emissions can be considered part of the climate change problem, municipal action may also be part of the solution. Municipal governments have a (highly variable) level of influence over GHG emissions through their roles in energy supply and management, transport, land-use planning, and waste management. Some local authorities focus on emissions over which they have direct control (municipal emissions), whereas others focus on so-called community-wide emissions. In general, municipal emissions account for only a small percentage of the overall GHG emissions from a city, though where a municipality owns the energy or water supply company, such as is the case in Los Angeles, this proportion can rise considerably (Schroeder and Bulkeley 2008). Schreurs (2008, 353) finds that "the kind of climate change initiatives that local governments can most easily do appear to be such activities as climate change and renewable energy target setting, energy efficiency incentive programs, educational efforts, green local government procurement standards, public transportation policies, public-private partnership agreements with local businesses, and tree planting."

Although some municipalities have developed a systematic approach to climate policy through the stages of undertaking inventories of GHG emissions and determining emissions reduction targets, climate change action plans, and various implementation plans, "numerous cities, which have adopted GHG reduction targets, have failed to pursue such a systematic and structured approach and, instead, prefer to implement no-regret measures on a case by case basis" (Alber and Kern 2008, 4; see also Jollands 2008). Despite the range of GHG emissions reduction activities that municipalities could engage with, research has found that "attention remains fixed on issues of energy demand reduction" (Betsill and Bulkeley 2007, 450; see also Bulkeley and Kern 2006), and primarily orientated around municipal emissions.

Particularly significant are issues of governance capacity, in terms of the ability to regulate GHG emissions, to provide services and infrastructure, and to work with others, enabling action to take place. We find that the literature suggests that policy entrepreneurs, access to additional sources of finance, municipal competencies, the framework established by national (and regional) levels of government, the support offered by transnational networks, and the ability to reframe the issue of climate change within the local context are most critical in building this governance capacity. These factors vary in their significance in relation to the different "modes" of governance under consideration.

For example, municipal competencies are critical with respect to the regulating and provision modes, and sources of additional finance and involvement with transnational networks are critical in terms of an enabling mode of climate governance. In the case studies that follow, we consider how these different "modes" of governing climate change have been deployed and with what effect.

Adapting to Climate Change

Adaptation policy is crucial for dealing with the unavoidable impacts of climate change, but this has so far been underemphasized at the urban level around the world. The economic cost of adapting to the effects from climate change will be significant; in Organisation for Economic Co-operation and Development (OECD) countries alone, making new infrastructure and buildings resilient to climate change is estimated to cost around $15 to $150 billion a year (0.05 to 0.5 percent of gross domestic product; Stern 2006). Adaptation addresses the consequences of climate change, such as heavy rainfall, flooding, or extreme temperatures. These are issues already affecting societies, independent of their role in causing climate change. As a result, the benefits from urban adaptation can be direct for a city, in contrast with the rather indirect benefits felt in the case of mitigation in the form of political or economic gains or improvements in the local environment. Not only does adaptation provide many local benefits, it can also be realized without long lead times (Stern 2006). Even though the impetus for economic development has traditionally been viewed as incompatible with considerations for environmental protection or climate change policies, mitigation and adaptation are increasingly being reframed as economic opportunities (Halsnæs and Verhagen 2007; Hay and Mimura 2006; Tanner and others 2008; UK WGCCD 2007).

Although the notion that adaptation and mitigation can be pursued simultaneously is increasingly being advocated, important trade-offs must also be considered when devising mitigation and adaptation strategies. Some mitigation options may exacerbate urban vulnerability to climate change. For example, although increasing urban density may contribute toward reducing emissions from transport, this will have negative implications for adaptation, such as intensifying the urban heat island effect and posing problems for urban drainage. Improving our understanding of the synergies, conflicts, and trade-offs between mitigation and adaptation measures would enable more integrated and effective urban climate policy (McEvoy, Lindley, and Handley 2006).

In addition, adaptation-specific challenges make urban governance and planning in this area particularly challenging. The lack of data and expertise at the local level is perhaps even more critical when it comes to adaptation than mitigation. There is a lack of scientific assessment as to what impacts might be expected and of social, economic, and scientific research as to potential impacts and implications of different measures of climate change adaptation in cities (Qi and others 2008; Satterthwaite 2008a; Tanner and others 2008). A lack of municipal capacity exists with respect to the most vulnerable populations in cities because such groups tend to live outside the formal jurisdictions of municipal governments, are ill-served by urban infrastructures, and may be subject to forms of discrimination and exclusion (Satterthwaite 2008b; Tanner and others 2008). At the same time, municipal governments have lacked the resources and the wherewithal to fund projects, to engage partners, and to involve communities in responses to climate change. We find a lack of coordination between departments at the municipal level and a strong dependence of local government on the policies and actions in this field by national authorities (Adger, Arnell, and Tompkins 2005; McEvoy, Lindley, and Handley 2006).

These specific challenges mean that, as well as similarities, crucial differences are found between the drivers and challenges for adaptation and mitigation at the urban level. Most important, although leadership has been identified in the literature as critical for municipal action on mitigation, this is not the same for adaptation. Municipal leaders can create significant political capital on the issue of mitigation, but addressing adaptation requires a different kind of leadership—based on inclusive or good governance, that is, foresight and the willingness to develop a safety net for citizens, especially for the urban poor. In adaptation, as with mitigation, we find that access to resources to make the necessary structural and capacity investments is crucial. However, as far as adaptation is concerned, municipalities are often starting from an infrastructure deficit—of basic provisioning, especially to the urban poor—that greatly exacerbates the challenge of adapting to climate change.

Rather than being framed as an opportunity—for green growth or addressing other urban environmental problems—we find that adaptation is often a marginal concern on the political agenda, given the challenges of meeting basic needs and everyday survival. At the same time, with limited implementation of adaptation policies and measures documented in the literature, to date little evidence is found of political conflicts emerging over climate adaptation in the same manner as is the case for mitigation. However, the research community acknowledges that the "political economy" of adapting to climate change may soon become a critical factor, as contests emerge about how, and for whom, climate change adaptation should take place (Huq and others 2007).

Urban Climate Change Policy and Action in Cities in the +8 Countries

In this section, we examine the current state of urban climate change policy and action by drawing on 10 case studies of cities in the "+8" countries—those considered most likely in academic and policy circles to be faced with some form of emissions reduction target in the post-2012 era and where many of the world's largest and potentially most vulnerable cities are located. This focus directs our attention to what is taking place in cities in the global South and newly industrialized and non–Annex I countries under the United Nations Framework Convention on Climate Change (UNFCCC) (Brazil, China, India, Indonesia, Mexico, South Africa, and the Republic of Korea), as well as in Australia, a country that joined the Kyoto framework in late 2007. The case studies—conducted in Beijing, Cape Town, Hong Kong, Melbourne, Mexico City, Mumbai, New Delhi, São Paulo, Seoul, and Yogyakarta—therefore provide important evidence about the drivers and challenges facing cities in rapidly industrializing countries in addressing climate change. Given the range of cities included, and the differences in socioeconomic context, insights can be gained from these cases that have broader applicability, though it is recognized that these insights may have limited validity for cities in low-income countries.

Climate Change and the Built Environment

The built environment—comprising domestic, commercial, and public buildings—is a significant contributor to global GHG emissions. The building sector consumes roughly one-third of the final energy used in most countries, and it absorbs an even more significant share of electricity. Electricity use in commercial buildings is driving peak demand in Japan, the United States, and some of the wealthier countries in the global South. As a result of concerns about the implications for climate change, and historical concerns about energy costs and security of supply, governments in both industrialized countries and the global South have initiated policies to reduce energy consumption in buildings. Most of these policies can be grouped into one of the following three categories: economic incentives (such as taxes or energy pricing), regulatory requirements (such as codes or standards), or informational programs (such as energy awareness campaigns or energy audits). More recently, growth in voluntary public-private partnerships (such as Energy Star in the United States and the Carbon Trust Standard in the United Kingdom) and the role of private actors (such as the C40 and the Clinton Climate Initiative) have changed the landscape for improvement by setting more ambitious "stretch" goals for the building industry and its clients and by resetting norms for how energy is used in buildings.

Although historically the main focus of action with respect to climate change and the built environment has been on issues of mitigation, the challenges posed by adaptation are increasingly being recognized. Such challenges are usually framed in terms of "resilient" buildings. One such example is buildings designed to recover quickly from the impact of flooding through ensuring that essential services (power, water, and sanitation) experience minimal disruption (such as by placing power sockets above likely flooding levels). Although to date little literature on resilient buildings is available, what such buildings might require is subject to significant debate, with some researchers favoring passive low-energy buildings and others placing faith in "smart" buildings (for example, Adaptive Building Initiative 2009; Roaf, Crichton, and Nicol 2005). Equally, minimal policy initiatives have been taken to realize either of these approaches; achieving adaptation to climate change in the built environment is likely to involve a combination of regulation, financial incentives, information, and voluntary approaches.

Self-governance

The mode of "self-governance" has been central to municipal efforts to address climate change, particularly in cities in the global North. In the sector of the built environment, one popular approach has been to increase the energy efficiency of municipal operations, either through retrofitting buildings or through improving the energy efficiency of appliances (such as office equipment and lighting) used by the municipality. In Cape Town, a target of increasing energy efficiency within the municipality by 12 percent by 2010 was set. In Yogyakarta, since 2003 a program to retrofit lights and reduce air-conditioning hours and bulbs in government buildings has been undertaken, and in Beijing, a program of energy efficiency improvements to government buildings was due to be completed by 2010. In Melbourne, energy-saving behavior among municipal staff members has been encouraged by the promise of a 0.5 percent performance-related pay increase if environmental targets are met; this demonstrates that climate change issues are being mainstreamed within the local authority. In contrast, action in Delhi has been primarily driven by power shortages in the city rather than concerns for climate change per se. Nonetheless, this has led to a comprehensive effort at energy conservation, including the banning of incandescent lighting in government buildings and a mandatory requirement for new government buildings to adopt green building technology, including efficient lighting, heating, ventilation, air conditioning, and water usage (DTL 2008). These initiatives demonstrate the potentially powerful effect that reframing climate change concerns with respect to other issues affecting energy conservation in the built environment can have in motivating action at the local level.

As research elsewhere has found, our case studies demonstrate that municipal initiatives in the self-governing mode have also involved the development of "exemplar" or best practice buildings to showcase the possibilities of new technologies and energy efficiency standards. In Seoul, the municipal government has consulted the German Fraunhofer Solar Research Institute on recycled heat in the new 26-story city hall. In Melbourne, the recently completed Council House 2 building has been recognized as a leading example of what can be achieved within the confines of inner-city building sites, reaching the top six-star rating on the Green Star rating scale.

Regulation

Across different countries, research suggests that the built environment is one sector in which the regulatory mode of governing climate change is prominent (Janda and Busch 1993, 1994). Energy standards for buildings range from voluntary guidelines to mandatory requirements, which may apply to one or many building types.[1] Although mandatory standards are embedded in structures of formal regulation, voluntary standards provide a form of "soft" regulation, often used to direct changes in practice on the implicit or explicit assumption that without such improvements mandatory measures will be implemented. Such standards are usually set at the regional or national level. To understand the potential for action with respect to energy standards in the built environment in our case-study cities, a literature review and online survey were conducted to gather information on standards in 81 countries.[2]

In terms of the countries in which these case-study cities are based, Australia, China, and Korea have mandatory standards for residential and commercial buildings; Mexico has mandatory standards for nonresidential buildings; and India, Indonesia, and South Africa have voluntary standards for nonresidential buildings, but there are currently no standards in place in Brazil. With its historic independence, Hong Kong SAR, China, has been in a position to implement its own building energy standards. A decade ago, the voluntary Hong Kong Energy Efficiency Registration Scheme for Buildings was established, which promotes the application of a comprehensive set of building energy codes—for building energy services and setting efficiency standards for lighting, air conditioning, electrical, elevator, and escalator installations.[3] In 2008, a public consultation on the mandatory building energy codes was conducted, and the necessary legislation was introduced in the Hong Kong Legislative Council during 2010. Despite the prevalence of building energy standards, it is important to note that their effectiveness varies greatly from country to country (Koeppel and Ürge-Vorsatz 2007). Koeppel and Ürge-Vorsatz suggest that effectiveness of energy standards may be particularly low in developing countries, given difficulties with enforcement and even corruption. Even in developed countries, the estimated savings from energy codes range from 15 to 16 percent in the United States to 60 percent in some countries in the European Union.

One problem with national energy standards is that they are usually set at a level to avoid worst practice rather than to encourage best practices. Although municipal governments usually have little influence over the levels of improvement set by national building energy standards, our case studies show that they can mandate additional measures for the built environment within their jurisdiction that can have an impact on GHG emissions. In Melbourne, a mandatory energy performance requirement of 4.5 stars for office developments greater than 2,500 square meters has been introduced under the municipality's planning powers. In New Delhi, solar water heating systems have been made mandatory in certain categories of buildings, including government offices, hospitals, educational institutions, and the hospitality sector, and the use of incandescent bulbs in all new and existing government establishments has been banned (DTL 2008). Similar standards have been established in São Paulo, where, since 2007, buildings with more than three bathrooms, whether they are homes, apartments, trade, services, or industrial buildings, must use solar water heating systems (TCG 2008). Mexico City has devised a new "Clean Building Label" for all new construction required as part of its Plan Verde (Mexico City 2008). These examples show that, even where direct municipal competencies for establishing building standards may be missing, local governments motivated to go beyond standard practice have a range of tools at their disposal to augment the energy performance of the built environment.

Provisioning

In contrast with the use of a regulation mode of governing, we find that governing through "provisioning"—of infrastructures or services, which shape behavioral choices and restructure markets—has been limited with respect to the built environment. We find only one example across our case studies where a municipal authority is involved in directly providing energy-efficient infrastructures and services, and this is Mexico City. Here the municipality is installing 30,000 square meters of green roofs each year until 2012. It is also launching a new social housing model that integrates green areas, public spaces, and environmental design (Mexico City 2008). Although formulated as mitigation strategies, these moves address adaptation as well through enabling residents to better cope with extreme temperatures indoors, especially in housing that lacks heating or cooling devices or for residents with limited income. The lack of evidence from the other cases of municipalities adopting this role suggests either that municipal governments have a limited role in the provisioning of built environments (such as social housing) in these cities or that they are engaged in other means of providing low-energy services, including enabling and partnership approaches, which we will discuss further.

Enabling

Our case studies show that providing information, reward, and recognition are key means through which municipal governments can enable action by private sector organizations and by individuals. The government of Hong Kong SAR, China, has been involved with a program to promote energy efficiency in homes through reducing the demand for cooling by keeping indoor environments at 25.5 degrees Celsius. In Mumbai, an eco-housing program that has been introduced to encourage environmental efficiency in residential buildings is a voluntary building certification program for new and existing housing. It is proposed that developers as well as consumers participating in this program will be offered incentives, and although the incentivization scheme is yet to be finalized with the state government, rebates in the form of reduced development charges and assessment taxes have been approved by the Municipal Corporation of Greater Mumbai in principle (MCGM 2008). As this example demonstrates, financial incentives are also an important element of enabling action to reduce GHG emissions from the built environment. In Delhi, the state government established an Energy Efficiency and Renewable Energy Management Centre, which provides partial monetary aid to domestic users for the installation of solar water-heating systems, and in Seoul incentives are offered to buildings with high levels of energy efficiency.

Our case studies also show that other forms of reward and recognition can be successful in enabling other actors to respond to mitigating climate change in the built environment. In Melbourne, the Savings in the City program involved 30 city hotels in a milestone and reward program to reduce energy and water use and to avoid waste. By providing these businesses with independent recognition of their success—and setting up a degree of competition between them to achieve results—significant savings of GHG emissions have been achieved. This example shows that, in addition to providing information and financial incentives, establishing the right frameworks through which communities and businesses can act on climate change is an important aspect of the role of municipal governments.

Partnership

As well as enabling others to act, our case studies suggest that, increasingly, acting on climate change in cities is dependent on a range of partnership and private sector initiatives. In Beijing, somewhat surprisingly given the city's otherwise limited role in climate change policy and the nature of the state, nongovernmental organizations (NGOs) have been important actors in raising awareness about the possibilities of behavioral change for reducing GHG emissions from the built environment through a joint campaign to maintain a 26 degrees Celsius room temperature led by Friends of Nature Beijing. In 2008, the Environmental Protection Department and the Electrical and Mechanical Services Department in Hong Kong SAR, China, drew up a set of "Guidelines to Account for and Report on Greenhouse Gas Emissions and Removals for

Buildings (Commercial, Residential or Institutional Purpose) in Hong Kong" (EMSD and EPD 2008). These guidelines will identify areas for energy efficiency improvement as part of voluntary programs to reduce or offset emissions arising from buildings. Since its introduction, 37 institutions have signed up as Carbon Audit Green Partners, including private corporations, public hospitals, and universities. One further example of this sort of public-private partnership is in Mumbai, where in February 2008 Mumbai-based K Raheja Corp, one of the biggest real estate developers in India, signed the first agreement with Johnson Controls to retrofit the largest mall in Mumbai under the aegis of Mumbai's membership in the C40 network and with funding provided through the Clinton Climate Initiative (Sinha 2008).

Two projects from Cape Town also illustrate the growing importance of nongovernmental actors in addressing climate change in the built environment at the municipal level. The Kuyasa Low-Income Housing upgrade is the first African project under the Clean Development Mechanism and attained the first Gold Standard status in the world (SSN 2008). The project started in June 2008, with the intention of installing solar water heaters, efficient lamps, and insulated ceilings in 2,300 existing low-income housing in Khayelitsha, Cape Town, over the next 21 years. These retrofits are expected to reduce about 2.85 tons of CO_2 per household per year, and the revenue gained from the selling of emissions credits will be channeled back to setting community-owned energy services and microenterprises, which in turn create local employment (SSN 2008). At a smaller scale, Sustainable Energy Africa's commercial office built in 2004 has demonstrated the potential of "green buildings" in Cape Town. It was designed to incorporate passive solar design, low energy- and water-use considerations, and maximized recycled building materials; it has been positively evaluated for its low environmental footprint.[4]

Transportation

The transport sector is a significant contributor to GHG emissions, representing 23 percent (worldwide) and 30 percent (OECD countries) of CO_2 emissions from fossil fuel combustion in 2005 (Kahn Ribeiro and others 2007). These shares have risen over the past three decades and are expected to continue to increase (Kahn Ribeiro and others 2007). From 1990 to 2004, CO_2 emissions from the transport sector rose by 36.5 percent (Kahn Ribeiro and others 2007). In developing countries, especially China, India, and other Asian countries, although transport's share of GHG emissions is low, the transport sector is growing much faster than other sectors (Karekezi, Majoro, and Johnson 2003). Increasing demand for fossil fuels and automobile-oriented infrastructure is leading to greater GHG emissions and deteriorating air quality. Thus, urban transport has become an important sector for achieving GHG emissions reductions targets, although issues of adapting transport infrastructures to climate change have yet to feature substantially on the urban policy agenda.

The mitigation strategies taken by cities that have reduced carbon emissions include promoting the capacity and quality of public transport systems, integrating transport and urban planning to facilitate efficient and low-carbon modes of transport, strengthening transport demand management, increasing investment in cleaner or alternative fuel vehicle technologies, tightening vehicle emissions and efficiency standards, and encouraging nonmotorized transport, such as biking and walking. The governance approaches adopted by municipalities include forms of self-governance (such as staff travel planning, vehicle fleet fuel switching), regulation (such as emissions standards, planning laws), provisioning (such as of public transport services or of infrastructures for alternative modes of travel), enabling (such as information), and partnerships (such as public-private financing for new modes of transportation).

Self-governance

One of the most common policies with respect to transportation has been for municipalities to replace their vehicle fleets with alternative fuels. Alternative fuel vehicles are vehicles powered by substantially non–petroleum-based fuels, including compressed natural gas (CNG), methanol, ethanol, propane, liquefied petroleum gas (LPG), biodiesel, and electricity. This approach has been popular among our case studies, although it should be noted that although these measures are often framed in terms of their potential impact in terms of mitigating climate change, there is uncertainty about whether some alternative fuels will in fact lead to a meaningful reduction in GHG emissions. Beijing has about one-third (4,158) of 20,000 buses powered by CNG. Three fuel-cell buses began operations in June 2006, and a hydrogen refueling station began operating in November 2006 within the Beijing Hydro Demo Park. About 500 advanced alternative fuel vehicles were used by the Beijing Organizing Committee for the 2008 Beijing Olympic Games and Paralympics, including 20 fuel cell cars, 50 lithium-ion battery-powered electric buses, 25 hybrid buses, and 75 hybrid cars (Zhao 2008). The hybrid vehicles and natural gas–powered vehicles around the village all meet Euro IV emission standards and helped achieve "zero emissions" in the central Olympic area. These vehicles were developed and supported by China's national research and development program, for which the Beijing Olympics was used as a testing ground.

In Seoul, the metropolitan government plans to replace government vehicles with hybrids and to increase the number of CNG buses (SMG 2008; SMG News 2008), and in Mexico City there is a plan to replace the entire city government car fleet with low-emission vehicles. In Delhi, the government has also introduced new vehicles in its fleet, in the form of modern low-floor CNG buses in the city, with plans in place to phase out the existing bus fleet in the coming years. This move follows a 1998 order of the India Supreme Court that all the buses in New Delhi be converted from diesel fuel to CNG and its further decision, despite opposition by the Delhi government, that Delhi's entire public transport fleet (buses, taxis, and auto-rickshaws) should be converted to CNG by 2003 (Rosencranz and Jackson 2003). This was hailed as a major success for the environmental lobby. As of 2008, there were more than 130,000 vehicles running on CNG in the city (GoD 2008).

Municipal governments can also seek to improve their own impact on climate change through the transport sector by seeking to change the travel behavior of employees. Usually this is pursued through staff travel plans or education campaigns. One of our case studies provides an example of a more rigorous approach. In early 2008, the mayor of Yogyakarta passed a resolution that forbids city workers living within a 5-kilometer vicinity of municipal buildings to commute to work in motor vehicles, forcing them to use public transportation (Bailey 2008). This approach is unique among our case studies but points to the potential impact that municipalities might be able to have on the culture of transportation in their cities.

Regulation

The regulation of emissions and energy efficiency of vehicles is viewed as the most prominent and widely used tool to improve vehicle fuel consumption and to reduce carbon emissions (Sperling and Cannon 2007, 259). These standards focus on vehicle efficiency and emissions for traditional pollutants, such as particulate matter, Nitrogen oxide, and carbon monoxide, but do not include CO_2 explicitly. Nonetheless, reducing such air pollutants can have a positive effect on GHG emissions, although this is by no means a certainty. Our case studies show that this has been a popular regulatory measure, reflecting the connections between transportation, air quality, and health. Since 2005, all new vehicles registered in Mumbai have to comply with Bharat Stage III (equal to Euro III) efficiency norms, and by 2010, they will have to be Bharat Stage IV compliant (equal to Euro IV). Older vehicles are being taken off the road or being converted to CNG (Takeuchi and others 2007). In Delhi, all new four-wheeled vehicles have to meet Bharat Stage III norms for emission control. From 2010, this bar will be raised, and vehicles will have to meet Bharat Stage IV norms. The implementation of these standards originates in the 1995 Clean Air Campaign by the Centre for Science and Environment, one of India's leading environmental NGOs (Véron 2006), with the result that, in compliance with India Supreme Court orders, between 1994 and 1996 new fuel-quality standards were introduced in India's four major cities, including Delhi.

In Hong Kong SAR, China, vehicles meeting the energy efficiency and exhaust emission criteria can have the First Registration Tax reduced.[5] In Delhi, a similar mixture of standard setting and incentives is seen. The state government also has initiated a program to provide a 30 percent subsidy on the purchase of battery-operated vehicles in the city. It is funding this subsidy from the diesel tax it has levied since early 2008. The program, which is also supported by a subsidy provided by the central Ministry of New and Renewable Energy, was introduced at a time when the price of crude oil was skyrocketing. The government is keen on encouraging the use of alternate fuel and is particularly eager to reduce the number of diesel vehicles, which currently account for 30 percent of the city's automobiles population of the city (MNRE 2008). These examples suggest that regulation may be most effective when it is combined with other, more enabling, modes of governing.

Beyond regulating vehicle standards and emissions, there is little evidence that our case-study cities deploy the regulatory mode of governing in the transport sector. One exception is Mexico City, where restrictions are placed on a car one day per week, based on a car's license plate number. In 2008, these restrictions were extended to include Saturdays. Mexico City also introduced a pilot scheme for mandatory school bus transportation in 2008 with 34 schools that will enforce the use of school buses for all private school students by 2012. Another example is Beijing, which had a two-month-long vehicle control program in place based on odd-even license plate numbers for the Olympic Games in 2008. Beginning in October 2008, the city started a vehicle-driving control based on the last digit number of license plate numbers so that each vehicle can drive only four days out of every five working days (Xinhua News 2008).[6]

Provisioning

Improving the efficiency and coverage of public transportation is critical for encouraging the public to change their travel mode to reduce energy use and emissions associated with the growth of private motorized transport. In this context, many municipalities are playing critical roles in providing infrastructures that promote less carbon-intensive travel. For example, large-capacity buses, light-rail transit, and metro or suburban rail are increasingly being used for the expansion of public transport. In some cases, municipalities are the direct providers of such services, and elsewhere they are critical actors in building the necessary infrastructure for their operation.

Providing a higher-quality public transport system is regarded by our case-study cities as an efficient and effective approach to reducing traffic jams, air pollution, and carbon emissions. Most cities have made enormous investments in public transport infrastructure and plan to continue doing so. Hong Kong enjoys a well-developed mass transit system; 90 percent of the 11 million commuter trips each day are made on the public transport system,[7] and plans are under way for five different extensions in the next five years. The state of São Paulo invested $7.285 billion during 2007–10 to upgrade the metropolitan subway and other public transport systems, using funds from the Inter-American Development Bank (SSP 2008). These investments will help modernize train lines and build 100 kilometers of new lines for buses in the city of São Paulo, Santos, and Campinãs (TCG 2008). By 2010, these upgrades were expected to have reduced 700,000 tons of GHGs, generating credits that can be sold in the clean development mechanism (CDM) markets (SSP 2008).

Over the past decade, Beijing has invested heavily in public transport infrastructure such as buses, bus rapid transit (BRT) lines, subways, and public transport transfer systems to improve air quality to meet the requirements of the 2008 Olympic Games. Beijing had only two subway lines, 54 kilometers long, in 2001 when the city won its bid for the Olympics. By 2008, six more lines had been built, extending the network to 200 kilometers and establishing new subway networks in north and central Beijing. Three BRT lines have been built in Beijing to link the center of the city to the east and north (Greenpeace 2008).

Similarly, in Delhi, the first phase of the Delhi metropolitan railway system (metro) came into operation in December 2002. The second phase of the system has been under construction with completion in 2010, in time for the Commonwealth Games. The project is a combination of surface and over-ground trains. At the same time, BRT lines also have been opened in some parts of Delhi. The BRT system has exclusive bus lanes operating in the central verge of the road. It also dedicates a lane for cyclists and improves pedestrian crossings and paths. Bus travelers, cyclists, and pedestrians are reported to be satisfied with the new system, but there has been major criticism of severe traffic congestion in some areas caused by the reduction in the number of lanes for other vehicles (Hidalgo and Pai 2009). BRT systems (MyCiTi bus services) were also introduced in Cape Town in time for the 2010 World Cup to reverse a recent trend toward the use of private motorized vehicles and informal minibus taxis. These last three examples demonstrate the importance of global events in shaping urban transport infrastructures, a point to which we will return.

As well as providing for public transport, municipalities can also develop infrastructures for alternative modes of transport, a less common approach in our case studies. One example is in Seoul, where a free bike program was launched in August 2007 following the example of Paris (SMG 2008). Approximately 200 bike stations will be provided in the Songpa-gu area, where cycle routes are well established, and there are about 5,000 bikes. The project will be expanded to other areas of the city but to a degree remains hampered by the lack of infrastructure such as cycle routes and bike racks. Mexico City has a plan to build about 300 kilometers of bicycle highways by 2012 to help reach the government target of at least 5 percent of person-trips to be made by bike. Primarily, though, it is clear that across our case-study cities, the provision of public forms of transportation is favored over nonmotorized alternatives.

Enabling

A key aspect of the enabling mode of governing for transportation has been the use of incentives. One approach has been to adopt economic incentive policies such as pricing policies to encourage the shift to public modes of transport. To resolve the problem of public transport use being well below capacity, the Beijing municipal government started an integrated circuit (IC) card ticket system, replacing the paper tickets used for more than 50 years (Li, Yunjing, and Yang 2008). The IC card can be used for both buses and subways, and there is a discount for using IC cards on buses and BRT lines. It currently costs 1 yuan ($0.13) for a regularly priced bus ticket; therefore, with an IC card, an adult need pay only 0.4 yuan ($0.06) and a student 0.2 yuan ($0.03) per trip. The price subsidies for public buses and subways are financed by the Beijing municipal government and have led to increased use of these services, especially by senior retired persons. The Seoul government encourages citizens to travel on public transport by charging a price for travel anywhere within Seoul of approximately $1 (SMG 2008; SMG News 2008). Incentive programs have also been used to encourage the use of alternative fuels. In 2000, Hong Kong SAR, China, introduced an incentive program to replace diesel with LPG, and by the end of 2003, nearly all taxis had switched to LPG, although this may not in fact reduce GHG emissions. A similar scheme was adopted in 2002 for light buses to replace diesel with LPG or electricity, and thus far, 2,500 light buses have done so (EMSD 2008). In Mexico City, the use of nonmotorized transport is also promoted through the use of incentives.

A second set of strategies for enabling the governance of transportation systems relies on information. Some cities, working with national governments or on their own, adopt public campaigns to increase public awareness and knowledge of cleaner transportation. China launched its first nationwide urban public transport week in September 2007, with 108 cities participating (including Beijing) and a theme of "Green Transport and Health" to raise residents' awareness of energy savings and environmental protection. The campaign encouraged people to walk, ride bicycles, and take public transport. Along with other cities, Beijing set September 22 as No Car Day for one area of the city, which was opened only to pedestrians, bicycle riders, and taxi and bus passengers between 7 A.M. and 7 P.M.[10] Seoul also held a Car Free Day on September 22, 2008, which was estimated to reduce CO_2 emissions by 10 percent. Similar awareness-raising initiatives have also been developed in Melbourne, and in the Greater Melbourne area, the city of Darebin promotes "living locally" through informing residents of the services available locally to reduce demand for travel.

Partnership

In contrast with the built environment sector, in the arena of transportation, we find few examples of partnerships between municipalities and nonstate actors seeking to address climate change. One exception is in the state of São Paulo, where the flex-fuel technology, which enables vehicles to run either ethanol, gasoline, or a mix, has been developed in collaboration with international manufacturers such as Fiat, GM, Peugeot, and Volkswagen. On this basis, the state-led Motor Vehicle Pollution Control Program (PROCONVE) sets standards for gasohol, ethanol, CNG, and diesel vehicles. Although it does not cover CO_2, nitrous oxide, or sulpher oxide directly, between 2010 and 2020 cumulative CO_2 emission reductions in the state resulting from this program are expected to be between 2.6 to 57.2 million tons of CO_2 (Hewlett Foundation 2005).

Another case is that of the Delhi Metro Rail Corporation (DMRC), which has registered a project based on regenerative braking in trains as a CDM project with the UNFCCC in 2007. This is an example of a "partnership" between a municipal government and the international regime, orchestrated by the CDM board, which also includes private actors. It is expected to earn 400,000 certified emissions reductions (CERs) over a 10-year period beginning December 2007. The DMRC will earn Rs. 12 million ($240,000) each year from this project, which will be used to offset additional investment and operatign costs. Another CDM project is being planned wherein the DMRC will claim CERs for the reduction of tailpipe emissions as commuters switch to the metro. These sorts of projects could potentially pave the way for significant sources of finance for public transport infrastructures in the global South, though they do, of course, come with all the usual caveats about CDM projects and the benefits (environmental, social, or economic) that they may be able to realize in practice.

Urban Infrastructures

Urban infrastructures—for example, energy (electricity and gas networks), water and sanitation systems, urban flood drainage, and coastal defenses—are critical in mediating the relation between climate change and cities. On the one hand, inadequate provision of infrastructure or its poor maintenance can exacerbate the impacts of climate change and the vulnerability of urban populations. On the other hand, the nature of utility provision—for example, fossil fuel–based or renewable energy—can influence the GHG intensity of daily decisions and the cumulative impact of the city on the global environment. Governing urban infrastructures is, however, a complex matter. Frequently, such systems lie outside the direct control of municipal governments, or, even where they are supposedly the responsibility of local authorities, inadequate funding combined with a lack of recognition of the rights of those living in informal settlements (Satterthwaite 2008b, 11) can lead to their neglect. The significant sums of money involved in developing urban infrastructure systems often require municipal governments to work in partnership with national governments, private sector actors, and donor organizations, leading to potential conflicts among priorities and problems of interagency coordination. In addition, the planning and development of urban-scale infrastructure systems can take several decades to come to fruition and is frequently unable to predict or track the sorts of social, economic, and environmental changes that might be witnessed over such timescales.

Because of the long time horizons and large financial investments involved, issues of social and environmental justice are particularly pertinent in responding to climate change in the infrastructure sector. As Huq and others (2007, 14) have argued, the "kinds of changes needed in urban planning and governance to 'climate proof' cities are often supportive of development goals. But … they could also do the opposite—as plans and investments to cope with storms and sea-level rise forcibly clear the settlements that are currently on floodplains, or the informal settlements that are close to the coast." In equal measure, mitigation strategies, such as smart meters for demand reduction or the embedding of energy-generation technologies in household infrastructure, could open up new divides between those who are able to pay and participate in mitigation measures and those for whom they will lead to new forms of social and economic exclusion.

Self-governance

In general, the urban infrastructures that municipalities have direct control over tend to be those through which the mitigation of climate change can be addressed, and even here they remain rather small in scale. Some municipalities have sought to shift their reliance on fossil fuel–based electricity provision through national grids through the development of small-scale, decentralized (off-grid) low-carbon or renewable energy systems. One example we find in our case studies is Melbourne, where, in addition to the Council House 2 project already discussed, which involves the production of renewable energy, demonstration photovoltaic cells have been built on the roof of the city center's Queen Victoria Market—providing some electricity for the municipality but also acting as a demonstration project as to what it might be possible to achieve.

Similarly in New Delhi, solar hot water systems have been made mandatory for government buildings, displacing conventional fuels used for this purpose.

Street lighting represents a kind of infrastructure that is the direct responsibility of municipal authorities. One of the most ambitious projects to address mitigation found in our case studies lies in this domain. Over the period 2001–06, under the auspices of the CCP program, Yogyakarta developed a streetlight management program, which involved the retrofit of 775 light bulbs and the installation of 400 energy meters at a cost of $1.7 million, resulting in an annual saving of 2,051–3,170 tons of carbon dioxide (annual energy savings 4,278,408 kilowatt-hours) and an estimated $211,765 (ICLEI 2004). In Beijing, a "green lighting" project has been implemented to promote a more efficient, energy-saving lighting system for the entire city. Similar projects have also been advanced by local authorities across Greater Melbourne, who have in the main found their efforts frustrated by the private companies involved in providing energy and maintaining the street lighting system, together with the long time horizons (20 years) over which bulbs are replaced. Missing the "window of opportunity" to effect change now can therefore result in significant avoidable emissions of GHGs over the next two decades, suggesting that advanced planning and gathering sufficient political momentum is particularly important in this area of urban governance.

Regulation

Our case studies demonstrate that where regulation is being used to shape the development of urban infrastructures, this is mainly through the use of planning requirements rather than the direct regulation of, for example, water provision or energy services. Several of our case studies have integrated environmental and urban planning in place, particularly with regard to water, urban green spaces, and environmental health (Melbourne, Mexico City, and São Paulo). One example of where the planning system has been used to improve the resilience of a city to climate change is in Seoul and the restoration of the Cheong Gye Cheon River for flood-risk management (Kim 1999). The project, which dismantled a highway and allowed the channel to revert back to its original natural course, ran from July 2003 to September 2005, covering 5.84 kilometers and with an estimated cost of 390 billion won (approximately $300 million).

Although the aim of the project was flood aversion, benefits included biodiversity restoration, decrease in ambient temperature, reduction of health risks on floodplains, and increased number of visitors (Pitts and Kim 2005). More explicitly directed at concerns for climate change have been efforts to shape the development of coastal areas. Cape Town commissioned a Framework for Adaptation to Climate Change study in 2006 and conducted a comprehensive risk assessment of sea-level rise as a port city in 2008 (CCT 2006, 2008a).

The 2005 Vulnerability Assessment of Western Cape proposed creation of a 5-meter buffer zone along the coast (Midgley and others 2005). In Mumbai, climate change is also beginning to have an effect on coastal zone planning. In 1991, the union government issued regulations to demarcate coastal areas as coastal regulation zones (CRZs), and restrictions were placed on the nature and extent of development that could take places in such zones. In May 2008, the government issued a notification proposing amendments to the 1991 regulations, which would in effect make the restrictions stricter. Because Mumbai lies in one of the CRZs, the 2008 notification, if approved, is likely to improve the management of the coastal resources and to protect the city from extreme weather events.

Provisioning

Until the mid-1990s, many municipal authorities around the world owned their energy generation, water provision, and waste services. In effect, they provided utilities for their communities. In this manner, "local governments were able to control the nature of infrastructure development and to influence practices of public consumption and waste in such a way as to limit emissions of greenhouse gases" (Bulkeley and Kern 2006, 2245) and potentially to enhance their resilience to the impacts of climate change. With the rising tide of neoliberalism in the utilities sector, many such municipally owned companies in Europe and Australia were sold during the 1980s and 1990s, though in parts of the United Kingdom and United States this took place much earlier, so that the direct provisioning of services has declined (Bulkeley and Kern 2006; Schroeder and Bulkeley 2009). Nonetheless, our case studies indicate that municipalities still play a critical role in the provisioning of urban infrastructures and services. These roles include the maintenance of existing systems and the development of new forms of infrastructure.

Water supply is one area of infrastructure maintenance that is critical for both climate change adaptation (in terms of reducing vulnerability to water shortages) and mitigation (given the energy-intensive nature of cleaning and distributing water for drinking and sanitation systems). For example, the Delhi Jal Board, the government agency responsible for water supply in Delhi, has estimated that distribution losses approach 40 percent of the total water supplied, due to leakages and unauthorized use. The board is in the process of replacing parts of the water mains because significant portions of the pipelines are 40 to 50 years old. In Cape Town a similar program of water system repair is also under way.

In terms of the development of new infrastructures, policies and projects are few and far between, and attention in our case studies has focused primarily on low-carbon and renewable energy. In Beijing, renewable energy currently provides only 1 percent of the electricity supply. A pilot Guanting Windfarm (first phase) was established to generate electricity and supply electricity to all of the 2008 Olympic Games venues, and 15 more renewable energy pilot villages and 10 to 15 biomass pilot projects are planned. In 2008, the Seoul metropolitan government devised a New Town Development Plan, which aims to build 277,000 new apartments with district heating, estimated to cost $2.6 billion. Although the energy and carbon dioxide savings, and propriety of the process, have been called into question, it demonstrates that making large-scale infrastructure changes to the provision of energy are on the agenda in Seoul in a way that is not yet apparent in most of the other case studies included in this report.

Enabling

In the main, strategies for enabling action by communities and stakeholders with respect to urban infrastructures are focused at the level of individual buildings and have already been discussed here. However, our case studies do reveal examples of more comprehensive approaches aimed at reducing the use of resources to tackle issues of poverty as well as energy and water shortages (with consequent implications for climate change mitigation and adaptation). In Delhi, rainwater harvesting is being promoted in the city, and monetary assistance is being given to individuals, resident organizations, and institutions to put in place the required system (GoD 2008). In Cape Town, two innovative schemes have been developed to address the combined effects of poverty and resources shortages. The city was the first to launch a "poverty tariff," where 50 kilowatt-hours of free electricity per month was being provided to households using below 400 kilowatt-hours per month on average over the 12 months up to May/June 2008 (CCT 2005; 2008b). To address future water shortages and stressed wastewater treatment rather than climate change, the city of Cape Town devised a Water Conservation and Water Demand initiative, which won an award from the national Department of Water Affairs and Forestry in May 2008 (CCT 2007; 2008c). The initiative involved installing advanced meters programmed to dispense a pre-agreed-upon amount of water each day, as little or as much as the householder can afford. Any unused amount will be carried over to the next day, but once the agreed-upon daily allocation has been reached, the flow stops until the next morning (CCT 2007). By 2009, more than 30,000 water management devices had been installed. The city will repair all internal leaks before the meter is set, with the intention of protecting both the consumer and water resources. This example does, however, raise concerns about issues of justice and access to resources and whether these should be determined by price alone. Furthermore, with respect to energy, in May 2008, South Africa's ruling part, the African National Congress, agreed that power prices will double to about R 46 cents per kilowatt-hour by 2012. Hence, Cape Town faces considerable challenges as it attempts to juggle energy and water poverty, the rising energy prices demanded by industry, power shortages, and environmental objectives in the future.

Partnership

Across our case studies, two forms of partnership are involved in the urban governance of infrastructures in response to climate change. The first involve CDM projects, facilitated through the international climate change agreements and overseen by the CDM board composed of state and nonstate actors. In Delhi, a CDM project was registered in 2007, which processes municipal solid waste to produce fuel that would then be used to generate electricity. The project is expected to earn 2.6 million tons of CERs over the next 10 years. In Delhi, at least four other similar projects have applied for registration under the CDM, and in Mumbai, a further project has been registered. This type of CDM project is also taking place in São Paulo, with energy being sourced from two of the largest landfills in the world, Bandeirantes and São Joao, which receive CDM credits (TCG 2008). Although Attero São Joao reached its full capacity in 2007, Aterro Bandeirantes continues to receive half of the waste (7,000 tons) from São Paulo every day. At the end of 2008, 7 percent of the city of São Paulo households were supplied by energy generated at both landfills. However, Bandeirantes is scheduled to close, and hence the city is planning to transport waste to neighboring municipalities by December 2010, meaning that the energy supplied will also no longer be available (Keith 2007).

The second set of partnership projects take place on a smaller scale and usually involve the private sector working with the municipality to develop new forms of infrastructure rather than in maintaining existing systems or working to improve their resilience for climate change adaptation. Several of these types of projects are taking place in Hong Kong SAR, China, including the HSBC project to install renewable energy in schools and the development of offshore wind farms by two power utilities that are currently under review. Similar strategies to develop the energy base of the city are being developed elsewhere but have reached a more advanced stage. In April 2007, Oh Se-hoon, Seoul's mayor, signed a memorandum of understanding with Korean Midland Power to expand the city's green energy. In Cape Town, to meet its target of producing 10 percent of electricity from renewable energy by 2020, the municipality has entered into a power purchase agreement with the Darling Wind Farm. The agreement provided financial and risk assurance for the generator whereby the city guarantees purchase for the next 20 years and plans to sell the green electricity at a premium price (R 22 cents per kilowatt-hour above current electricity rates) (CCT 2008b). However, Cape Town has yet to secure willing buyers. Meanwhile, Darling Wind Farm had not been able to attract investors in view of potential technical and legal complexities in contractual arrangements with the National Energy Regulator of South Africa and the electricity utility Eskom. This example shows that as such partnerships scale up from individual buildings to broader scale, the technical, legal, and financial challenges involved can be substantial.

Case-Study Findings and Implications

On the basis of the evidence from the case studies, we now consider the broader implications of our findings for the governing of climate change mitigation and adaptation at the municipal level.

Modes of Governing Climate Change in the Case Studies

Overall, we find across our case studies an increasing engagement with the issue of climate change, though primarily action remains focused on issues of mitigation rather than of adaptation. Given the dominance of cities from the global South in this selection, and the long-running argument that mitigation should be an issue addressed in the North before countries in the global South should take on such responsibilities, this may be a somewhat surprising finding. It suggests that climate change mitigation is becoming part of a discourse about the responsibilities of global and megacities, for reasons that we will discuss, despite the continuing international conflicts over what "common but differentiated responsibilities" might entail.

In terms of the sectors covered, we can see that action for climate change mitigation is taking place across the built environment, transport, and urban infrastructure domains, but that action for climate adaptation is primarily related to infrastructures and that both are usually as a side benefit of policies to address issues of air and water pollution, green space, and urban development more broadly. In contrast with previous studies based on cities in the North that have suggested that self-governance and enabling modes dominate urban responses to climate change, our case studies suggest that regulation and provision, together with partnership initiatives led by other actors, are also important. The use of the regulation and provision modes in the transport sector is particularly prominent; although even in regard to the built environment— where self-governance and enabling modes might be easier to implement— regulation still has an important role.

In terms of the specific focus of policies and measures, as has been found in other research, efforts with respect to energy efficiency dominate (Bulkeley and Kern 2006). As Rutland and Aylett (2008, 636) have argued in the analysis of the development of climate change policy in Portland, Oregon, energy efficiency is a particularly powerful mobilizing device because it can "advance diverse (and often divergent) goals in tandem," serving to translate various interests into those concerning climate change and effectively forging new alliances. In our case studies, concerns over energy security and the economic benefits of energy savings are serving to push energy efficiency actions up the climate change agenda. At present, this effort appears primarily directed toward corporate and government buildings rather than the domestic housing stock, which suggests that our case studies reflect a difference in approach from that which dominates municipalities in Australia, Europe, and North America where interventions in the domestic sphere have been much more common. This focus could bring a distinct politics to energy efficiency in the built environment in cities in the global South, resting more on the involvement of corporate partners and their corporate social responsibility agendas than the involvement of individual householders, reflecting a different "geography" of responsibility for emissions reductions in these places. With respect to urban infrastructures, notable mainly for their absence in the efforts to date to mitigate climate change across these case studies are initiatives to promote or develop sizable renewable energy installations. This may reflect the finding by Lasco and others (2007, 17) that a "discourse of unrealism" with respect to renewables that is more extreme than is warranted appears to have taken hold and be widely accepted. Also in contrast with research on cities in other parts of the world, attempts to address GHG emissions from the transport sector are more common than might be expected, though here the predominant motivations are addressing air quality and health concerns and reducing congestion. Nonetheless, potential is seen for considerable side benefits in terms of reductions of GHG emissions to be realized as municipalities in the global South seek to tackle this most prominent of local environmental concerns.

Drivers for Action

In common with previous research, our case studies suggest that the four factors of leadership, the authority of local governments, resources, and issue framing have been critical drivers for climate policy and action.

In terms of leadership, we find that individual political champions, such as the mayor of Yogyakarta, have been important in terms of driving initiatives forward. More important, though, have been opportunities for the municipality to display "global" leadership on issues of climate change and environment. In three of our case studies (Beijing, Cape Town, and Delhi), the window of opportunity created by global sporting events has been used as a vehicle for promoting action on climate change within the city. In Seoul, membership in the C40 network and the forthcoming meeting in May 2009 were also seen to be important in galvanizing action. Such "trigger events" provide the motivation, and physical opportunity, for intervening in the urban landscape (for example, transportation systems, housing) to address climate change.

We found that adaptation measures often get adopted only in response to specific local or regional natural disasters, which may or may not be climate related. For example, in Mumbai, after the 2005 deluge flooding, the Greater Mumbai Disaster Management Plan was revised in 2007, strengthening the Municipal Corporation of Greater Mumbai's Disaster Management Committee and raising disaster preparedness of the city (Gupta 2007). In Yogyakarta, the 2006 earthquake highlighted the lack of government management capacity and understanding of disaster response. Consequently, a Disaster Management Bill and a National Action Plan for 2007–09 were enacted (Hadi 2007b). At the local level, Yogyakarta's provincial and local agencies conducted a damage loss assessment and formulated a local action plan, including regulatory, institutional, and funding frameworks and recognizing the need to enhance institutional capacity and networks among government, the private sector, and civil society (Hadi 2007a).

With regard to the authority of municipal governments, the impetus of national government action (in China and Korea, in particular) has been an important factor in creating the political space for local government action on climate change. Municipalities that have a broader range of competencies (such as for street lighting or the provision of public transport) have been able to intervene across the different modes of governing for climate change, whereas those with more restricted authority have had less scope to become directly involved.

Seoul is one case study in which numerous significant initiatives have taken place, made feasible partly by the availability of funding. In August 2007, Seoul expanded the scope of the City Gas Business Fund to a broader climate change fund with a goal to raise more than $100 million by 2010 to finance research, technological development, and mitigation projects; to support renewable energy; to improve energy accessibility to the poor; and to promote energy-efficient appliances (SMG News 2008). The country's private sector also raised six funds totaling about $100 million in 2007 for climate change purposes (Oh 2008). Such resources are scarce among our case-study cities. One means through which additional resources have been garnered is the CDM, with projects in the transport and infrastructure sectors in Delhi, Mumbai, and São Paulo. This suggests that the CDM could be an important mechanism for addressing climate change in cities in the future.

Issue framing has also been important. We earlier outlined the importance of both "localizing" climate change and "issue bundling," both strategies that serve to make climate change an important issue on local agendas and that cuts across other (priority) sectors. Our case studies suggest that issue framing has been very important in moving climate action forward: first, with respect to energy security, energy efficiency, and fuel poverty, which have proved to be driving factors in almost all the case studies, and second, with respect to air quality and health, which have provided the impetus for action in the transport sector in all of the case studies. The exception in both cases is Melbourne, which is located in a region with abundant coal resources and where issues of local air pollution, although important, have not served to drive climate change action.

Barriers

The factors that have driven climate change action in some of our case studies—opportunities for leadership, the authority to tackle the issue, access to resources, and issue framing that has attracted political support—can also serve to hamper efforts for governing climate change in cities. This may account for why climate change adaptation is relatively low on the agenda, with few opportunities to demonstrate leadership (repairing water systems is hardly headline grabbing), a lack of an explicit remit to address climate adaptation, limited access to resources to repair infrastructure systems or enhance the resilience of the urban environment, and an absence of issue framing that has linked adaptation to pressing urban social, economic, and environmental issues. It also explains why some cities—such as Mumbai in our case—have to date taken little action to mitigate climate change. In the midst of other pressing environmental, health, and economic concerns, the issue does not have the traction or the support required to ensure that it is on the urban agenda.

In addition, however, we find one other obvious set of issues that have acted as a barrier to further action at the municipal level: the relation between continued fossil fuel use and economic growth. In most of our case-study cities, demands for travel and energy consumption are increasing exponentially, and the majority of these needs will be met through the continued provision of fossil fuel–based energy.

Lessons

By disaggregating urban climate change governance across different sectors and in relation to the different "modes" of governing employed, we can identify specific lessons from the built environment, transportation, and urban infrastructures that may be applicable beyond the case studies considered here. As has been noted earlier in this chapter, the cases from which these lessons are derived represent a particular subset of cities in rapidly industrializing countries and in which there is both a capacity to govern at the urban level and a growing impetus to address climate change. The relevance for cities in low-income countries or where urban governance capacity is virtually nonexistent will therefore be limited.

Built environment

1. Energy conservation is a critical local "hook" for municipal action on climate change, and the built environment is a key sector in which such approaches can be put into action. Significant opportunities exist to pursue this agenda, especially in the commercial sector.

2. Municipal governments have the capacity to go beyond national building standards and to adopt additional means of regulating energy use in the built environment. Forms of "soft" regulation can be effective in this regard.

3. Municipal governments have various means of enabling action by stakeholders and communities in reducing energy use in the built environment through the provision of information, recognition, and reward for achievement.

4. Stakeholders outside local government are important drivers of action in this sector. This is particularly the case in the commercial built environment. Potential is seen for further partnership work and for action on climate change mitigation and adaptation in the absence of significant municipal capacity for climate governance.

Transportation

1. In the transportation sector, action on climate change benefits from a strong link to issues high on the agenda of rapidly expanding cities—air pollution, congestion, sprawl—but is reliant on the planning and governance capacity of municipalities as well as the availability of funding from national governments or external agencies.

2. Municipalities have been able to use various forms of regulation, predominantly concerning efficiency and emissions standards but also relating to behavioral change, to address transport issues in ways that could have benefits for GHG emissions.

3. Municipal provision of low-carbon transport infrastructures is another key means through which local governments can combine local priorities and climate change agendas.

4. Our cases also suggest that a number of incentives are available that municipalities can deploy to achieve behavioral change, though these are underdeveloped compared with regulatory and service provision modes of governing.

Urban infrastructure

1. Primarily, addressing climate change is a marginal issue in the development and maintenance of urban infrastructures, and any benefits that arise in terms of mitigation and adaptation are incidental.

2. Street lighting is one important arena in which municipal governments have been taking action to reduce energy use and save money, but this requires significant investment, and the timing of intervention is crucial.

3. One case, that of Cape Town, shows that addressing climate change in terms of reducing energy use and securing water supplies can go hand in hand with development goals of meeting basic needs, but this faces considerable challenges in a context of rising energy costs and inadequate infrastructure provision.

4. The availability of carbon finance—in the form of CDM projects and voluntary offsetting schemes—may provide a resource that municipalities can use to deliver low-carbon infrastructures and meet sustainability goals, but the potential impacts of such programs on different sectors of society will need to be carefully considered.

Conclusions

Our review of the evidence on urban climate change mitigation and adaptation strategies found a strong bias toward the former, a history of engagement primarily by cities in the North, and a focus on issues of energy conservation. Although there is evidence of a new "wave" of urban climate change response, encompassing a broader geographical range of cities and placing adaptation on the agenda, the emphasis remains on mitigation in both research and policy. Our case studies confirmed this finding, with evidence of action to mitigate climate change across the built environment, transportation, and urban infrastructure sectors, whereas action on climate adaptation has remained marginal and is usually a secondary impact of policies designed to tackle other urban problems. We found evidence that municipalities are deploying multiple modes of governing climate change, with more emphasis on regulation and provision than is the case in many cities in the North, and that there is evidence, especially with respect to the built environment, that urban responses to climate change are being undertaken by other stakeholders. Across all three sectors, concerns for energy efficiency—rather than the provision of alternative sources of energy or demand management—dominate.

In terms of the key drivers and challenges for climate change at the urban level, our literature review and case-study research concur that the key factors shaping responses to mitigation are the following:

- Effective policy entrepreneurs
- Municipal competencies in critical areas such as transportation, infrastructure, energy. and planning policy
- Access to additional financial resources, and flexibility in their deployment
- An enabling policy framework at national and regional levels
- The fit between jurisdictional areas and problem boundaries
- The ability to engage partners to achieve action beyond the municipality
- The knowledge and resource capacity, as well as political support, generated by networks and partnerships
- The reframing of climate change as an issue of local importance and the absence of conflict between addressing climate change and other local priorities.

In terms of adaptation, we find the following key factors:

- Availability of data and information about local impacts from climate change
- Good governance
- Access to financial and human resources provided by the national government or international donors
- Coordination of policies and measure across both local agencies and levels of government
- Empowerment and training of civil society to help strengthen service provision, environmental management, and the livelihoods of the most vulnerable people
- Nurturing a sense of readiness for disaster emergency.

In part, the differences in the drivers and the challenges faced reflect the different type of city upon which the research base has been built. In relation to climate change mitigation, our case studies and most of the available evidence, relate to cities that have at least a minimal level of governance capacity and often quite significant resources for regulating, providing services, and enabling stakeholder engagement. In low-income countries and cities with minimal if any urban governance capacity, the challenges of addressing climate change are of a different order. This is reflected in our review of urban responses to adaptation in which the literature stresses the importance of basic governance functions and the provision of infrastructure to meet basic needs. Nonetheless, our case-study findings suggest that even where governance capacity exists, climate change adaptation remains marginal. We suggest that this could derive from the relative lack of action by transnational networks on climate adaptation to date, a lack of opportunities for leadership, limited knowledge on which to base decisions, a lack of resources for the provision and maintenance of infrastructure systems, and an absence of issue framing that has linked adaptation to pressing urban social, economic, and environmental issues, with the result that adaptation has limited traction or support on a local scale.

Notes

1. We use the word "standard" to refer interchangeably to what also might be called codes, criteria, guidelines, norms, laws, protocols, provisions, recommendations, requirements, regulations, rules, or standards. Depending on the country, the "standard" may be contained in one document, be part of another larger document (such as a general building code), or comprise several documents.
2. This research updates a similar study completed in 1994 on the worldwide status of energy standards for buildings (Janda and Busch 1993, 1994).
3. See http://www.arch.hku.hk/research/BEER/besc.htm.
4. See http://www.sustainable.org.za/greenbuilding/index.htm.
5. Eligible car list (subject to question because preparers rely on automakers to provide information): http://www.epd.gov.hk/epd/english/environmentinhk/air/prob_solutions/environment_friendly_private_cars.html#3.
6. Also see http://auto.sohu.com/20081013/n260001979.shtml.
7. Hong Kong Environmental Protection Department website, http://www.epd.gov.hk/epd/english/climate_change/transport.html.
8. See http://en.beijing2008.cn/bocog/environment/sports/n214159224.shtml.

References

Adaptive Building Initiative. 2009. http://adaptivebuildings.com/.

Adger, W., N. Arnell, and E. Tompkins. 2005. "Successful Adaptation to Climate Change across Scales." *Global Environmental Change* 15: 77–86.

Alam, M., and M. Rabbani. 2007. "Vulnerabilities and Responses to Climate Change for Dhaka." *Environment and Urbanization* 19: 81–97.

Alber, G., and K. Kern. 2008. "Governing Climate Change in Cities: Modes of Urban Climate Governance in Multi-Level Systems." OECD International Conference, Competitive Cities and Climate Change, 2nd Annual Meeting of the OECD Roundtable Strategy for Urban Development, Milan, October 9–10. http://www.oecd.org/document/32/0,3343,en_21571361_41059646_41440096_1_1_1_1,00.html.

Allman, L., P. Fleming, and A. Wallace. 2004. "The Progress of English and Welsh Local Authorities in Addressing Climate Change." *Local Environment* 9 (3): 271–83.

Bai, X. 2007. "Integrating Global Environmental Concerns into Urban Management: The Scale and Readiness Arguments." *Journal of Industrial Ecology* 11 (2): 15–29.

Bailey, J. 2008. "Do Cities in Developing Countries Respond to the Global Call for Climate Protection? A Case Study on Yogyakarta, Indonesia." M.Sc. dissertation, University of Oxford, United Kingdom.

Betsill, M. 2001. "Mitigating Climate Change in US Cities: Opportunities and Obstacles." *Local Environment* 6 (4): 393–406.

Betsill, M., and H. Bulkeley. 2007. "Guest Editorial: Looking Back and Thinking Ahead: A Decade of Cities and Climate Change Research." *Local Environment* 12 (5): 447–56.

Bulkeley, H. 2000. "Down to Earth: Local Government and Greenhouse Policy in Australia." *Australian Geographer* 31 (3): 289–308.

Bulkeley, H., and M. Betsill. 2003. *Cities and Climate Change: Urban Sustainability and Global Environmental Governance.* London: Routledge.

Bulkeley, H., and K. Kern. 2006. "Local Government and the Governing of Climate Change in Germany and the UK." *Urban Studies* 43 (12): 2237–59.

CCT (City of Cape Town). 2005. *Cape Town Energy and Climate Change Strategy.* Cape Town: City of Cape Town.

———. 2006. *Framework for Adaptation to Climate Change in the City of Cape Town (FAC4T).* Cape Town: City of Cape Town.

———. 2007. *Long-Term Water Conservation and Water Demand Management Strategy.* Cape Town: City of Cape Town.

———. 2008a. *Global Climate Change and Adaptation—A Sea-Level Rise Risk Assessment.* Cape Town: City of Cape Town and SEI.

———. 2008b. "Schedule of Electricity Tariff Effective by 1 July 2008," http://www.capetown.gov.za/en/electricity/tariffs/Pages/default.aspx.

———. 2008c. "Water Awards Obtained by the City of Capetown." http://www.capetown.gov.za/en/Water/Pages/Awards.aspx.

Collier, U. 1997. "Local Authorities and Climate Protection in the European Union: Putting Subsidiarity into Practice?" *Local Environment* 2 (1): 39–57.

Davies, A. 2005. "Local Action for Climate Change: Transnational Networks and the Irish Experience." *Local Environment* 10 (1): 21–40.

DeAngelo, B., and L. Harvey. 1998. "The Jurisdictional Framework for Municipal Action to Reduce Greenhouse Gas Emissions: Case Studies from Canada, the USA and Germany." *Local Environment* 3 (2): 111–36.

DTL (Delhi Transco Ltd). 2008. "Energy Efficiency and Renewable Energy Management Centre: Context." http://www.delhitransco.gov.in/EnergyEfficiency/Context.htm.

Dhakal, S. 2004. "Urban Energy Use and Greenhouse Gas Emissions in Asian Mega Cities: Policies for a Sustainable Future." Institute for Global Environmental Strategies, Kanagawa, Japan.

———. 2006. "Urban Transportation and the Environment in Kathmandu Valley, Nepal: Integrating Global Carbon Concerns into Local Air Pollution Management." Institute for Global Environmental Strategies, Hayama, Japan.

EMSD (Electrical and Mechanical Services Department). 2008. "LPG Vehicle Scheme." http://www.emsd.gov.hk/emsd/eng/sgi/lpg.shtml.

EMSD and EPD (Electrical and Mechanical Services Department and Environmental Protection Department). 2008. "Guidelines to Account for and Report on Greenhouse Gas Emissions and Removals for Buildings (Commercial, Residential or

Institutional Purpose) in Hong Kong." http://www.epd.gov.hk/epd/english/climate_change/files/CAGuidelines_Eng.pdf.

GoD (Government of Delhi). 2008. "Economic Survey of Delhi 2007–2008." http://delhiplanning.nic.in/Economic%20Survey/ES2007–08/ES2007–08.htm.

Greenpeace. 2008. "China after the Olympics: Lessons from Beijing." July. Greenpeace, Beijing.

Gupta, K. 2007. "Urban Flood Resilience Planning and Management and Lessons for the Future: A Case Study of Mumbai, India." *Urban Water Journal* 3 (3): 183–94.

Hadi, S. 2007a. "The Country Perspective on Emergency Preparedness: Case of Indonesia." Powerpoint presented at the ADB Small Group Workshop on Preparing for Large-Scale Emergencies, Manila, July 5–6. http://www.adb.org/Documents/Events/2007/Small-Group-Workshop/PPT-Hadi.pdf.

———. 2007b. "ADB Country Perspective: Indonesia." ADB Small Group Workshop on Preparing for Large-Scale Emergencies, Manila, July 5–6. http://www.adb.org/Documents/Events/2007/Small-Group-Worksho/Paper_Hadi.pdf.

Halsnæs, K., and J. Verhagen. 2007. "Development Based Climate Change Adaptation and Mitigation—Conceptual Issues and Lessons Learned in Studies in Developing Countries." *Mitigation and Adaptation Strategies for Global Change* 13 (2): 105–30.

Harvey, L., and D. Danny. 1993. "Tackling Urban CO_2 Emissions in Toronto." *Environment* 35 (7): 16–20, 38–44.

Hay, J., and N. Mimura. 2006. "Supporting Climate Change Vulnerability and Adaptation Assessments in the Asia-Pacific Region: An Example of Sustainability Science." *Sustainability Science* 1: 23–35.

Hewlett Foundation. 2005. *No Reason to Wait: The Benefits of Greenhouse Gas Reduction in São Paulo and California.* Menlo Park, CA: Hewlett Foundation.

Hidalgo, D., and M. Pai. 2009. *Delhi Bus Corridor: An Evaluation.* Washington, DC: World Resources Institute; Delhi: Centre for Science and Environment.

Holgate, C. 2007. "Factors and Actors in Climate Change Mitigation: A Tale of Two South African Cities." *Local Environment* 12 (5): 471–84.

Huq, S., S. Kovats, H. Reid, and D. Satterthwaite. 2007. "Editorial: Reducing Risks to Cities from Disasters and Climate Change." *Environment and Urbanization* 19 (3): 3–15.

ICLEI. 2004. Yogyakarta Case Study in Local Energy Efficiency. SEA-CCP Case Outline 4. ICLEI Southeast Asia, Manila.

IEA (International Energy Agency). 2008. *World Energy Outlook 2008.* Paris: IEA.

Janda, K., and J. Busch. 1993. *Worldwide Status of Energy Standards for Buildings. LBL-33587.* Vols. 1 and 2. Berkeley, CA: Lawrence Berkeley National Laboratory.

———. 1994. "Worldwide Status of Energy Standards for Buildings." *Energy* 19 (1): 27–44.

Jollands, N. 2008. "Cities and Energy—A Discussion Paper." OECD International Conference, Competitive Cities and Climate Change, 2nd Annual Meeting of the OECD Roundtable Strategy for Urban Development, Energy Efficiency and Environment Division, International Energy Agency, Milan, October 9–10. http://www.oecd.org/dataoecd/23/46/41440153.pdf.

Kahn Ribeiro, S., S. Kobayashi, M. Beuthe, J. Gasca, D. Greene, D. S. Lee, Y. Muromachi, P. J. Newton, S. Plotkin, D. Sperling, R. Wit, and P. J. Zhou. 2007. "Transport and its infrastructure." In *Climate Change 2007: Mitigation. Contribution of Working*

Group III to the Fourth Assessment Report of the Intergovernmental Panel on Climate Change, B. Metz, O.R. Davidson, P.R. Bosch, R. Dave, and L.A. Meyer, eds. Cambridge and New York: Cambridge University Press.

Karekezi, S., L. Majoro, and T. Johnson. 2003. "Climate Change and Urban Transport: Priorities for the World Bank." Working paper, World Bank, Washington, DC.

Keith, R. 2007. "Serra's 21 Strategic Environmental Projects for São Paulo." The Temas Blog, April 9. http://www.temasactuales.com/temasblog/environmental-protection/serras-21-strategic-environmental-projects-for-sao-paulo/.

Kern, K., and H. Bulkeley. 2009. "Cities, Europeanization and Multi-Level Governance: Governing Climate Change through Transnational Municipal Networks." *Journal of Common Market Studies* 47 (2): 309–32.

Kim, K.-G. 1999. "Flood Hazard in Seoul: A Preliminary Assessment." In *Crucibles of Hazard: Mega-Cities and Disasters in Transition,* ed. J. K. Mitchell, 92–118. New York: United Nations University Press.

Koeppel, S., and D. Ürge-Vorsatz. 2007. "Assessment of Policy Instruments for Reducing Greenhouse Gas Emissions from Buildings." Report for the United Nations Environment Programme–Sustainable Buildings and Construction Initiative. Central European University, Budapest. http://web.ceu.hu/envsci/projects/UNEPP/index.html.

Kousky, C., and S. Schneider. 2003. "Global Climate Policy: Will Cities Lead the Way?" *Climate Policy* 3 (4): 359–72.

Lambright, W., S. Chagnon, and L. D. Harvey. 1996. "Urban Reactions to the Global Warming Issue: Agenda Setting in Toronto and Chicago." *Climatic Change* 34: 463–78.

Lasco, R., L. Lebel, A. Sari, A. Mitra, N. Tri, O. Ling, and A. Contreras. 2007. "Integrating Carbon Management into Development Strategies of Cities—Establishing a Network of Case Studies of Urbanisation in Asia Pacific." Final Report for Asia-Pacific Network project 2004-07-CMY-Lasco.

Li, Q., W. Yunjing, and Z. Yang. 2008. "Readjustment Effect Analysis of Public Bus Network in Beijing." *Journal of Transportation Systems Engineering and Information Technology* 8 (2): 27–33.

Lindseth, G. 2004. "The Cities for Climate Protection Campaign (CCPC) and the Framing of Local Climate Policy." *Local Environment* 9 (4): 325–36.

McEvoy, D., S. Lindley, and J. Handley. 2006. "Adaptation and Mitigation in Urban Areas: Synergies and Conflicts." *Municipal Engineer* 159 (4): 185–91.

Mexico City. 2008. "Plan Verde." http://www.planverde.df.gob.mx/planverde/.

Midgley, G. F., R. A. Chapman, B. Hewitson, P. Johnston, M. de Wit, G. Ziervogel, P. Mukheibir, L. van Niekerk, M. Tadross, B. W. van Wilgen, B. Kgope, P. D. Morant, A. Theron, and R. J. F. Scholes. 2005. "A Status Quo, Vulnerability and Adaptation Assessment of the Physical and Socioeconomic Effects of Climate Change in the Western Cape." Stellenbosch, CSIR Report ENV-S-C 2005–073, Report to the Western Cape Government, Cape Town, South Africa.

MCGM (Municipal Corporation of Greater Mumbai). 2008. "Eco-Housing Incentives." http://www.mcgm.gov.in/irj/portalapps/com.mcgm.ecohousing/docs/Eco_Housing_Brochure.pdf.

MNRE (Ministry of New and Renewable Energy). 2008. "Need for Rigorous Marketing of Battery-Operated Vehicles." http://mnre.gov.in/press-releases/press-release-17062008.pdf.

Oh, L.-Y. 2008. "Status of Climate Change Policies in South Korea." In *Proceedings of the EU-Korea Conference on Science and Technology*, Springer Proceedings in Physics, vol. 124, part 4, 485–93. New York: Springer.

Pitts, A., and K. Kim. 2005. "Planning and Design Strategies for Sustainable Low Energy Development in Seoul, Korea." Paper presented at Passive and Low Energy Cooling for the Built Environment Conference, May, Santorini, Greece.

Qi, Y., L. Ma, H. Zhang, and H. Li. 2008. "Translating a Global Issue into Local Priority: China's Local Government Response to Climate Change." *Journal of Environment and Development* 17 (4): 379–400.

Roaf, S., D. Crichton, and F. Nicol. 2005. *Adapting Buildings and Cities for Climate Change*. Amsterdam: Elsevier.

Romero-Lankao, P. 2007. "How Do Local Governments in Mexico City Manage Global Warming?" *Local Environment* 12 (5): 519–35.

Rosencranz, A., and M. Jackson. 2003. "The Delhi Pollution Case: the Supreme Court of India and the Limits of Judicial Power." *Columbia Journal of Environmental Law* 28: 223–54.

Rutland, T., and A. Aylett. 2008. "The Work of Policy: Actor Networks, Governmentality, and Local Action on Climate Change in Portland, Oregon." *Environment and Planning D: Society and Space* 26 (4): 627–46.

Satterthwaite, D. 2008a. "Cities' Contribution to Global Warming: Notes on the Allocation of Greenhouse Gas Emissions." *Environment and Urbanization* 20: 539–49.

————. 2008b. "Climate Change and Urbanization: Effects and Implications for Urban Governance." United Nations Expert Group Meeting on Population Distribution, Urbanization, Internal Migration and Development Paper UN/POP/EGM-URB/2008/16, United Nations, New York.

Satterthwaite, D., S. Huq, M. Pelling, H. Reid, and P. Romero-Lankao. 2008. "Adapting to Climate Change in Urban Areas: The Possibilities and Constraints in Low- and Middle-Income Nations." http://www.iied.org/pubs/pdfs/10549IIED.pdf.

Schreurs, M. 2008. "From the Bottom Up: Local and Subnational Climate Change Politics." *Journal of Environment and Development* 17 (4): 343–55.

Schroeder, H., and H. Bulkeley. 2008. "Governing Climate Change Post-2012: The Role of Global Cities, Case-Study: Los Angeles." Tyndall Working Paper 122, Tyndall Centre for Climate Change Research, University of East Anglia, Norwich.

————. 2009. "Global Cities and the Governance of Climate Change: What Is the Role of Law in Cities?" *Fordham Urban Law Journal* 36 (2): 313–59.

Sinha, N. 2008. "Clinton Climate Initiative Joins Hands with Indian Group to Retrofit Buildings." *Indian Express*, June 13. http://www.indianexpress.com/news/clinton-climate-initiative-joins-hands-with-indian-group-to-retrofit-buildings/322155/0.

SMG (Seoul Metropolitan Government). 2008. "What We Do: Seoul's Response Measures to Climate Change." C40 Seoul Conference Division, Seoul. http://www.c40seoulsummit.com/eng/about/whatwedo_02.html.

SMG News. 2008 "Designing a Beautiful Future." Special Report, January 10. http://english.seoul.go.kr/today/infocus/specialreport/1252626_5093.php.

Sperling, D., and J. Cannon. 2007. *Driving Climate Change: Cutting Carbon from Transportation*. Burlington, MA: Academic Press.

SSN (SouthSouthNorth). 2008. "Kuyasa Low-Income Housing Upgrade Project." http://www.southsouthnorth.org.

SSP (State of São Paulo). 2008. São Paulo Case Study. http://www.theclimategroup.org/major_initiatives/states_and_regions/sao_paulo_state.

Stern, N. 2006. "Stern Review on the Economics of Climate Change, HM Treasury and Cabinet Office." http://www.hm-treasury.gov.uk/sternreview_index.htm.

Sugiyama, N., and T. Takeuchi. 2008. "Local Policies for Climate Change in Japan." *Journal of Environment and Development* 17 (4): 424–41.

Takeuchi, A., M. Cropper, and A. Bento. 2007. "The Impact of Policies to Control Motor Vehicle Emissions in Mumbai, India." *Journal of Regional Science* 47(1): 27–46.

Tanner, T., T. Mitchell, E. Polack, and B. Guenther. 2008. "Urban Governance for Adaptation: Assessing Climate Change Resilience in Ten Asian Cities." Institute of Development Studies. http://www.ids.ac.uk/UserFiles/File/poverty_team/climate_change/IDS_Climate_Resilient_Urban_Governance_RF_report_2008_2.pdf.

TCG (The Climate Group). 2008. "São Paulo Case Study." http://www.theclimategroup.org/major_initiatives/states_and_regions/sao_paulo_state.

UK WGCCD (UK Working Group on Climate Change and Development). 2007. "Up in Smoke? Asia and the Pacific: The Threat from Climate Change to Human Development and the Environment." http://www.oxfam.de/download/up_in_smoke.pdf.

Véron, R. 2006. "Remaking Urban Environments: The Political Ecology of Air Pollution in Delhi." *Environment and Planning A* 38 (11): 2093–109.

Xinhua News. 2008. "Beijing Starts 2-Month-Long Vehicle Use Control for Olympic Games." http://news.xinhuanet.com/english/2008-07/20/content_8576632.htm.

Yarnal, B., R. O'Connor, and R. Shudak. 2003. "The Impact of Local versus National Framing on Willingness to Reduce Greenhouse Gas Emissions: A Case Study from Central Pennsylvania." *Local Environment* 8 (4): 457–69.

Zhao, J. 2008. "Can the Green Olympics Help Beijing Create a More Sustainable Transport System?" NECTAR (Network on European Communications and Transport Activities Research) cluster conference, "Integrated Transport: From Policy to Practice," Oxford University, 12–13 September 2008.

6

Viral Governance and Mixed Motivations: How and Why U.S. Cities Engaged on the Climate Change Issue, 2005–2007

Toby Warden

Cities are often considered a valuable starting place for reducing greenhouse gas emissions to address global warming. As primary actors on urban policies, city leaders are also responsible for decisions on local land-use planning and waste management—domains essential to the implementation of environmentally sustainable policies (Betsill 2001; Bulkeley 2000). In addition, mayors and city officials are often the first responders when a natural disaster or an extreme weather event has urgent local consequences.

Yet municipalities might abstain from efforts to reduce greenhouse gas emissions for numerous reasons. Betsill (2001) identified the challenge of allocating scarce local resources for a problem that was largely framed as a global issue. Additionally, questions have been posed as to whether there can be successful locally based mitigation without wide-scale national and international participation. DeAngelo and Harvey (1998) pointed out that although a community may strive to control emissions locally, the resulting impact may not be felt where the mitigation efforts have taken place, thereby decreasing tangible incentives for action.

Furthermore, global warming has been largely considered to be a "creeping" problem; people have had a tendency to feel removed from the problem in "space and time" (Betsill 2001; Wilbanks and Kates 1999). Turnpenny and

The research for this paper was made possible through fellowships from the Newkirk Center for Science and Society, the University of California's School of Social Ecology Dean's Dissertation Writing Fellowship, and the generous support of the Department of Environmental Health, Science, and Policy at the University of California, Irvine.

others (2005, 11) summarized this prominent challenge: "Ultimately, climate change is rather peripheral to mainstream policies such as pursuance of economic growth or housing development, mainly because of its overwhelmingly long-term nature and lack of tangible current pressures for action"

In 2005, in an effort to inspire U.S. cities to address the climate change resulting from global warming, Mayor Greg Nickels of Seattle, Washington, launched the U.S. Mayors Climate Protection Agreement (USMCPA) via the City of Seattle's Office of Sustainability and Environment. The agreement encouraged U.S. municipalities to take action to reduce greenhouse gas emissions. The four-page written pledge asked mayors to "strive" to meet or exceed the guidelines for emissions reduction for a developed country as set forth in the Kyoto Protocol. Simply, a mayoral signature in support of this mission earned participation in the USMCPA (USCOM 2005).

Mayor Nickels's goal was to enlist 141 U.S. cities, a number that symbolically paralleled the amount of participating nations required to enter into force the Kyoto Protocol. In February 2005, when Mayor Nickels launched his nationwide campaign, the required 141 nations as signatories (less the United States) had been secured, and the protocol went into effect.

Within a few months, Mayor Nickels exceeded his goal of enlisting 141 cities; 400 U.S. mayors signed the USMCPA. Participation in the agreement and municipal engagement on the issue of climate change grew rapidly thereafter. This chapter examines how and why this widespread and rapid engagement took place.

Methods and Analysis

The data analyzed for this investigation included 200 archival sources of news articles, government documents, conference summaries, and websites. Direct statements capturing motivations for participation in the USMCPA were analyzed from 125 U.S. cities. In-depth, semistructured interviews conducted with key informants (mayors, city officials, and representatives of relevant organizations) from nine cities and eight organizations served to triangulate the findings as well as to offer deeper insight into the outcome under investigation.

The primary analysis applied to the data was Policy Network Analysis (PNA), an analytical framework developed and refined by political science scholars Rhodes, Marsh, and Smith (Marsh and Smith 2000; Rhodes 1997; Rhodes and Marsh 1992). The PNA model explains policy outcomes through an iterated analysis of the actors, contexts, and interactions tied to an issue area. The key policy network under investigation for this study was the core group of individuals and organizations coalescing and interacting around the issue area of U.S. cities and climate change as anchored by the USMCPA from 2005 to 2007.

The analysis of the data revealed that the rapid policy momentum and municipal engagement of U.S. cities on the climate change issue from 2005 to 2007 evolved from a set of factors. The engagement is explained by (1) examining the actions and interactions of a group of key organizations and mayoral actors, (2) considering the context of an emerging national awareness of climate change, and (3) investigating the nature of cities.

The Agreement

The initial four-page agreement described the need for governmental involvement from the federal, state, and municipal levels (USCOM 2005). The agreement outlined various steps that cities could take to reduce their emissions. This mayoral effort grew quickly to become the largest coordinated U.S. municipal undertaking to address climate change. By February 2007, more than 400 U.S. mayors, representing nearly 60 million U.S. citizens, had signed the agreement.

Although the agreement's success called attention to the role that cities play in addressing the climate change, groundwork had begun over a decade earlier by ICLEI. In 1990, ICLEI, a membership association of local governments and regional and national-level organizations committed to sustainable development, was established at the inaugural World Conference of Local Governments for a Sustainable Future at the United Nations. ICLEI's mission was to target local governmental action as a prescription for complex, global environmental problems.

In 1993, ICLEI created Cities for Climate Protection (CCP), a campaign to enlist municipalities from around the world to commit to a five-step process to reduce greenhouse gas emissions in their communities. CCP provided technical tools and support to cities and counties to develop targets, to implement timelines, and to monitor progress for reducing greenhouse gas emissions. U.S. participation in the program grew steadily from 10 local governments in 1995 to more than 160 U.S. cities and counties by February 2006 (ICLEI 2006). When the USMCPA was launched in 2005, CCP had already established itself as the leading organized, municipal-centered climate change program in the United States.

The USMCPA, however, presented a less structured platform for coalescing cities on the issue of climate change; participation was flexible, nonbinding, and without a formal enforcement mechanism. Cities were presented with an opportunity to easily and quickly join a broad effort to address a global issue with local dimensions. The policy landscape for U.S. cities and climate change is in no way confined to the USMCPA (one example being the longevity of the work of ICLEI's CCP campaign). In addition, from 2005 to 2007, many actors were active in the global warming policy arena, from local to international levels (see Selin and VanDeveer 2007). This study focuses primarily on U.S. cities and climate change anchored by the USMCPA, as the agreement presents a valuable focal point from which to consider the rapid engagement of U.S. cities on the climate change issue from 2005 to 2007.

Interactions and Influence: Key Policy Network Actors

The engagement was influenced by a decentralized cooperative policy network of five key actors: (1) Mayor Nickels and the Seattle Office of Sustainability and the Environment, (2) the U.S. Conference of Mayors (USCOM), (3) ICLEI and the CCP Campaign, (4) the Sierra Club Cool Cities Campaign, and (5) Mayor Rocky Anderson of Salt Lake City, Utah. All five actors have been investigated for their catalyzing contributions that served to spur municipal engagement on the climate change issue. They are described in greater detail in table 6.1.

TABLE 6.1
Key Policy Network Actors

Actor	Description
Mayor Greg Nickels of Seattle	Creator of the U.S. Mayors Climate Protection Agreement
USCOM	The U.S. Conference of Mayors is the official nonpartisan association of U.S. cities with a population of 30,000 or more. The conference endorsed the USMCPA in June 2005 and created the U.S. Mayors Council on Climate Protection in 2006.
ICLEI/CCP	ICLEI is a nonprofit membership association of local governments committed to furthering worldwide sustainability development. In 1993, the organization launched the Cities for Climate Protection Campaign, a city-centered effort to address climate change from the local level.
Sierra Club Cool Cities Campaign	The Sierra Club, one of the country's oldest environmental organizations, launched the Cool Cities Campaign in October 2005 to increase participation in the USMCPA and to provide a platform for citizen involvement with the climate change issue.
Mayor Rocky Anderson of Salt Lake City	Notable leader in the area of cities and global warming, organized catalyzing conferences with ICLEI and the Sundance Preserve, an environmental nonprofit organization led by Robert Redford

Source: Warden 2007.

These actors were linked through a shared urgency about the climate change issue, a shared mission to engage cities in action, and the mutual desire to see the federal government generate a robust regulatory action plan to reduce greenhouse gas emissions. The result was an informal, decentralized policy network. Network-based policy structures have been described as "characterized by high levels of interdependence involving multiple organizations, where formal lines of authority are blurred and where diverse policy actors are knitted together to focus on common problems" (Schneider and others 2003, 143–44).

A collection of conferences, summits, and interactions by and among the key policy network actors served as catalysts in two significant ways. The activities contributed to the premise that cities play a central role in addressing the climate change challenge. The gatherings served as points of "contagion" and reinforced the policy network's shared mission.

The inaugural Sundance Summit: A Mayors' Gathering on Climate Protection was held in July 2005. The event was cohosted by ICLEI, Salt Lake City mayor Rocky Anderson, and actor and director Robert Redford (his nonprofit conference organization is called Sundance Preserve). In addition to Redford, former vice president Al Gore was in attendance. Several participants identified the summit as a valuable platform for creating both awareness of the issue and generating interaction among stakeholders; the second Sundance Summit took place in the fall of 2006 and similarly fostered generative and generous exchange among attendees, which furthered municipal engagement on the climate change issue (Warden 2007).

In 2006, ICLEI held a separate mayoral summit in Alaska titled "Strengthening Our Cities: Mayors Responding to Global Climate Change, Anchorage." In attendance were more than 30 mayors from 17 states (Municipality of Anchorage 2006). The Alaskan backdrop was a powerful platform to host a conference on climate change; mayors visited a native village facing relocation because of the effects of global warming.

Also in 2006, USCOM held an event titled "Emergency Summit on Energy and the Environment" in May as a response to rising energy costs. Nearly 40 mayors as well as some of the key policy network actors (Michelle Wyman of ICLEI and Anderson, a keynote speaker) were present. The attendees, who also included experts on the global warming issue, gathered to discuss national energy policy and the role of cities in taking action.

A month later, the U.S. Mayors Council on Climate Protection was formed at the conference's annual June meeting. Mayor Greg Nickels and Mayor James Brainard of Carmel, Indiana, were appointed cochairs of the council. In September 2006, the conference held a second summit focusing on the environment. In January 2007, USCOM held their annual winter meeting in Washington, D.C., with a plenary session on global warming. It was here that

Mayor Nickels, as cochair of the council presented a request for a $4 billion energy and environmental block grant from Congress (USCOM 2007). The mayors presented a unified voice in addressing the federal level of government.

The Cool Cities Campaign, a separate Sierra Club initiative inspired by the USMCPA, was launched in October 2005, just four months after the mayors agreement was endorsed by USCOM. The campaign's mission was to encourage mayors to join the USMCPA, to highlight the successes of participating mayors, and to encourage citizens to hold their mayors and cities accountable for their commitments (O'Malley 2005).

This collection of interactive municipal gatherings and activities served to further engage mayors and their cities on the global warming in tandem with the USMCPA. Participants identified an acquired sense of municipal self-efficacy toward tackling the problem, inspiration from other cities to take action, and the formation of valuable networks among municipal actors as valuable outcomes of these gatherings (Warden 2007).

Municipal engagement was also fostered by the design of the mayors agreement, which was basic, flexible, and nonbinding: Download the form from the website, sign it, and submit it. Soon after, the name of city and the name of the mayor would be posted on Seattle's promotional website for the agreement. Some mayors were required to gain approval from their city councils; other mayors signed it and submitted it on their own accord. There were no follow-up requirements or accountability mechanisms. The flexibility of the agreement meant that cities could develop their own approach to participation and in some cases their own interpretations of what the agreement meant (Warden 2007). Participation was easy, and the cost was low.

The Context for Engagement

Municipal engagement was also nurtured by a fertile societal context; the issue of climate change caused by global warming was rising on the agenda of the U.S. collective consciousness. Although the federal government remained inactive in terms of regulatory policies, global warming became a pressing concern in the public and private sectors. A shift was taking place from "Should we do anything?" to "What should we do?" (Selin and VanDeveer 2007, 4).

Following the Kyoto Protocol ratification in February 2005, multiple contextual elements emerged that served to emphasize the urgency of the need to address global warming. The issue received extensive press with cover stories in prominent news outlets such as *Time, Newsweek,* and the *Economist.* During the fall of 2005, the *New York Times* ran a series of print and online articles, alongside a multimedia presentation titled "The Big Melt" on the *New York Times* website, depicting the multifaceted issues surrounding global warming and the melting Arctic (Kraus and others 2005; Myers and others 2005; Revkin 2006). Other magazines, such as *Vanity Fair,* followed suit with "green" editions, often mentioning both Mayor Nickels and the mayors agreement.

In 2006, the documentary film *An Inconvenient Truth,* featuring Al Gore, told the global warming story and explained the climate science (Guggenheim 2006). At the conclusion of the film, Gore praised cities for taking action on the issue and provided a list of the hundreds of mayors who had signed on to the initiative by the time of filming. The USMCPA generated direct, ongoing press coverage as well, with sustained media coverage nationally and internationally.

The energy crisis in the spring of 2006 contributed to municipal awareness of the issue, one example being a mayoral summit on energy and the environment hosted by USCOM. Other contextual catalysts included a campaign to place the polar bear, whose threatened existence became symbolic of the dangers of global warming, on the endangered species list. In 2006, "carbon neutral" was voted "word of the year" by the *New Oxford American Dictionary.*

Notable celebrities and established corporations had solutions for global warming high on their agendas. Richard Branson of Virgin Records pledged $3 billion to alternative fuels research. General Electric launched its pro-environment "Eco-magination" campaign, which linked the company's mission to the concept of sustainability.

Leading energy corporations, such as Duke Energy, formed the U.S. Climate Action Partnership to present a unified business voice to Congress on the need for greenhouse gas regulation. Former President Clinton, through the Clinton Foundation, launched the Clinton Climate Initiative in September 2006. This initiative reinforced not only the urgency of the issue, but also the discourse that placed cities at the core of the solution; the initiative's focus was to reduce greenhouse gas emissions for the 40 largest cities in the world. Hurricane Katrina propelled the concept of an "extreme weather event," often mentioned as a future consequence of global warming, to the forefront of the national consciousness. Nearly a year after the hurricane, an overwhelming majority of respondents to a Zogby America telephone poll (74 percent) said they were now more convinced that global warming was real than they were two years earlier (Zogby International 2006).

A congressional investigation to address charges that federal officials had manipulated climate science findings in governmental reports to decrease the severity of the global warming issue made headline news. In the fall of 2006, Nicholas Stern, noted British economist and former chief economist of the World Bank, released a report commissioned by the British prime minister that concluded the cost of global inaction on global warming would be devastating (Stern 2006).

Rounding out this two-year awareness-generating period, the first install-ment of the 2007 Intergovernmental Panel on Climate Change report was released in February 2007, which created an even greater consensus on the scientific aspects of the issue (IPCC 2007). The report, and the lead-up during the few months before its release, generated more press on the problem. Global warming was less thought of as a "creeping problem." It was here.

This broad collection of influential contextual factors, or the "effective context" (Stokols 1996), contributed to a more fertile environment for mayors and cities across the United States to engage. From a decision-making perspective, a "policy window" was open (Kingdon 1995).

The Nature of Cities

In addition to the open "policy window," the catalyzing activities of the key policy network actors, and the simple design of the USMCPA, common municipal themes also served as catalysts for engagement. The sharing of useful information between cities and a spirit of friendly competition triggered municipal engagement across the United States.

When questioned for this study, city representatives often cited a moral imperative to help other cities by sharing information on how best to address climate change. This recurring and prominent practice has been conceptualized under the concept of *city solidarity,* or camaraderie among cities. Additionally, these findings were supported by responses from key informants from leading green cities who described a duty to help other cities take action (Warden 2007).

Friendly competition to be the greenest city also served to further amplify engagement (Warden 2007). In this study, the phrase *green capital* has been applied to describe the desired outcome of friendly competition. The greener city may promote itself as such when striving to keep its city healthy in terms of business and resident retention. As promotional benefits accrue from engagement on the global warming issue, a positive green image creates incentive for that city and other cities to be green. Green action—in this case, engagement to address climate change—spread as cities promoted themselves (and were promoted by policy actors), competed with each other, and inspired other cities to go green.

For the mayors agreement, city solidarity and green capital fueled a self-replicating policy effort through the sharing of information and friendly competition. Participation was amplified as the media publicized mayoral and municipal activity to address climate change and as the collective consciousness of the United States became more aware of global warming.

Thematic Categories for Participation

An analysis of the archival data in terms of the question "Why are cities participating in the USMCPA?" yielded 10 thematic categories. These categories reveal ways in which mayors and municipal officials understood their participation in the USMCPA while speaking as representatives of their cities. Descriptions of these themes and occurrence levels are provided in table 6.2.

These 10 themes demonstrate that mayors and city officials were thinking about the global warming issue in different ways when making public statements on behalf of their cities. Two of these leading themes—city solidarity and green capital—have been identified as sources of "contagion" for the overall policy

TABLE 6.2

Occurrence Levels and Thematic Categories for Participation in the U.S. Mayors Climate Protection Agreement

Why and How Cities Participate in the USMCPA, 2005–07

Occurrence levels[a]	Emergent themes	Emergent theme description
25	Local urgency	Local consequences make action urgent
8	Global urgency	Global consequences make action urgent
18	Moral urgency	There is a moral imperative to act now
27	Future generations	Intergenerational equity, sustainability, and responsibility for future generations (keyword: future)
33	Environmental protection	Responsibility to the environment, stewardship
26	Economic incentive	Economic rationales for environmental policy citing either past or future financial benefits
14	Absence of federal action	Failure of the federal government to take sufficient action
31	Green capital	Desire to be a green leader among cities; green leadership by example to encourage action by constituent base
10	Power in numbers	The more, the better—number of participants is important for solutions
35	City solidarity	Cities and mayors are part of collective group; cities and mayors work together; cities have a collective strength and share information; cities draw strength from unity; cities are at the center of global warming solutions

Source: Warden 2007.

[a]n = 125 cities (227 thematic occurrences).

effort, addressing the "how" of engagement. Of additional interest is that the diversity of the statements suggests city representatives had their own, different reasons for participation.

Across the United States, cities differ in many ways. They vary, for example, across population, governance structures, global warming consequences, capacity for implementing policy, economic resources, and stage of development. As already noted, the cities had not only different understandings of the global warming issue and motivations for participation, but also different interpretations of what the USMCPA meant.

Viral Governance

The interactions, activities, and shared mission of the key policy network when combined with an open policy window, city solidarity, quest for green capital, simple policy design of the USMCPA, and differentiated nature of cities contribute to the proposal of a theory of governance, identified here as *viral governance*. This explanation of viral governance draws from the principles of viral marketing; viral marketing refers to the use of preexisting social networks to rapidly and cheaply create brand awareness (Domingos 2005; Jurvetson 2000; Wilson 2000). The word "viral" was used, "not because any traditional viruses were involved, but because of the pattern of rapid adoption through word of mouth networks" (Jurvetson and Draper 1997, 1).

In viral marketing, the infected "host" passes on the message to others: "each new user becomes a company salesperson, and the message spreads organically" (Jurvetson and Draper 1997). With the USMCPA, each city became a promoter of taking action on the issue. As noted, once a mayor officially signed on, the names of the city and mayor were shortly thereafter posted on the agreement's promotional website. Participation was amplified among the broader target population by the concept of city solidarity. Some mayors and city representatives adopted the practice of sharing information, which served to inspire more participation. Additionally, "friendly competition" made cities strive to outdo one another and created a platform for the accrual of green capital. City solidarity and quest for green capital became vessels of contagion through positive feedback, in a viral fashion, in the broader social ecosystem of U.S. cities.

A relevant viral marketing principle is to "minimize the friction of market entry" by generating a simple message that has a low participation cost and compelling reason for involvement (Jurvetson and Draper 1997). The mayors agreement was simple, had a low cost to participate, and drew on the compelling reason that cities were at the center of global warming solutions.

In summary, viral governance captures the spreading of a policy measure wherein the key policy network actors, those executing the governance, begin an effort fueled by positive feedback that then takes on a momentum of its own. Because participation in the USMCPA was simple, low cost, and had a compelling reason behind it, it was easy for cities to participate, and as a consequence, more cities were compelled to engage on the issue. The simple and flexible nature of the agreement also made it accessible to a diverse group of potential municipal participants. Different cities could attach their own meanings to participation based on their individual resources, needs, and capacities, which can vary greatly across the municipal population.

Since 1997, as strategies of viral marketing have evolved in the business sector, one of the downsides of the strategy has emerged. In some circumstances, strategists may successfully execute a viral strategy wherein a viral message spreads rapidly and cheaply, without giving adequate forethought to the next strategic step.

Jurvetson and Draper highlighted the potential for missing this step: As more companies can grow more rapidly than ever before, they can also die out quickly if they have not established "switching barriers." According to these authors, switching barriers are the mechanisms that bring the customer to the next step, past engagement and to the retention phase (in the case of business, where income is generated). Jurvetson and Draper further warned that "rapid growth is of no value without customer retention."

This admonition parallels a key finding from this study. Although "engagement" on the issue spread, the next step of implementation and turning engagement into action was not adequately addressed at the outset. Key informants pointed out that that if cities were not brought to the next step, damage could be done to the overall policy effort (Warden 2007).

A viral outcome of engagement has limitations. The rapid growth of the USMCPA must be tempered with an awareness of the challenges of the next step: translating engagement into concrete implementation for reducing greenhouse gases. Viral solutions must be coordinated with solid next steps or else the viral outcome may lead to unfulfilled expectations. Nearly all of the key policy network participants and municipal representatives interviewed for this study expressed awareness of the challenges ahead. They identified the USMCPA as an important "first step," but only a "first step."

Implications for Policy and Future Research

This study contains numerous implications for policy and practice. A viral solution can have tremendous merit, especially because it has the capacity to rapidly canvass a diverse policy issue landscape of a complex problem area. The rapidity hails not only from the simplicity of the strategy, but also from the participant as promoter model, wherein members of the target populations—in this case, cities—become primary points of contagion. However, forethought must be given to "customer retention"—or, in this case, policy action—moving cities past engagement and to concrete implementation strategies. In particular, as novel governance structures continue to emerge, it is important to examine how, why, and if these strategies are successful.

Conclusion

The rapid and widespread engagement of U.S. cities and the climate change issue between 2005 and 2007, as anchored by the USMCPA, has been explained by (1) examining the actions and interactions of a group of key organizations and mayoral actors, (2) considering the context of an emerging national awareness of climate change, and (3) investigating the nature of cities. A theory of viral governance has been proposed as an explanatory concept to better understand how and why U.S. cities engaged with the climate change issue. Participation in the USMCPA spread in viral fashion even without additional effort by the key policy actors. The flexible and nonbinding design of the mayors agreement served to facilitate widespread engagement with a simple design that accommodated the nuances of dissimilar cities.

The overall consensus of participants in this study was that the U.S. Mayors Climate Protection Agreement, from 2005 to 2007, remains valuable because of its ability to generate awareness and to engage a large number of cities on the issue of climate change. However, the agreement must be considered only a first step. The agreement lacks accountability mechanisms that lead to tangible reductions in greenhouse gas emissions. There is still much work to be done to ensure that cities have the will, capacity, and action to follow through on their climate change mitigation commitments. Furthermore, although cities have presented a collective stance, solidarity must not overshadow the complexity of concrete solutions. Individually, cities have vastly different needs and situations that must be both acknowledged and addressed in the development and implementation of future policy measures. Continued coordinated dialogue between multiple stakeholders and an increase in resources are essential to realizing the commitments of so many U.S. cities to reduce greenhouse gas emissions.

References

Betsill, M. M. 2001. "Mitigating Climate Change in U.S. Cities: Opportunities and Obstacles." *Local Environment* 6 (4): 393–406.

Bulkeley, H. 2000. "Discourse-Coalition Approach and the Australian Climate Change Policy Network." *Environment and Planning C: Government and Policy* 18 (6): 727–48.

DeAngelo, B., and L. D. Harvey. 1998. "The Jurisdictional Framework for Municipal Action to Reduce Greenhouse Gas Emissions: Case Studies from Canada, USA and Germany." *Local Environment* 3 (2): 111–36.

Domingos, P. 2005. "Mining Social Networks for Viral Marketing." *IEEE Intelligent Systems* 20 (1): 80–82.

Guggenheim, D., director. 2006. *An Inconvenient Truth.* Hollywood, CA: Paramount Classics.

ICLEI. 2006. *Cities for Climate Protection, ICLEI International Progress Report.* Oakland, CA: ICLEI.

IPCC (Intergovernmental Panel on Climate Change). 2007. "Climate Change 2007: The Physical Science Basis. Summary for Policymakers." Geneva: IPCC Secretariat/World Meteorological Organization. http://www.pnud.cl/recientes/IPCC-Report.pdf.

Jurvetson, S. 2000. "From the Ground Floor: What Exactly Is Viral Marketing?" *Red Herring* (May): 110–11.

Jurvetson, S., and T. Draper. 1997. "Viral Marketing." Netscape M files, 1997, and edited version Business 2.0, 1998. http://www.dfj.com/news/article_26.shtml.

Kingdon, J. 1995. *Agendas, Alternatives, and Public Policies.* New York: HarperCollins College.

Kraus, C., Myers, S. L., Revkin, A. C., and Romero, S. 2005. "The Big Melt: Pt. 1. As Polar Ice Turns to Water, Dreams of Treasure Abound." *New York Times,* October 10. http://www.nytimes.com/2005/10/10/science/10arctic.html?ex=1187582400&en=282e5823e29e03f1&ei=5070.

Marsh, D., and M. Smith. 2000. "Understanding Policy Networks: Toward a Dialectical Approach." *Political Studies* 48: 4–21.

Municipality of Anchorage. 2006. "Mayors Meet in Alaska to Tackle Global Climate Change: Bipartisan Group of 30 Mayors Represent Next Wave of Climate Leaders." http://www.akcf.org/pages/release.doc.

Myers, S. L., A. C. Revkin, S. Romero, and C. Kraus. 2005. "The Big Melt: Pt. 2. Old Ways of Life Are Fading as the Arctic Thaws." *New York Times,* October 20. http://www.nytimes.com/2005/10/20/science/earth/20arctic.ready.html?ex=1187582400anden=368637483953717fandei=5070.

O'Malley, B. 2005. "Sierra Club Launches National Cool Cities Campaign." http://www.sierraclub.org/pressroom/releases/pr2005-10-12a.asp.

Revkin, A. C. 2006. "The Big Melt: Pt 3. No Escape, Thaws Gain Momentum." *New York Times,* October 25. http://www.nytimes.com/2005/10/25/science/earth/25arctic.html?ex= 1187582400anden=b1e83adc39a12320andei=5070.

Rhodes, R. A. W. 1997. *Understanding Governance: Policy Networks, Governance, Reflexivity and Accountability.* Buckingham U.K.: Open University Press.

Rhodes, R. A. W., and D. Marsh. 1992. "New Directions in the Study of Policy Networks." *European Journal of Political Research* 21: 181–205.

Schneider, M., J. Scholz, M. Lubell, D. Mindruta, and M. Edwardsen. 2003. "Building Consensual Institutions: Networks and the National Estuary Program." *American Journal of Political Science* 47 (1): 143–58.

Selin, H., and S. D. VanDeveer. 2007. "Political Science and Prediction: What's Next for U.S. Climate Change Policy." *Review of Policy Research* 24 (1): 1–27.

Stern, N. 2006. "Stern Review on the Economics of Climate Change, October 30, 2006. Report Presented to the Prime Minister and Chancellor Exchequer, HM Treasury." http://www.hmtreasury.gov.uk/Independent_Reviews/stern_review_economics_ climate_change/sternreview_ index.cfm.

Stokols, D. 1996. "Translating Social Ecological Theory into Guidelines for Community Health Promotion." *American Journal of Health Promotion* 10: 282–98.

Turnpenny, J., A. Haxeltine, I. Lorenzoni, T. O'Riordan, and M. Jones. 2005. "Mapping Actors Involved in Climate Change Policy Networks in the UK." Working Paper 66, University of East Anglia, Tyndall Centre for Climate Change, Norwich, England. http://www.tyndall.ac.uk/publications/working_papers/ wp66.pdf.

USCOM (U.S. Conference of Mayors). 2005. "USMCPA Endorsed Resolution, 2005." http://www.seattle.gov/mayor/climate/PDF/Resolution_FinalLanguage_061305. pdf.

———. 2007. "Mayors Call for $4 Billion in Energy and Environmental Block Grant at 75th Winter Meeting of the U.S. Conference of Mayors. Mayors Launch Campaign to Create a 'Climate of Change' in Washington, Urge Congress to Act Now." http:// www.usmayors.org/ 75thWinterMeeting/eebg_012507.pdf,

Wilson, R. F. 2000. "The Six Simple Principles of Viral Marketing." *Web Marketing Today* 70 (February 1). http://www.wilsonweb.com/ wmt5/viral-principles.htm.

Warden, T. 2007. "The Engagement of U.S. Cities and the Global Warming Issue, 2005–2007." Doctoral dissertation, School of Ecology, University of California, Irvine.

Wilbanks, T. J., and R. W. Kates. 1999. "Global Change in Local Places: How Scale Matters." *Climatic Change* 43: 601–28.

Zogby International. 2006. "Americans Link Katrina, Global Warming." http://www. zogby.com/News/ ReadNews.dbm?ID=1161.

7

Urban Heat Islands: Sensitivity of Urban Temperatures to Climate Change and Heat Release in Four European Cities

Mark P. McCarthy and Michael G. Sanderson

Introduction

It has long been recognized that urban areas have their own climates (Howard 1818; see also Arnfield 2003 and Oke 1982) and are generally warmer than surrounding rural areas. The urban environment has the capacity to store heat during the day, which originates from both absorption of solar radiation and human activity (for example, exhaust gases from traffic, heating and cooling of buildings, and human metabolism). This absorbed heat is then released at night. Many buildings are designed to take account of this phenomenon as a means of keeping their interior temperatures within defined limits. Because of this heat release, night-time air temperatures in urban areas are higher than surrounding rural areas. The temperature difference between the urban and rural area is referred to as the "urban heat island" (UHI). The UHI is also sensitive to the ambient weather and climate. Urban populations are therefore exposed to both urban-induced climate modification and larger-scale climate change resulting from increasing greenhouse gas concentrations. An understanding of current and possible future changes in the magnitude of the UHI is therefore necessary for planning and developing of adaptation and mitigation strategies.

Mark P. McCarthy was supported by the EU/FP6 integrated project CIRCE (Climate Change and Impact Research: the Mediterranean Environment; http://www.circeproject.eu/) (contract number 036961), and by the Joint DECC and Defra Integrated Climate Programme, DECC/Defra (GA01101). Michael G. Sanderson was funded under the EPSRC project "The use of probabilistic climate data to future proof design decisions in the buildings sector" (PROMETHEUS) under grant no. EP/F038305/1.

■ **175**

Many different models have been developed to model and understand the UHI. These can be broadly categorized as *empirical* models based on relationships between observed temperatures and various characteristics of the urban environment (Unger 2006), key atmospheric variables (Wilby 2003), or *physical* models that attempt to simulate the important heat and moisture exchanges above an urban area (Best 2006; Masson 2006). However, not all of these models are suitable for estimating future UHI intensities. Empirical models are specific to certain cities or climate domains, and statistical relationships between atmospheric variables and the UHI may change in the future. Representing cities within climate models is therefore necessary to study climate impacts on urban populations and understand the links between the UHI and the climate of the surrounding areas. This is the objective of this chapter.

The Met Office Hadley Centre in Exeter, England, has developed a land-surface scheme, which can be used within a climate model to represent surface heterogeneity at scales smaller than the model's resolution. This scheme (MOSES2; Essery and others 2003) operates at the same spatial scale as the climate model and divides each surface grid square of the climate model into up to nine different surface types (called tiles), of which one represents urban areas and the others represent grass, trees, and other surfaces. This surface scheme has been used in a global climate model (GCM) to simulate the UHI of London.[1] An additional heating term may be added to the surface energy balance equation of the urban area, which represents the anthropogenic heat source present in all cities. More recently, MOSES2 has been implemented into a regional climate model (RCM) that has a much higher horizontal resolution than the GCM. The RCM and the land surface scheme are described here. The model simulations presented explore the sensitivity of urban temperatures to the location of the urban area, climate change, and anthropogenic heat release. The simulations do not represent a robust projection of future climate in any given location.

The Met Office Hadley Centre Regional Climate Model (HadRM3) and Land Surface Scheme (MOSES2)

At the scale of a GCM, which generally has a horizontal resolution of the order of hundreds of kilometers, the influence of urban areas on the simulated climate is negligibly small and has generally been ignored within the climate change–modeling community. Limited-area RCMs are now available that have much higher spatial resolutions. The Met Office Hadley Centre RCM HadRM3 (Buonomo and others 2007) uses a horizontal resolution of 25 kilometers. However, even this resolution is not sufficient to explicitly capture UHIs. Urban areas are poorly resolved, but a methodology has been developed to capture the city-scale impacts of urbanization on climate. The urban tile within MOSES2 is used to provide a representation of cities, and a more complete description of the urban model is given elsewhere (Best 2005; Best, Grimmond, and Villani 2006). Another tile within MOSES2 is classified as grass (and represents boreal grasslands). For all model grid cells, the UHI is calculated using surface air temperatures of the boreal grass and urban tiles.

In the RCM simulations, the urban surface properties are not modified geographically. Consequently, the urban tile represents a hypothetical city with identical surface properties located within each grid cell of the climate model. Determining and validating appropriate parameter settings for the urban model at different locations is beyond the scope of this study. For example, details of the surface albedo, thermal properties of buildings, ratios of building heights to street widths, and orientation of streets would be needed (Unger 2006). The implementation of MOSES2 within the RCM means that the climate of all nine tiles is calculated for every model grid square, regardless of whether that land type is present. The climate of each tile is not used further in the model unless it is present in the model grid square. This feature is useful because it allows potential UHIs to be calculated at all locations in a consistent way within the model domain.

The area studied with the RCM is Europe and the Mediterranean coastal areas of North Africa (see figure 7.1 for a map of this area). The influence of global climatic change is introduced at the boundaries of the regional model by prescribing temperatures, winds, and other key meteorological variables. The climate projections from the RCM are therefore consistent with the driving GCM projections and add realistic detail at the finer spatial scales.

As mentioned in the introduction, an additional and well-documented driver of urban climate is anthropogenic heat released through human activity in cities, such as heating and cooling of buildings, exhaust gases from traffic, and even human metabolism. Energy-use statistics for London and Manchester have been analyzed to estimate the heat flux for these cities (GLA 2006). The results suggest that heat fluxes averaged over a 25-kilometer RCM grid cell located over the city centers to be about 25 W m^{-2}, and for urban areas excluding the center to be approximately 15 W m^{-2}. Based on these estimates, a value of 15 W m^{-2} has been used as a default heat flux for the urban tile at the RCM resolution except for a small number of cities (including London, Moscow, and Paris) with 25 W m^{-2}. Estimates of energy consumption and heat released in these latter cities support the higher value. Two additional sets of climate simulations have been conducted, with the heat flux set to 0 and 45 W m^{-2} (75 W m^{-2} for the larger cities). It is outside the scope of this chapter to assess future energy use for cities, but these experiments will provide a quantitative assessment of the sensitivity of urban areas to changes in the anthropogenic heat flux. It might be expected that the heat release during winter will fall as temperatures warm, whereas it may rise

Figure 7.1 Comparison of Modeled and Observed Daily Mean 1.5-Meter Temperatures for Winter and Summer over Europe

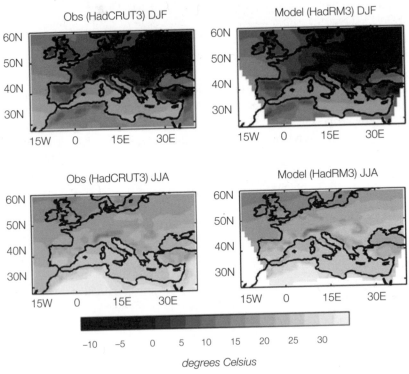

Source: Authors.

Note: The model data have been averaged over the period 1971–90, and the observations 1961–90.

in summer owing to increased cooling demands. These potential changes in the seasonality of the anthropogenic heat release could impact on the modeled urban temperatures. In the present study, the anthropogenic heat release was assumed to be uniform throughout the year and is included as an additional source term to the surface energy balance equation of the urban tile.

Model Experiments

The different experiments performed with the RCM are listed in table 7.1. In total, seven different experiments have been carried out to validate the regional model and to test the sensitivity of the simulated urban and rural temperatures to climate change and, in the case of urban areas, to different assumptions regarding anthropogenic heat release. For all the regional climate simulations, suitable boundary conditions were supplied from a climate projection for the period 1950–2099 created with the global model HadCM3 (Collins and others 2006). This global model simulation used greenhouse gas emissions from a medium-high emissions scenario (A1B; Nakićenović and Swart 2000). This scenario assumes rapid introduction of new and efficient technologies, with a balance between fossil fuel use and alternative energy sources (IPCC 2007).

Results

The results obtained from the model experiments are discussed next.

Validation of Modeled Temperatures

Simulations of surface air temperatures from run (a) (see table 7.1) are compared with observations in figure 7.1 to validate the model. These observations have

TABLE 7.1
Regional Climate Model Experiments

Run name	Period	Anthropogenic heat flux (W m^{-2})	Notes
a	1971–90	0	Urban fractions set to zero; urban temperatures calculated at every location within the model domain, but only nonurban tile climates feed back onto the modeled atmosphere
b	1971–90	0	Fully coupled urban areas
c	1971–90	15/25	As run (b) plus anthropogenic heat flux
d	1971–90	45/75	As run (b) plus tripled anthropogenic heat flux
e	2041–60	0	Fully coupled urban areas
f	2041–60	15/25	As run (e) plus anthropogenic heat flux
g	2041–60	45/75	As run (e) plus tripled anthropogenic heat flux

Note: RCM control run with rural surfaces only feeding back to modeled climate. Urban climate calculated but not used in the simulation. The urban fractions have all been set to zero, so surface fractions of rural tiles have been increased where necessary so they sum to 1. (b) Same as run (a) but urban areas included fully in simulation. A comparison of runs (a) and (b) allows any feedbacks between the urban climate and the larger modeled climate to be quantified. Run (c) as (b) but with an anthriopogenic heat source to the urban tile included. Run (d) as (c) but the anthropogenic heat source is tripled. Runs (e), (f), and (g) are repeats of runs (b), (c), and (d), respectively, for the future period 2041–2060.

had any influence of urban areas removed (Brohan and others 2006) and so are representative of rural temperatures. The data shown are daily mean surface air temperatures averaged over the period 1961–90; for the model results, temperatures averaged over all rural tiles are shown. A visual comparison of the observed and modeled daily mean temperatures suggests that the model reproduces the observed temperature patterns in both winter and summer very well, although a quantitative comparison has not been performed. The model does overestimate summer temperatures by approximately 2 degrees Celsius over parts of Europe. This overestimation is not significant for the purpose of this study.

Urban and Rural Temperature Differences

The differences between the urban and nonurban surface daily minimum and maximum temperatures averaged over the period 1971–90 are shown in figure 7.2, using results from run (a). In run (a), although the urban fractions are zero, the surface temperatures of the urban tiles are still calculated (table 7.1). The temperature differences between the urban and grass tiles from run (a) are shown in figure 7.2. It is clear that the urban areas surface characteristics have a large impact on daily minimum temperatures in both seasons, which are 1 to 4 degrees Celsius larger than the rural areas, but with a larger heat island overall in summer than winter. Daily maximum temperatures are 0.5 to 2.0 degrees Celsius higher in summer and 0 to 1 degrees Celsius higher in winter. This result is in qualitative agreement with observations of urban temperatures. The simulated UHI for London has been compared with the UHI calculated using measured temperatures from two locations within the city and a suitable rural location (data not shown). Using monthly mean values, the modeled heat island lies between the two heat islands calculated from observations. However, no comparison of modeled and observed urban climates was conducted for other cities. The model experiments are designed to explore the sensitivity of urban temperatures to the location of the urban area, anthropogenic heat release, and climate change.

Impact of Climate Change on Modeled Urban and Nonurban Temperatures

The impact of climate change on modeled urban and nonurban temperatures is shown in figure 7.3. These results are the differences in temperatures between runs (e) and (b). Both runs used fully coupled urban areas but no anthropogenic heat source. A positive value indicates that the temperatures for the period 2041–60 (run [e]) are warmer than those for the period 1971–90 (run [b]). Panels (a) through (d) show the changes in minimum temperatures (T_{min}), and

Figure 7.2 Mean Difference in Daily Minimum (T_{min}) and Maximum (T_{max}) Temperatures between Urban and Nonurban Areas for Summer and Winter

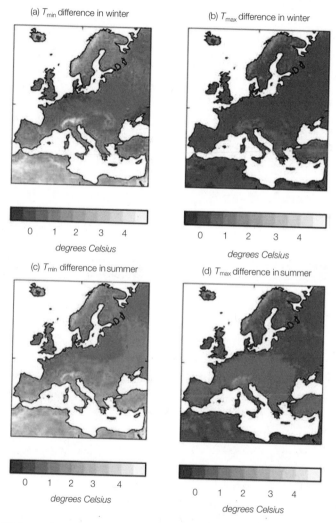

(a) T_{min} difference in winter

(b) T_{max} difference in winter

0   1   2   3   4
degrees Celsius

0   1   2   3   4
degrees Celsius

(c) T_{min} difference in summer

(d) T_{max} difference in summer

0   1   2   3   4
degrees Celsius

0   1   2   3   4
degrees Celsius

Source: Authors.

Note: A positive value indicates that the urban temperatures are higher than the rural temperatures. The daily minimum temperatures are between 1 and 4 degrees Celsius higher in both winter and summer, but overall are larger in summer. Daily maximum temperatures in summer are higher by 0.5–2.0 degrees Celsius and in winter are 0–1 degrees Celsius higher in the urban tile. The warmer temperatures of the urban tile are an addition to the modeled climate. The warm bias in the modeled climate for summer means that the urban temperatures could be overestimated very slightly, but not by enough to change the conclusions of this study.

Figure 7.3 Impact of Climate Change on Maximum and Minimum Daily Temperatures for Urban and Nonurban Surfaces for Summer and Winter

(a) Urban T_{min} change in winter

(b) Urban T_{min} change in summer

(c) Nonurban T_{min} change in winter

(d) Nonurban T_{min} change in summer

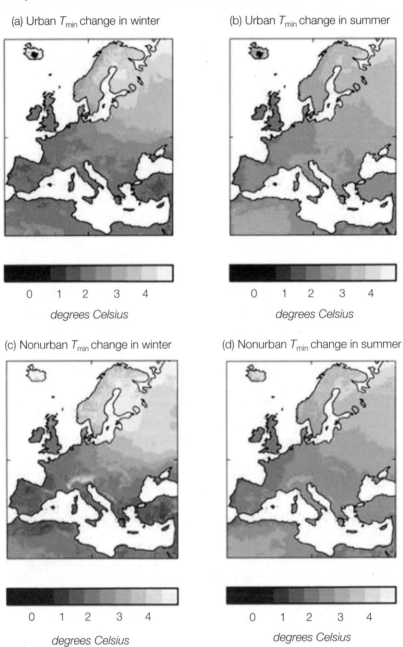

Figure 7.3 Impact of Climate Change on Maximum and Minimum Daily Temperatures for Urban and Nonurban Surfaces for Summer and Winter *(continued)*

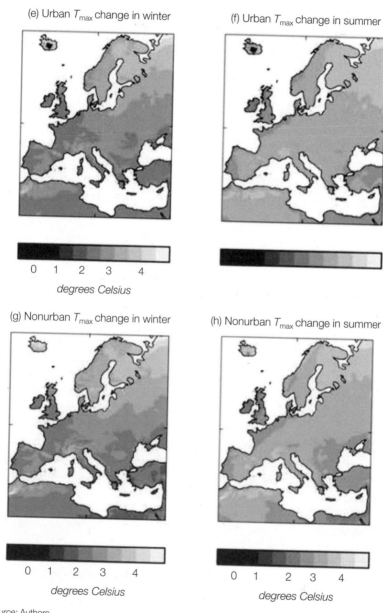

(e) Urban T_{max} change in winter

(f) Urban T_{max} change in summer

0   1   2   3   4
degrees Celsius

(g) Nonurban T_{max} change in winter

(h) Nonurban T_{max} change in summer

0   1   2   3   4
degrees Celsius

0   1   2   3   4
degrees Celsius

Source: Authors.

Note: Panels show the mean temperature differences between the periods 1971–90 and 2041–60. A positive value indicates that temperatures in the future period are warmer than those for the present.

the panels (e) through (h) show the differences in maximum temperatures (T_{max}). In all cases the differences are positive, indicating that temperatures in the future are warmer than those in the present. Minimum temperature changes in winter are similar for the urban and nonurban tiles except for northwestern Europe, where a larger increase occurs on the nonurban tiles. For summer, the patterns and magnitudes of the increases in T_{min} (between 2 and 4 degrees Celsius) are similar for the urban and rural tiles, but overall the urban tiles are warmer.

The winter changes in T_{max} are between 1.5 and 4.0 degrees Celsius, and summer changes lie between 2.5 and 3.5 degrees Celsius, for both urban and nonurban tiles; the summer temperature increases are fairly uniform across the model domain. These results suggest that climate change is the main driver of increases in daily maximum temperatures, whereas increases in daily minimum temperatures are caused by the properties of the urban area itself.

Impact of Anthropogenic Heat Release on Future Urban Temperatures

As previously discussed, the release of heat within urban areas could have a significant impact on urban temperatures. The set of experiments listed in table 7.1 assesses the possible impact of this heat release on future urban temperatures. In this section, results from runs (b), (e), and (g) are compared. In these three runs, a fully coupled urban tile was included in the model, allowing any feedbacks between the urban environment and the atmosphere to be simulated. The model will still calculate a temperature for the urban tile at all locations in the model, even if the urban fraction is zero. Subtracting the temperatures in run (e) from run (g) gives the size of the temperature increase for the future period (2041–60) caused by the anthropogenic heat release. The simulation using the tripled heat flux (run [g]) was chosen because it is assumed that the heat flux will increase in the future. Only changes in urban minimum temperatures are shown in figure 7.4; minimum temperatures increase by the largest amounts, as has been shown previously. The urban temperature increases from figures 7.3(a) and 7.3(b) have been repeated here, so the temperature increases due to climate change can be compared with those from the anthropogenic heat release.

A comparison of figures 7.4(b) with 7.4(a) and 7.4(e) with 7.4(d) shows that the anthropogenic heat release has increased minimum temperatures in both winter and summer, and the greater impact is seen in winter, particularly over northern Europe. The increases in urban tile minimum temperatures resulting from the anthropogenic heat release only are shown in panels (c) and (f) for winter and summer, respectively. The anthropogenic heat release is responsible for increases in urban temperatures between 0.2 and 1.0 degrees Celsius, again with a larger impact in winter than summer. This increase is significant

Figure 7.4 Impact of Climate Change and Climate Change +45 W m⁻² Anthropogenic Heat Flux on Minimum Temperatures of the Urban Tile, for Winter and Summer, between 2041–60 and 1971–90

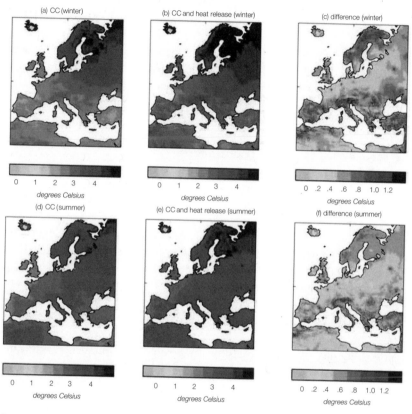

Source: Authors.

Note: Panels (a) and (d) show temperature differences between runs (e) and (b), and panels (b) and (e) show the temperature differences between runs (g) and (b). The impact of the heat release only is shown in panels (c) and (f), which are the differences between panels (b) and (a) and (e) and (d), respectively.

compared with the magnitude of the modeled UHI with no heat release of 1 to 4 degrees Celsius. A detectable feedback is seen between the urban areas of the largest cities and the atmosphere at the scale of the RCM, resulting in further elevation of the UHIs. For example, in panels (c) and (f), small circular areas with temperature increases of approximately 0.6 to 0.8 degrees Celsius are located over London, Moscow, and Paris, indicating that these urban areas (which are represented in the model) are warmer than identical urban areas where no feedback occurs.

Case Study: Simulations of UHIs of Athens, Cairo, London, and Moscow

The separate impacts of climate on the maximum and minimum temperatures of the four cities Athens, Cairo, London, and Moscow, and on their respective UHIs, is now assessed. These four cities were chosen because they lie in very different parts of Europe. Two lie in the north of Europe, and the other two are located in the Mediterranean area and have hotter climates. First, the seasonal cycles in minimum and maximum temperatures for each city are shown, together with the sizes of the modeled UHIs. Next, the occurrence of extreme temperatures for the present day and future are calculated and discussed.

Seasonal Cycles of Surface Temperatures

Figure 7.5 depicts the seasonal temperature cycles for each city. The data shown are monthly mean values averaged over the period 1971–90 from urban areas in run (b) and rural areas in run (a) (see table 7.1). First, the cycles of maximum and minimum temperatures for urban and rural areas are considered. In all four cases, the lowest temperatures are found in winter and the highest in summer. The temperature range is greatest for Moscow and Athens. The UHI is defined as the difference in temperature between the urban and rural tiles associated with each city and is shown in the lower two panels of figure 7.5. Considering the UHI T_{min} data, it can be seen that the largest UHI is seen during the summer months for London and Moscow, but little seasonality is seen for Athens and Cairo. The modeled seasonal cycle for London (using T_{min}) agrees well with an observed cycle based on temperature measurements within the city and a rural location. The seasonal cycle of the UHI T_{max} values are broadly similar for all four cities. The largest UHIs are seen during the summer months and are greatest for London and Moscow. The UHI T_{max} cycle for Cairo also peaks during summer, but the peak is very broad. The UHI T_{max} for Athens does not display a clear seasonal cycle. This behavior might be due to the proximity of Athens to the Mediterranean Sea.

Frequency of Extreme Hot Temperatures

Finally, the occurrence of extreme hot temperatures is calculated for the four cities. The cumulative effects of the UHI (that is, the characteristics of the urban areas), climate change, and anthropogenic heat release are assessed. For this analysis, daily maximum and minimum temperatures for the summer period only (defined as June, July, and August) are considered, because the highest temperatures are simulated for this period. Extreme temperatures for each city were defined as those exceeding the 95th percentile of the T_{min} and T_{max} values of the urban tile from run (a), over the period 1971–90. Run (a) had all surface

. **Figure 7.5 Seasonal Cycles of Minimum and Maximum Temperatures for the Urban and Rural Tiles Associated with Each of the Four Cities Athens, Cairo, London, and Moscow**

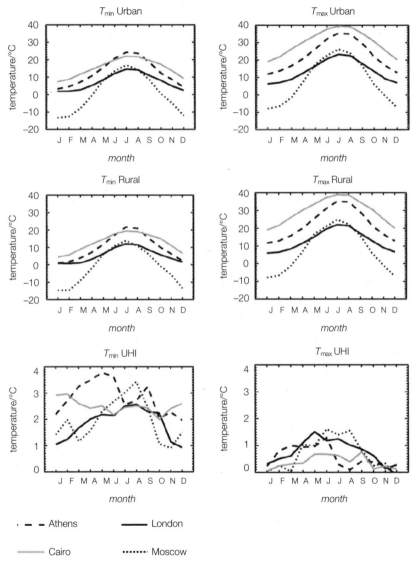

- – – Athens   —— London

   Cairo   ········ Moscow

Source: Authors.

Note: The UHI is the temperature difference between the urban and rural tiles.

urban fractions set to zero. Thresholds were calculated separately for each city. Figure 7.6 shows the number of days when these threshold temperatures are exceeded under runs (b)–(g). Exceeding the T_{min} threshold is classed as a hot night, and exceeding the T_{max} threshold is classsed as a hot day.

Simulated hot nights for London and Moscow exhibit similar behavior. For the period 1971–90, the number of hot nights increases with the sequence rural, urban, and urban +25 W m^{-2} heat release, although the rural-to-urban increase in hot nights is larger than that caused by the addition of the anthropogenic heat release. In the future (2041–60), the UHI is projected to result in considerably more hot nights for both London and Moscow, with further increases resulting from the low and high values of the heat release. For London, urban areas experience up to three times more hot nights (40 days) than rural areas, and for Moscow, the figure is slightly smaller, at 30 days. For the other two cities, Athens and Cairo, the impact of urbanization on the number of hot nights for present day values is smaller than for London and Moscow but is significant for the future. The heat release has a relatively smaller impact on the number of hot nights for Athens and Cairo than for London and Moscow. The assumed anthropogenic heat release for London and Moscow is larger than that for Athens and Cairo. However, this heat release is a larger proportion of the energy budget for London and Moscow, because these cities receive much less solar energy than Athens and Cairo. These results show that the characteristics of the urban area itself are responsible for the majority of the increases in hot nights, with the anthropogenic heat release having a smaller but significant effect.

The UHI does not have a significant impact on the frequency of hot days in all four cities for the control period (1971–90). However, it does result in additional hot days for the future, although the impact for Moscow is small. In all four cases, the addition of either magnitude of anthropogenic heat release to the urban area produces little or no increase in the number of hot days.

Overall, these results show that the characteristics of the urban areas are responsible for a large proportion of the increases in the number of hot days and nights in the future, with the anthropogenic heat flux having a smaller but often significant impact. The number of hot nights projected for the two cooler northern cities (London and Moscow) appears to be more sensitive to the anthropogenic heat flux than the two warmer Mediterranean cities (Athens and Cairo), as we have discussed. If the same-sized heat fluxes had been used for all four cities, this conclusion would still be true. It should be noted that a comprehensive comparison of the simulated climate against observations for each of these cities has not been conducted (except for London). The main emphasis of these results is on the sensitivity of urban temperatures to climate change and anthropogenic heat release. They do not represent a robust prediction of future climate change in any of these four locations.

Figure 7.6 Occurrence of Extreme Temperatures During the Day and Night for Athens, Cairo, London, and Moscow during Summer (June, July, and August)

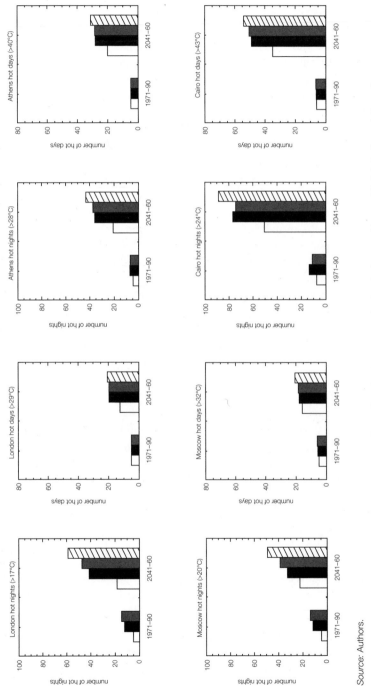

Source: Authors.

Note: A hot day or night is defined as the 95th percentile of the T_{max} or T_{min} urban temperatures for that city from run (a); see table 7.1. Each panel shows the average number of times that the 95th percentile temperature is exceeded for the periods 1971–90 and 2041–60, for rural areas (white), urban (black), urban +15/25 W m⁻² heat release (gray), and urban +45/75 W m⁻² heat release (pattern). For the period 1971–90, the rural and urban data were calculated from run (b), and the urban +15 W m⁻² data from run (c). For 2041–60, the rural and urban data were calculated from run (e), the urban +15 W m⁻² from run (f), and the urban + 45W m⁻² from run (g).

Conclusions

This chapter presents an analysis of regional climate change in Europe, with a focus on the influence of the urban environment and urban anthropogenic heat release. The regional model used reproduces observed surface temperatures in nonurban areas well for both winter and summer. The results indicate that the UHI has the largest impact on minimum temperatures during winter and a smaller but significant impact on summer maximum temperatures. Projected changes in temperature by the decade of 2050 are similar for urban and non-urban surfaces. The model shows that climate change itself is the main driver of increases in daily maximum temperatures, but the urban area characteristics are the main cause of increases in daily minimum temperatures. However, regional variations are apparent. The model also simulates the interactions between the urban area and the atmosphere, resulting in larger UHIs compared with a simulation in which the urban temperatures were calculated in isolation. These results show that the UHI is likely to change over time, and so a present-day UHI cannot be added to a future climate.

The UHI also responds significantly to changes in the anthropogenic heat emissions of a city. The sensitivity study has shown that including this heating (at the high value of 45/75 W m^{-2}) can increase temperatures by as much as 0.5 degrees Celsius. The heat emission values are probably reasonable at the scale of the RCM, but within the core of large cities, heat emissions can be considerably larger.

As for the cumulative impact of climate change and UHIs on the frequency of extreme temperature events, it is apparent that the UHI itself will be the main cause of an increase in extreme temperatures during both day and night in a city, with the anthropogenic heat release having a smaller effect. It is essential to consider the dual role of global warming and local urban warming for assessing potential risks to people and infrastructure within cities.

Note

1. R. Betts and M. Best, "Relative Impacts of Radiative Forcing, Landscape Effects and Local Heat Sources on Simulated Climate Change in Urban Areas," Betwixt Technical Briefing Note 6, version 1, http://www.cru.uea.ac.uk/cru/projects/betwixt.

References

Arnfield, A. J. 2003. "Two Decades of Urban Climate Research: A Review of Turbulence, Energy Exchanges of Energy and Water, and the Urban Heat Island." *International Journal of Climatology* 23: 1–26.

Best, M. J. 2005. "Representing Urban Areas within Operational Numerical Weather Prediction Models." *Boundary Layer Meteorology* 114 (1): 91–109.

———. 2006. "Progress towards Better Weather Forecasts for City Dwellers: From Short Range to Climate Change." *Theoretical and Applied Climatology* 84 (1–3): 47–55.

Best, M. J., C. S. B. Grimmond, and M. G. Villani. 2006. "Evaluation of the Urban Tile in MOSES Using Surface Energy Balance Observations." *Boundary Layer Meteorology* 118 (3): 503–25.

Brohan, P., J .J. Kennedy, I. Harris, S. F. B. Tett, and P. D. Jones. 2006. "Uncertainty Estimates in Regional and Global Observed Temperature Changes: A New Data Set from 1850." *Journal of Geophysical Research* 111, D12106, doi:10.1029/2005JD006548.

Buonomo, E., R. Jones, C. Huntingford, and J. Hannaford. 2007. "On the Robustness of Changes in Extreme Precipitation over Europe from Two High Resolution Climate Change Simulations." *Quarterly Journal of the Royal Meteorological Society* 133 (622): 65–81.

Collins, M., B. B. B. Booth, G. Harris, J. M. Murphy, D. M. H. Sexton, and M. Webb. 2006. "Towards Quantifying Uncertainty in Transient Climate Change." *Climate Dynamics* 27: 127–47.

Essery, R. L. H., M. J. Best, R. A. Betts, P. M. Cox, and C. M. Taylor. 2003. "Explicit Representation of Subgrid Heterogeneity in a GCM Land-Surface Scheme." *Journal of Hydrometeorology* 4 (3): 530–35.

GLA (Greater London Authority). 2006. "London Energy and CO_2 Inventory (LECI) 2003." Greater London Authority, London.

Howard, L. 1818. *The Climate of London, Deduced from Meteorological Observations, Made at Different Places in the Neighbourhood of the Metropolis.* 2 vols. London: W. Phillips.

IPCC (Intergovernmental Panel on Climate Change). 2007. "Summary for Policymakers." In *Climate Change 2007: The Physical Science Basis. Contribution of Working Group I to the Fourth Assessment Report of the Intergovernmental Panel on Climate Change,* ed. S. Solomon, D. Qin, M. Manning, Z. Chen, M. Marquis, K. B. Averyt, M. Tignor, and H. L. Miller, 1–18. Cambridge: Cambridge University Press.

Masson, V. 2006. "Urban Surface Modeling and the Meso-Scale Impact of Cities." *Theoretical and Applied Climatology* 84 (1–3): 35–45.

Nakićenović, N., and R. Swart, eds. 2000. *Special Report on Emissions Scenarios.* IPCC Special Report. Cambridge: Cambridge University Press.

Oke, T. R. 1982. "The Energetic Basis of the Urban Heat Island." *Quarterly Journal of the Royal Meteorological Society* 108: 1–44.

Unger, J. 2006. "Modelling of the Annual Mean Maximum Urban Heat Island Using 2D and 3D Surface Parameters." *Climate Research* 30 (3): 215–26.

Wilby, R. 2003. "Past and Projected Trends in London's Urban Heat Island." *Weather* 58: 251–60.

8

Adapting Cities to Climate Change: Opportunities and Constraints

Dirk Heinrichs, Rimjhim Aggarwal, Jonathan Barton, Erach Bharucha, Carsten Butsch, Michail Fragkias, Peter Johnston, Frauke Kraas, Kerstin Krellenberg, Andrea Lampis, Ooi Giok Ling, and Johanna Vogel

Introduction

Adaptation of cities to climate change had not been a prominent issue in academic and political debate on societal responses to global climate change for a long time (IIED 2007). The associated concern is that increased attention on adaptation would reduce the pressure for mitigation action—and thus foster (or at least indirectly allow) the continuing emission of anthropogenic greenhouse gases (GHGs) into the atmosphere. This perspective is starting to change. Today adaptation is increasingly seen as an essential and integral part of proposed and implemented climate policy. The recent Intergovernmental Panel on Climate Change (IPCC) Report (IPCC 2007, 7) states: "There is high agreement and much evidence that with current climate change mitigation policies and related sustainable development practices, global GHG emissions will continue to grow over the next few decades." In the meantime, cities and their residents have no choice other than to adapt to the impacts of climate change. This view coincides with a growing political voice for adaptation mainly in countries and cities that are likely to be affected most severely (Pielke and others 2007).

Cities around the world have started to design and implement adaptation strategies, often independent of existing national planning frameworks. These

This work was a collaborative initiative by associates of the Urbanization and Global Environmental Change Core Theme of the International Human Dimensions Programme. It was supported by the German Federal Ministry for Economic Cooperation and Development and the Initiative and Networking Fund of the Helmholtz Association "proactive" experiences have been studied and documented to some extent (see the special issues of *Environment and Urbanization* [2007] and *Habitat Debate* [2009]). This chapter goes beyond the investigation of "good practices" and explores the variety of adaptation options that cities have started to implement. It draws on the experience of eight cities—Bogota, Cape Town, Delhi, Pearl River Delta, Pune, Santiago de Chile, São Paulo, and Singapore—and compares their progress toward adaptation. The chapter focuses on two related questions: What motivates early adaptors to develop and implement adaptation plans? and What obstacles may explain the reluctance of some cities to take on the adaptation challenge? The eight cities were selected to reflect a diversity of conditions, including climatic zones, political-administrative organization, steering capacity, and state of progress toward adaptation planning and action. At the same time, they are large urban agglomerations that can be expected to play an important role in further advancing the global adaptation agenda.

The concept of *coping capacity*, defined as the ability to manage both the causes of environmental change and the consequences of that change, is central to this study (Tompkins and Adger 2005). Coping capacity is dependent on the availability of resources, authority, human capital, and social capital, as well as the ability to manage information, the availability of technological innovation, and public perception of attribution (Yohe 2001). It also depends on normative or motivational contexts (Haddad 2005) as well as human behavior and choices (Burch and Robinson 2007). Based on this, we take the view that response action to climate change depends on both the ability and willingness of (single and collective) actors to take action. In this context, we explore coping capacity to better understand the opportunities and obstacles to adaptation and how they translate into scenarios of response or nonresponse.

The first section of this chapter provides relevant background information on the cases, including demographics, spatial location, administrative organization, annual temperature and precipitation, scenario trends, and whether the locations have national and local adaptation frameworks and action plans. The second section reports on the individual exposure of cities to climate change and shows the climate-related trends and existing local driving forces. As all the cases confirm, climate change exacerbates many existing vulnerabilities. In the third section, we turn to coping capacity and explore how and to what extent cities are integrating climate change into local strategies and action. This pertains to questions of temporal scales, multisectoral structures and coordination, strategic orientation, new priorities, and governance arrangements. The fourth section provides an analysis across all eight cases of the opportunities and motivating factors that drive or obstruct adaptation planning and action. In the final section, we elaborate on our recommendations for policy and research. The source papers (individual case reports) are available from the authors as separate documents (Aggarwal 2009; Barton 2009; Bharucha and others 2009; Fragkias 2009; Heinrichs, Krellenberg, and Vogel 2009; Johnston 2009; Lampis 2009; Ooi 2009).

Background of the Case Studies

As mentioned, eight cities and regions are included in this case study: Bogota, Cape Town, Delhi, Pearl River Delta, Pune, Santiago, São Paulo, and Singapore. All the cities are representative of large urban agglomerates (table 8.1). Their populations range from three to five million (Cape Town and Pune) to 19 million (São Paulo). Pearl River Delta, and the nine prefectures of its Guangdong province, are estimated to have a population of about 48 million people, including 12–14 million migrants from remote provinces. The population changes in the eight cities reflect various stages of urbanization. The Latin American cities have already passed their urbanization peak and show a rather consolidated status of urbanization. Annual increase in population has slowed to less than 2 percent and takes place mainly in the suburban and periurban areas. However, intense inner-city restructuring is still taking place. Asian cities are at a much earlier stage of urbanization and show an impressive annual increase in population of about 3 to 5 percent (UN 2008).

All eight cases bundle important political and administrative functions as national, regional, or provincial capitals or secondary centers. This generally creates more favorable conditions in terms of access and control over political, financial, and administrative resources. However, the internal political-administrative structures and distribution of power and capacity between local and regional bodies vary significantly from case to case.

Because of their different geographical locations and climatic zones, the average annual temperatures and precipitation levels in the case cities range from tropical climates in Singapore and Pune with seasonal monsoons; to subtropical climates in São Paulo, Bogota, and Pearl River Delta; to a mild Mediterranean climate in Santiago de Chile.

Cape Town, Singapore, and Pearl River Delta are the only three coastal city regions explored in this study. These cities are therefore the only three cities here at risk from the effects of sea-level changes. Because the other five cases are located in noncoastal areas, the study provides an opportunity to study anticipated changes and effects that go beyond the threat of sea-level rise. For example, other expected climate change–related challenges include temperature increases and changing precipitation rates and seasonality as well as extreme events such as storms and floods. Their impacts will increase over time and will contribute to severe risks (IPCC 2007). An increase in annual median

TABLE 8.1
Background Information

City	Projected average temperature change[a]	Projected annual rainfall change	Anticipated changes in extreme events	Sea-level change
Bogota	2–4°C increase	15% decrease	Increasing intensity of rainfall events, heat waves, electrical storms	Not applicable
Cape Town	2–3°C increase in maximum/ minimum temperatures (by 2050)	Up to 20% increase in winter months; 10% runoff decline by 2015	Increase of already significant number and intensity of storms	Rise by 2 cm per decade over the past decade, projected at 200–900 mm by 2100
Delhi	3–4°C increase (by end of century)	Predicted increase of about 10% in Gangetic plains; not quite clear from regional climate models	Increasing intensity of rainfall events and total rainfall, heat waves, increased drought, disease transmission	Not applicable
Pearl River Delta	3.5°C increase (by end of century)	1% increase per decade during the 21st century	Increasing intensity of heat waves (increase in number of very hot days and hot nights in summer)	Projected at 30 cm by 2030; 40–60 cm by 2050; the southern part of the delta lies between –0.3 and 0.4 m relative to mean sea level
Pune	2.5–5.0°C increase (by end of century)	Increase according to current regional climatic model; new data suggest there could be a decrease	Increasing intensity of rainfall events, local heat waves, disease transmission	Not applicable

National strategy for climate change	National climate change action plan	Local/city adaptation plan
Integrated National Adaptation Project, planned 2008–13, implemented only 2007 ($400,000 World Bank and Japanese cooperation)	Guidelines for a National Climate Change Policy (2002): estimate impacts, protect high mountain systems (water), adapt to sea-level rise and to changing epidemiological patterns	Nonexistent, planned in 2008, not yet included in the recently published environmental policy guidelines
The national climate plan flowed almost directly out of the Western Cape plan	Approved 2008	Approved 2006
National Environmental Policy 2006, National Action Plan on Climate Change passed in June 2008	Solar energy, energy efficiency, sustainable habitat, conserving water, sustaining the Himalayan ecosystem, green India, sustainable agriculture, and strategic knowledge platform for climate change	"Climate Change Agenda 2009–2012," approved in 2009
Nonexistent	National adaptation plan addressing regional adaptation in coastal zones	Nonexistent
National environmental policy 2006	Approved June 2008	Nonexistent

continued

TABLE 8.1, *continued*

City	Projected average temperature change[a]	Projected annual rainfall change	Anticipated changes in extreme events	Sea-level change
Santiago	2–4°C increase	40% decrease in lower lying areas, less in higher areas	Increasing intensity of rainfall events	Not applicable
São Paulo		No information	Increasing intensity of rainfall events	Not applicable
Singapore		Corresponding to IPCC projections; increase of annual rainfall	Increasing intensity of rainfall events	Corresponding to IPCC projections

Source: Authors' compilation.

Note: °C = degrees Celsius.

a. IPCC 2007.

temperatures has been projected for all regions where the case cities are located, ranging between 2 and 5 degrees Celsius. An increase in extreme events has been identified for all city cases, including intensity in rainfall, heat waves, and storm events.

Although climate action plans exist on the national level for all cases, only Cape Town, Delhi, and São Paulo have started to formally incorporate adaptation strategies into their local agendas through dedicated climate action plans.

Exposure to Climate Change and Anticipated Effects

This section summarizes the sectors or urban functions where impacts of climate change are anticipated. It summarizes local conditions and trends that reinforce local exposure to climate change impacts.

As a striking observation, all case cities are expected to face major stresses on water availability (table 8.2). Particular concerns relate to issues of supply scarcity, contamination and salt water infiltration, higher demands, and growing dependency on external supply. In various cases (Cape Town, Delhi, Santiago, and Singapore), there is explicit reference to potential distribution conflicts

National strategy for climate change	National climate change action plan	Local/city adaptation plan
Approved 2006	Approved December 2008	Nonexistent
Approved 2008	No information	Plano Municipal de Mudancas Climaticas; approved in June 2009
Approved March 2008	Sustainable Singapore Blueprint approved in 2009; several sector action plans	Not applicable

between sectors and population groups. The impacts of climate change on health are another area of concern, including air pollution (Pearl River Delta, Santiago, and São Paulo), heat island effects (Delhi, Pearl River Delta, Pune, Santiago, and São Paulo), and the spread of disease vectors (all cities). The consequences on human settlements due to sea-level rise or coastal and inland flooding in Pearl River Delta and Singapore are a further concern that could lead to serious disruption in the transportation and infrastructure service. As a consequence of increasing global temperatures, rising energy demands (in conjunction with heat island effects) are identified as an issue of concern primarily in tropical cities. Disruption of sensitive ecosystems (from fire or environmental degradation), loss of biodiversity (as in the case of Pune), and food security are most notably of concern in Bogota and Cape Town. Although they are quantified in only a few of the case cities, economic losses due to climate change are significant, cross-cutting impacts.

Interestingly, high convergence is seen in terms of the local conditions and trends that reinforce the anticipative impacts of climate change in the case cities (table 8.3). In-migration to ecologically sensitive areas and associated land-use changes are major issues. Another common factor is the adoption of western consumption patterns that increase per capita demands for water, energy, food, and land. This is mentioned in connection with the already high dependency on "external supply" of resources (such as drinking water or energy). A final aspect is the highly inequitable distribution of associated risks across population groups and locations, with rising vulnerability within marginalized populations.

TABLE 8.2
Exposure of Case Cities to Climate Change Impacts

Affected sector/service/use	Bogota	Cape Town	Delhi	Pearl River Delta	Pune	Santiago	São Paulo	Singapore
Water	✓	✓	✓	✓	✓	✓	✓	✓
Ecosystems	✓	✓	✓	✓	✓			
Food	✓	✓		✓	✓			
Health	✓	✓	✓	✓	✓	✓	✓	✓
Infrastructure		✓	✓	✓			✓	✓
Energy			✓	✓	✓	✓	✓	✓
Human settlement (floods, sea-level rise)		✓	✓	✓	✓	✓	✓	✓

Source: Authors' compilation.

TABLE 8.3
Exposure of Cities to Climate Change

City	Anticipated impacts, knock-on effects	Reinforcing local conditions
Bogota	Rise in fire risk, heat effects on population, disease vectors, changing crop patterns, and food security	In-migration due to civil conflict
Cape Town	Water scarcity and potential distribution conflicts, increased energy consumption, heat-related health risks, increased water use, flooding (beaches, shorelines, coastal areas, infrastructure), stresses (fire) on indigenous vegetation	High in-migration, adoption of western consumption patterns
Delhi	Water shortages, heat waves, higher energy demands, flooding, rise in disease vectors	Urbanization in vulnerable areas, rising in-migration, increasing poverty levels
Pearl River Delta	Haze pollution and air quality, regional air pollution exacerbated by (regional) climate change, contamination of local drinking supplies with salt water, flooding, water shortage (partly due to loss of mountain glaciers), heat island effects, food and energy security, urban infrastructure (transportation networks) risks	Regional land-use change due to rapid urbanization degrading ecosystem services, regional climate effects of urbanization, long-term droughts (generally anomalous wet and dry conditions)
Pune	Water shortages, energy security challenges, flooding, siltation, land-use transformation, biodiversity loss, disease risk	Urbanization in vulnerable areas, rising in-migration, increasing poverty levels
Santiago	Water scarcity, supply deficit and conflicts, flooding, heat island effects	Urbanization in vulnerable areas, inequitable exposure to climate change impacts across spatial scale and social groups
São Paulo	Spread of vector-borne diseases (dengue, malaria), higher water demand, higher energy demand (cooling), effects on infrastructure, flooding	Unregulated settlement leading to loss of green spaces and vegetation cover, loss of drainage/retention function of rivers, building materials in Favelas (corrugated iron roof heats up houses)

continued

TABLE 8.3, *continued*

City	Anticipated impacts, knock-on effects	Reinforcing local conditions
Singapore	Economic infrastructure (port, airport, petrochemical plants, refineries in coastal areas); water supply becomes threatened (water is already purchased from Malaysia), increase in the spread of vector-borne disease, energy demand	Land reclamation in the low-lying island state (addition of 10% to preexisting area)

Source: Authors' compilation.

Our findings support the hypothesis that climate change effects add to already existing inequalities and vulnerabilities that are connected to high dependency on scarce resources. These effects are not limited by far to coastal or deltaic cities alone. Clearly, effects need to be seen in connection with "reinforcing" local conditions and factors. Crucial across all cities is the issue of water scarcity, especially where existing supplies are running into deficits (Cape Town, Delhi, Pune, and São Paulo) and are leading to distributional conflicts.

City Adaptation Capacity and Response

This section examines the state of adaptation planning and action in the selected cities. First, we examine national-level actions. Then we examine the city or regional scale. Here our descriptions focus primarily on cases where local action plans have been approved, implemented (Cape Town and Singapore), or about to be approved (Delhi and São Paulo). This is complemented by information on the national-level experience for all eight cases.

We adopt three focal points for the discussion of responses. First, what action do cities take? Second, who are the main actors? Third, what tools and instruments are prescribed and used to implement adaptation action?

Actions

Our first question examines motivations for adaptation as well as the fields of urban policy in which cities decide in favor of dedicated action. We also explored what types of responses have been initiated in the sample cities (table 8.4).

Looking at national-level strategy and action-plan preparation, the city responses are largely driven by the will to comply with international commitments. In one case (Colombia), financial incentives and technical support have been available. In Delhi, Pearl River Delta, and Pune, the strategy formulation is used to demonstrate international "leadership." The case of Cape Town is probably somewhat different, because the preparation of the national action plan emerged almost directly from the Western Cape provincial plan.

At the city level, the driving factors of "early" action vary quite significantly. In Delhi, city managers emphasize the responsibility of the city as a global leader. At the same time, they see the opportunity to advance their existing development agenda (basic service provision) through strategically accessing financial instruments (Clean Development Mechanism). In Singapore, adaptation is taken as an opportunity for technological innovation with significant investment in research and development. In Cape Town, the preparation of the Western Cape provincial plan was largely driven by the experience with disasters and the anticipated worsening effects of climate change. In the case of São Paulo, a driving factor is the mayor's involvement in the C40 initiative. This highlights the potential for new ideas, networks, and leadership as well as, especially, the variety of motivations and incentives for different actors.

With regard to policy fields or sectors where adaptation actions are being implemented, plans at the national level normally break down the action plans and often quite generally prescribe guidelines for sectoral action. Surprisingly, no specific urban focus or agenda is found, except perhaps in those cases where frameworks and plans have identified coastal areas as a concern.

City-level actions concentrate on a range of sectors, including water, energy, waste, infrastructure, land use, human settlement, and disaster management. A concern across all cases is anticipated water supply scarcity. In Cape Town, this has led city managers to initiate a range of actions under the adaptation plan to address residential consumption patterns. Behavioral change is also a strong emphasis in Singapore with respect to energy consumption. The city also initiated several programs for technology development with regard to water (desalination and recycling) and energy (for example, solar energy). Aside from linking supply management with demand management, action in all cases displays an increasing awareness for integrating key sectors. Some examples include disaster management and land use (São Paulo) or land use and transportation (Singapore). In Cape Town, the framework for adaptation to climate change represents a citywide and coordinated approach that reviews direct impacts on natural resources as well as secondary impacts on the socioeconomic conditions and livelihood of communities, and it references specific strategies in response to these impacts (Mukheibir and Ziervogel 2007). In all cases, the actions formulated in the local action plans tie in to (preexisting) strategies and goals for sustainable development (Cape Town and Singapore) or global competitiveness (Delhi and Pune). Likewise, actions are legitimized by linking them to problems

TABLE 8.4
Response Capacity (Action)

City	What motivated action	Policy fields in which dedicated climate action has been introduced	Type of action
Bogota	External funding for the National Adaptation Project	No information	No dedicated action, preexisting sectoral initiatives
Cape Town	Existing threats, experiences with disasters	Water resources conservation and consumption, disaster management and preparedness	Adaptation linked to goal and ongoing initiatives of reducing vulnerability and sustainability, proactive and protecting, knowledge driven
Delhi	National Action plan, which underlies India's intention to be recognized as a key player in climate negotiations with Delhi playing a lead role domestically and seeking to enhance its global stature; need to address problems related to basic services provision and the opportunity to capitalize on CDM and other financial mechanisms	"Air Ambience Fund" to promote clean air policies, transportation (condensed natural gas buses), energy sector (greater reliance on solar, shutting down coal powered plants), water (rainwater harvesting, solar heaters), waste management (interceptor sewer canals)	Action plans primarily focused on mitigation, strongly driven by need to tap opportunities offered by CDM; adaptation linked to existing development concerns and largely follows a sectoral approach
Pearl River Delta	Scientific findings and consensus on climate change risks, international collaboration (UNFCCC [common but differentiated responsibilities], IPCC, DFID), participation in international environmental agreements	No urban policy but China's National Climate Change Program (national policy established by central government)	Ecosystem protection, disaster prevention and reduction, other key infrastructure construction (antiflood safety of large rivers, key cities and regions, guarantee safe drinking water and sound social and economic development), technological advancement

Pune	No climate change motivators, poverty alleviation, disaster management	No dedicated climate change action, sectoral interventions in flooding, water supply, and transport (mitigation: BRT)	No dedicated action, preexisting sectoral initiatives, shifting of slums along flood-prone river bed, BRT system
Santiago	On national level, response to international commitments (OECD, UN)	No dedicated plan of action	No dedicated action, preexisting sectoral initiatives
São Paulo	Mayor brought back the idea from a C40 meeting	Disaster management, vulnerability analyses, "Plan Parque Lineares," transportation, energy, waste management, health, building standards, land use, and resettlement	Adaptation linked to prominent concerns (transportation); mix of retreating, accommodating, and protecting; short-term and project orientation
Singapore	Adaptation as the continuation of a well-established long-term/coordinated planning approach	Infrastructure planning: drainage of recent tidal barrier and reservoir, transportation-coordinated land use, energy efficiency (technology, audits, standards, behavior change), water supply (desalination, recycling), urban greening	Protecting, linking with science and technology

Source: Authors' compilation.

Note: BRT = Bus Rapid Transit; CDM = Clean Development Mechanism; DFID = U.K. Department for International Development; OECD = Organisation for Economic Co-operation and Development; UNFCCC = United Nations Framework Convention on Climate Change.

that are "prominent" and debated in public. An example is São Paulo, where much of the rhetoric is linked to the transportation situation, which attracts much of the public debate. These two aspects (continuity of the agenda, public relevance of the topic) seem to be important "strategic" considerations in bringing adaptation action into the mainstream of local development.

With the exception of Cape Town and its clear focus on adaptation with a dedicated "framework for adaptation to climate change," the city-level action cases do not make explicit distinctions between adaptation and mitigation. In Delhi, there is some indication that a focus on mitigation, motivated by the opportunities offered by the Clean Development Mechanism, has thus far prevented a stronger consideration of adaptation measures.

Looking at the type of response, it is useful to differentiate between accommodating, protecting, or retreating action. Coastal cities facing sea-level rise and extreme events seem to favor "protective" approaches (Cape Town and Singapore). With respect to impacts that relate to resource availability and redistribution, accommodating responses are adopted (Cape Town), whereby a main instrument is to adjust (minimize) consumption or to seek technological solutions. For São Paulo, retreating options in the form of resettlement are discussed and written into the local adaption plan.

Actors

Our second question explores which actors have taken the lead on climate change adaptation, how responses are being coordinated (vertically and horizontally), and how public and local community participation is organized.

Across all eight case study cities, the lead responsibility for adaptation lies with governments. In China, a concerted top-down strategy has been developed with the establishment of a "regional administration system" to coordinate local responses to climate change. In all other cases, local or regional responsibility exists independently from national strategies. In cities with existing local action plans, three principal alternatives have materialized. (1) In Cape Town and Singapore, the lead responsible actor is the agency concerned with the environment (Environmental Resource Management section within the Department of Environmental Affairs, Development and Planning in Cape Town, and the National Environment Agency, Ministry of Environment and Water Resources in Singapore). This may correspond to the existence of a strong environmental sustainable development agenda. (2) In São Paulo, the lead initiative is more in the political domain of the mayor's office. Here this may be due to the strong personal interest and engagement of an individual leader. (3) In Delhi, the government of the National Capital Territory of Delhi is mandated to take up action in several core areas defined by a national plan.

At the city level, the Delhi climate action plan outlines different projects that are taken up by specific local departments.

In cities with dedicated local action strategies, the primary mechanism for coordination is the action plan or framework itself. The process of implementation, however, varies substantially (table 8.5). In some cases (Cape Town and Singapore), technical working groups took over the responsibility to advance specific projects such as the Western Cape Reconciliation Strategy Study (WCRSS) to facilitate the reconciliation of predicted future water requirements over a 25-year horizon. In the case of São Paulo, the local action plan prescribes the formation of a dedicated multistakeholder committee (Comite Municipal de Mudanca do Clima e Ecoeconomia) under the Environment Department.

The task of engaging private sector, civil society, and local community stakeholders is undertaken in different ways in each city. In Cape Town, the WCRSS involves citizens through newspaper advertisements, public meetings, capacity-building exercises, newsletters, and workshops with key stakeholders. The objective is to induce behavioral change in water consumption. In São Paulo, the dedicated multistakeholder committee invites the private sector, civil society, and science community to participate. Across almost all cases, participation is generally "top-down" oriented. This may be associated with the perception that action is primarily undertaken within the public sector domain. An important exception is Pune, in which a large number of nongovernmental organizations act as important drivers of change. A reason for strong public engagement is the limited civil society engagement and level of organization, either in general (Cape Town and Singapore) or with respect to adaptation in urban areas in particular. In São Paulo, a noticeable sensitivity for climate change and adaptation exists, but this is largely associated with the issue of the Amazon rainforest. With respect to local communities and individual citizens, some evidence across cities suggests that climate change adaptation is still only loosely connected to individual living conditions or lifestyles, especially in the emerging middle classes, which are becoming increasingly globalized as their resource demands and supply patterns change.

Tools and Instruments for Implementation

Our third question reviews the knowledge base and means of communication for planning efforts. More specifically, we ask: How do the actors communicate information and generate awareness, what measures are in place to ensure compliance and evaluation of action, and how are adaptation projects financed?

Not surprisingly, all existing local plans and resulting projects benefit somehow from research on the uncertainty of local climate change impacts

TABLE 8.5
Response Capacity (Actors)

City	Lead agency	Principal participants	Coordination mechanisms	How participation is organized
Bogota	Mayor, Regional Autonomous Corp. of Cundinamarca	National Environment Council, Environmental District Secretariat, Emergency Prevention and Attention Directorate		
Cape Town	City Environment Department	Local authority departments, provincial departments, consultant teams	Formation of technical working groups	Interactive workshops
Delhi	Government of National Capital Territory of Delhi, mandated to take up action in core areas defined by the National Plan	Department of Environment, Department of Power, Public Works Department, Delhi Jal board (autonomous water management agency), Delhi Transportation Corporation, NGOs	At national level, prime minister's advisory council on climate change provides overall coordination of action plans, lead agency for implementation is Ministry of Environment and Forests	Largely top-down, occasional meetings of core participants
Pearl River Delta	Top tier of the hierarchy (national government), National Leading Group to address climate change, headed by the Chinese premier, was set up in 2007 to draw up important strategies, policies, and measures related to climate change and to coordinate the solving of major problems	Supported by a regional governance system; in 2007, the state council called on all regions and departments to strictly implement the National Plan for Coping with Climate Change	Plan's presence and mandate for regional application will motivate action at the local level; establishment of a regional administration system for coordinating the work in response to climate change; building local expert group on climate change	

Pune	Pune Municipal Corp.	Pimpri Chinchwad Municipal Corp., cantonment administrations, Maharashtra State Electricity Board, Maharashtra Housing Development Agency, NGOs	Potential advisory by citizen groups to the Pune Municipal Corporation of environment-related NGOs	Meetings at the Pune Municipal Corp.
Santiago	National Environment Agency (CONAMA)	Government ministries and agencies	National Climate Change Committee under CONAMA, Agriculture and Climate Change Committee (Ministry of Agriculture)	Few meetings of core participants
São Paulo	City government (Prefeitura de Cidade de São Paulo), mayor's office, lead delegated to the Environment Department	ICLEI, Fundacao Getulio Vargas, FADESP (Research Institute), Ministerio de Saneamiento e Energia (Estado de São Paulo)	Comite Municipal de Mudanca do Clima e Ecoeconomia (municipal government, São Paulo state, civil society, private sector, science community)	Possibility to participate on the committee
Singapore	National Environment Agency	State agencies with authority over land use and transport development and building controls; civil society organizations tend to be small in terms of membership numbers and resources; public sector: strong support for state initiative as they converge with their own priorities		

Source: Authors' compilation.

Note: NGO = nongovernmental organization.

(table 8.6). The necessity of additional knowledge to identify the challenges of climate change therefore is highlighted in all national action plans. However, fundamental gaps exist in many action plans because proven local or regional climate scenarios are left out in all cases. Research action to close these gaps has been proven to be quite different. Cape Town and Singapore have engaged scientific expertise to study long-term local effects of climate change. In Delhi, efforts to improve the understanding of local climate effects are driven by national-level initiatives and involve both national and local research institutions. São Paulo engages in a process to elicit local knowledge through a series of stakeholder consultations with the assistance of the ICLEI and the Fundação Getulio Vargas, a local foundation. Obviously all cases (including those that have not yet formulated "formal" action plans) benefit from the research institutions in place.

The eight cities pursue options for communicating relevant information and creating awareness. The communication efforts include general information on climate change and the benefits of adaptation, increasing awareness about the implications of consumption patterns, and communication about the impacts of climate change–related events. Cape Town has taken the most extensive initiative in relation to its water demand management activities to gain collaboration by the citizens. The city has engaged in another project, which modeled the physical, biological, and social impacts arising from a "sea-level event" (inundation) in the city. The dramatic results were publicized widely through local media. The public response to the study has been vociferous on the one hand, where interest groups such as land owners have objected to the report as alarmist, and muted on the other hand, where the nonaffected population regards the scenarios as "someone else's problem." Looking across the eight cases, however, the entire field of communication, information, and awareness creation appears somewhat neglected even in cities where the topic of climate change has been picked up explicitly. More commonly, initiatives are developed in conjunction with related projects instead of linked directly to a climate change agenda. In Delhi, for example, the "Clean Yamuna" (river) water-harvesting and solar-heating projects are being implemented essentially as awareness campaigns.

What measures are in place to ensure compliance and assessment? Singapore has introduced such measures as the green mark standard for energy-efficient buildings and energy audits as well as encouraging households to conserve energy, for example, through the 10 percent energy challenge to encourage energy-efficient habits. This involves mandatory energy labeling for common household appliances to ensure that consumers can make efficient, well-informed choices when they decide on their purchases. Market-based instruments are likewise being introduced. The installation of water meters and sliding-scale water tariffs in Cape Town are two examples, complemented by regulatory measures such as comprehensive water by-laws, including the right to enforce water restrictions. The responsible agencies operate compliance teams to monitor and enforce water use.

All climate action plans carry or, in the cases where approval is pending, at least propose discretionary financing for climate action. In some cases, funding mechanisms have been put in place. An example is the Air Ambience Fund, financed through a fee on the sales of diesel fuel. The plan in São Paulo proposes to use 5 percent of the revenues from newly discovered offshore oil reserves for adaptation. Singapore practices copayment and cofinancing. The state sector in Singapore has always emphasized this form of financing for supporting programs from housing to transport and health care, among a range of social, environmental, and other policies. In Cape Town, the Environmental Resource Management Department has an annual locally funded budget, with contribution from the Danish International Development Agency.

Opportunities and Constraints

Finally, we discuss what motivates the nexus of actors and organizations in cities that have started to develop and implement adaptation plans. This is followed by an assessment of opportunities for local climate action. Moreover, we identify obstacles to adaptation in cities that have been more reluctant to take on the adaptation challenge as well as cities with local action plans in place.

Opportunities and Success Factors for Adaptation

One of the main drivers of adaptation action in the majority of the sample cities appears to be the clear *awareness* by local stakeholders of local vulnerability to climate change as well as perceptions of risk. Community safety and minimization of disaster impacts are major objectives in many surveyed adaptation plans (such as Cape Town, São Paulo, and Singapore). Initiatives are often linked to historical disaster experiences, which reinforces predictions about climate impacts and builds awareness of the need for adaptation. The creation of awareness and local knowledge is normally driven by locally relevant scientific *information*, which has to be communicated by adequate means. The identification of risks by downscaling climate models and by the analysis of vulnerability generate political interest in understanding how the local climate is likely to change, how the city will be affected, and what local response options seem appropriate to confront predicted impacts. In an attempt to address existing uncertainties about climate change impacts, significant reliance is put on university scholars, centers, and programs and on consensus-building processes with affected stakeholders.

TABLE 8.6
Response Capacity (Tools)

City	Information flows, awareness creation, and communication	Links to existing urban policy instruments	Knowledge basis on which plan was prepared	Implementation (compliance mechanisms, monitoring)	Financing
Bogota					Existing emergency funding budget
Cape Town	Dedicated awareness campaign: newspaper, advertisements, public meetings, capacity building, newsletters	For water, expansion of existing sector policies	Water: Western Cape Reconciliation Strategy Study (25-year horizon); sea-level rise: risk assessment project to model and understand impacts	Water: comprehensive water by-laws include a range of tools: right to set water price, install water meters, enforce water restriction; making use of breakwaters compulsory	Discretionary budget
Delhi	No dedicated climate change awareness programs, several "standalone" environmental awareness programs; National Action Plan proposed creation of	Delhi Master Plan 2021, JNNURM	IPCC reports, research at Tata Energy Research Institute, Indian Institute of Tropical Meteorology, National Mission on Strategic Knowledge to be set	Mix of regulatory instruments (such as solar water heaters made mandatory in all buildings on area of more than 500 square meters, digging of bore wells for individual use	Mitigation efforts funded through carbon market financing and CDMs, private participation to be encouraged through venture funds; Air Ambience Fund

	integrated National Knowledge Network ministries, experts from industry, academia, and civil society organizations	banned in Delhi, allowed only for community use); market-based instruments (such as fee on sale of diesel, proposed introduction of congestion fees)	financed through fee on sale of diesel; Transport Development Fund funded through tax receipts from registration charges and proposed congestion fees; funding for adaptation linked to existing urban development projects (such as JNNURM) and Department of Environment funding
Pearl River Delta	Chinese government set up special institutions to deal with climate change in 1990 and established the National Coordination Committee on Climate Change in 1998	Mentioned in the national plan but with no concrete strategy (the plan suggests a need for international technology transfers)	

continued

TABLE 8.6, *continued*

City	Information flows, awareness creation, and communication	Links to existing urban policy instruments	Knowledge basis on which plan was prepared	Implementation (compliance mechanisms, monitoring, and so on)	Financing
Pune	Experts from university environmental departments, NGOs	Annual Environment Status Report (JNNURM)	Fragmented research, such as urbanization; heat island; no local administration documentation	Not in place	JNNURM
Santiago	Limited to technical information; no regional/ local communication	National Action Plan links to water management, infrastructure, regulatory plans, and energy policy	No regional adaptation evaluation to date, no specific consideration of urban areas	Sectoral investment programs in flood mitigation, energy mix, biodiversity management	No dedicated budget for adaptation
São Paulo	Website by the municipal government, perception that information is accessible only if the user knows that it is there	Land-use plan	Plan based on a process of consultation, stakeholder participation, expert involvement, literature review, strong role of "external" support (ICLEI)		Fundo Municipal de Verde e Meio Ambiente

| Singapore | Link to research and development in water technologies (desalination, recycling of sewage water) and energy (focus on alternative energy technologies), urban greenery (rooftop) | Study on understanding long-term effects of climate change in 2007, led by the Tropical Marine Science Institute, contracted by the National Environment Agency | Various mechanisms |

Source: Authors' compilation.

Note: CDM = Clean Development Mechanism; IPCC = International Panel on Climate Change; JNNURM = Jawaharlal Nehru National Urban Renewal Mission; NGO = nongovernmental organization.

Second, adaptation plans are purposefully used to *support and prioritize already existing strategies*. As Cape Town and Singapore show, this ensures the integration and "mainstreaming" of adaptation action and serves as an opportunity to develop existing (local) development goals further. This guarantees continuity instead of radical change in local priorities. The focus of the adaptation strategy, however, seems to vary significantly between cases. In Cape Town, adaptation is connected strongly to existing environmental programs. In Singapore, it supports a strategy for building competitive advantages in technological advancement and innovation. This is an important lesson and a potential starting point for local action in other cities. Our study reveals that, although not explicitly declared as climate action, related initiatives exist in all cities to which local climate action can be tied. An open question, though, remains as to whether these actions are underlining general goals and priorities or serve more solely as artificial labels in the field of climate change.

Third, adaptation action requires *strong local leadership*, often motivated by opportunities to become recognized as innovative and future oriented. Local politicians or personalities, and often both, drive city adaptation actions. One objective is to raise visibility in regional, national, and international arenas, as the case of Delhi shows. Another objective is the intention to demonstrate "good governance" to the residents and to bring about innovation in local governance and administration. Cape Town and its slogan "The city is working for you" serves as an example.

Fourth, local adaptation action strongly builds on *interpersonal and interinstitutional interaction to establish confidence in priorities*. The transfer of ideas, knowledge, and insight through "external" networks, that is, international or cross-country cooperation (such as C40, ICLEI, and United Cities and Local Governments), as demonstrated in the case of São Paulo, is strong across early adaptors. Memberships in networks and attendance at conferences go beyond enhancing reputation, as these relationships and events are important sources of ideas and information for cities. Furthermore, early movers utilize diverse types of climate-related events, including "internal" networks in cities, so that information is shared among politicians and departments and fosters participation in events at regional, national, and international levels. This involves the strong presence and engagement of both nongovernmental and community-based organizations.

Fifth, a common practice in the implementation of adaptation plans is the creation of *dedicated climate teams* working within a centralized office and not attached to one specific sector. This appears to be an adequate treatment of the cross-cutting nature of adaptation and avoids confining adaptation to the responsibilities of one sector alone (most likely the Environment Department). An alternative is the creation of a Climate Protection Department within the office of the mayor, as discussed in the case of São Paulo. This reinforces the interdepartmental character of climate impacts.

Finally, *enhancing financial capacities* seems to play a role in driving adaptation responses, but to a lesser degree than one would have expected. Among the eight cases, none of the local action plans has relied on external financial assistance. Expanding financial capacity has been an issue in Delhi in relation to the Clean Development Mechanism. At the national level Colombia has benefited from financial assistance in drawing up the national framework.

Constraints on Adaptation

With respect to adaptation constraints, several lessons arise from the experiences of Bogota, Pearl River Delta, Pune, and Santiago, as well as from the "early" movers Cape Town, Delhi, and Singapore.

First, we observe *very limited levels of awareness* with regard to the relevance of climate change for local conditions. In addition, local officials contacted in surveys tend not to recognize or promote the potential connection between climate change and existing development goals. Nor do they make reference to the potential of adaptation planning to address other priorities. In general, adaptation to climate change is not seen as relevant for the local development agenda. Where these links are reported, they are related to carbon dioxide mitigation, which local officials view as the major response. Overall, adaptation does not play a prominent role. This perception is mirrored in the opinion held by the public. Awareness is low, and climate change, let alone the need to adapt to its consequences, is not viewed as a problem associated with local urban development or connected to personal consumption patterns, not even in the emerging middle classes.

Second, the existing definition and *distribution of political competences and responsibilities* are reported to be inadequate. This observation relates to the local versus national level and likewise to the distribution of responsibilities between the various subnational entities. In all cases, respondents report a multilevel coordination problem with overlapping competences resulting in weak political competences. Although numerous coordination units between these entities exist, they are not defined by a clear division of competences that empower the responsible level. Adaptation to climate change is harder to achieve in such a setting, because the interests of the different entities tend to ignore those of others or to create conflict—and do not allow an overall planning process.

A third obstacle is the limited *competence for managing financial resources* at the local level. Even in the cities where local action plans are in place, they do not (with the exception of Cape Town) contain dedicated financing mechanisms. More broadly, a mismatch is reported between the requirement of

TABLE 8.7
Opportunities and Constraints

City	Opportunities	Constraints
Bogota	• Strong emergency management structure • Clear territorial authority structure (role of mayor and regional corporation)	• Civil conflict and migration patterns • Vulnerability to wide range of natural disasters due to localization
Cape Town	• Motivation primarily internal: existing threats that will be exacerbated, experiences with disasters • Dealing with existing (but exacerbating) vulnerabilities in government is not actively seeking profile in this regard, but rather trying to develop a social conscience • Environmental awareness in the Western Cape has always been high • Very highly qualified academic base in the local universities; the city and province have in most instances been receptive to scientific input and have established committees and forums for discussing the issues	• Foresight required in terms of SLR: officials and politicians are less likely to respond to the threat of a distant disaster than a more immediate one • Citizens' involvement, "social component" largely unrepresented in Cape Town, thus there is little to build on, but public awareness and pressure from NGOs is growing
Delhi	• International role in climate change forums, building profile of a global city and leadership role in climate change • Strong motivation to tap financial opportunities through CDM • Links with existing urban renewal missions such as JNNURM • Existing Bhagidari initiatives in priority areas, increasing local awareness	• Rapid in-migration (20–25% slum dwellers, higher vulnerability) • Limited local revenue-raising capacity, complex relationship with neighboring states in National Capital Region, weak coordination among departments, climate change seen as a distant problem, development needs perceived to be more pressing

Pearl River Delta	• The national plan is advertised as the first climate plan from a developing country; its presence and mandate for regional application will motivate action at the local level	• National Plan has very few references to city adaptation action; suggested local government action is connected mostly to agricultural sector adaptation and the protection of coastal zones • Emphasis on mitigation action in National Plan • Emphasis on adaptation for agricultural production in National Plan (protecting yields for wheat, rice, and maize); strengthening forest/wetland conservation is also considered as enhancing adaptation capacities • Reduced governability capacity due to extremely rapid urbanization with limited control (comprehensive plans do not guide the observed levels of urbanization) • Top-down governance structure (a five-tier hierarchical structure) imposes limits for local action • Policies are implemented differentially at the local level (spatial differentiation of governance) • Lack of an independent budget for energy savings, environment protection, and adaptation at local level • Economic competition among regions and special economic zones increases the probability of no action (China insists on not sacrificing economic growth)
Pune	• Traditional water management systems (such as harvesting) • Investments through JNNURM • Strong engagement and involvement of NGOs • High level of civil society involvement • Strong reflection and discussion in local media	• High poverty levels, increasing vulnerability • Rapid in-migration and unplanned settlements (40% slum dwellers) • Weak coordination between local authorities • Low levels of climate change awareness • Rapid dynamics of change with low reaction time in a multistakeholder environment

continued

TABLE 8.7, *continued*

City	Opportunities	Constraints
Santiago	• Increasing (local) research awareness • Incorporation into (national) political discourse • Engagement within regional planning instruments	• Limited regional executive decision authority • Low awareness and communication • Nonurban bias in national adaptation
São Paulo	• Leadership (mayor) • Attach the issue of adaptation to "prominent" and cross-cutting problems (transportation, project "Parques Lineares")	• Adaptation is not a priority in relation to mitigation • National and regional levels not perceived as meaningful support for adaptation agenda, national level too concerned with international negotiations than with "local" concerns • Distribution of competences between municipality, state of São Paulo and national government • Lack of scientific knowledge on vulnerability • Lack of understanding of concept of adaptation and the potential to solve "other" priorities • Lack of knowledge on economic implications (action, inaction) • Conflict of interests (political leaders at local, regional, and national levels belong to different parties) • Short-term "project" orientation • General: lack of enforcement • Awareness (problems seen not related to climate change, and climate change not related to personal consumption patterns)
Singapore	• Technology development • "Tradition" of foresight planning	

Source: Authors' compilation.

Note: CDM = Clean Development Mechanism; JNNURM = Jawaharlal Nehru National Urban Renewal Mission; NGO = nongovernmental organization; SLR = Sea-level rise.

adaptation as a local challenge and the availability of local resources. The cases included in this study, despite having concentrations of a large population and oversight functions, mostly (with the exemption of Pune) have a limited degree of autonomy to decide on adaptation action according to administrative priorities. The examples of early adaptation we have discussed highlight that setting priorities is a decisive element for adaptation strategies. Setting priorities is primarily a political process, and it is more difficult to define priorities if the resources come from an external source, such as the national government.

A fourth factor relates to limitations in *administrative competences and fragmentation*. Developing adaptation strategies and implementing them are primarily tasks for the public sector. These responsibilities include the provision of public goods, such as infrastructure, sanitation, public transportation, housing, and social policy. Across cases, constraints relate to issues such as the lack of regulation compelling the private sector to meet minimum social goals and to share public-private planning. One prerequisite for fulfilling these tasks is adequate and state-of-the-art knowledge and information about (local) climate change impacts, including economic costs. The administrations in cities such as Pearl River Delta, Pune, or Santiago do not yet possess detailed and downscaled information about climate change impacts across sectors (such as infrastructure planning or water provision) and more important mechanisms for cross-sectoral coordination to properly address the problem of adaptation. Nor do mechanisms exist to capture and integrate existing local knowledge of adaptation that lies with affected stakeholders or organized community-based or nongovernmental organizations. As an aggravating factor, the current "fragmented" institutional structure prohibits a cross-cutting learning process.

A final obstacle relates to the *relevance of national climate action planning for local responses*. From the perspective of city representatives, national plans are prepared primarily as a response to the international negotiations and processes of the United Nations Framework Convention on Climate Change with a primary focus on mitigation (instead of adaptation). More important, for the most part they take a sectoral perspective and, with the exception of reference to coastal areas, have a nonurban bias. In some instances, the national plan has been "victimized" by conflicting political interests with contradicting and vague results. These arguments raise concerns about the adequacy and legitimacy of national plans in terms of guidance and support (table 8.7).

Conclusion

The examination of opportunities and constraints associated with the implementation of local adaptation measures and action plans provides insights on the capacity of local actors to internalize climate change into local responses. The exercise demonstrates that the challenge of climate change adaptation to a large extent connects to and emphasizes existing local development concerns that have been debated for quite some time. For example, the effects of sea-level rise, changes in temperature and rainfall, and changes in the intensity and frequency of extreme events add to existing vulnerabilities of populations or infrastructure. Likewise, they are inextricably linked with local driving factors that determine vulnerability. Examples include migration, land-use change, and the inequitable distribution of risks and opportunities across different population groups. Equally, many of the obstacles highlighted here with respect to the political, financial, and administrative capacity are not entirely new. They have been identified and discussed in previous contexts, for example, connected to decentralization or, more recently, "good urban governance."

Aside from reemphasizing existing necessities, what new insights do we derive?

The cases of Cape Town, Delhi, São Paulo, and Singapore show that cities (or city-states) can play a leading role as forerunners in designing local responses. They highlight the multitude of existing options, including the instruments needed to ensure compliance and fund sourcing. In addition, they show how the issue of climate change can be integrated into local development strategies. Even in the most proactive cases, the main emphasis is on mitigation action. However, all cases offer important lessons. In each city, opportunities exist for connecting local climate action to already ongoing activities or instruments in areas of major concern. Thus, a first lesson for applied research and policy is to better understand existing local opportunities and the ways to connect them to local climate action.

Although the cases highlight that local climate action is integrated in "established" policy fields or sectors, they demonstrate the need for applying holistic approaches, particularly in respect to consumption levels. As the water sector shows, individual and collective preferences can no longer be disconnected from the policy and practice of service delivery but, rather, need to be integrated. Thus, a second lesson is that a main strategy to confront the trend of growing scarcities will have to focus on adjusting consumption levels as a complement to reuse and recycling schemes.

Adaptation will invariably push concerns about the distribution of scarce resources across sectors (for example, domestic water use versus water use for agriculture) as well as across communities and locations further to the forefront of the adaptation debate. This will be particularly true and highly problematic in cities where scarce resources are linked with highly inequitable access of different population groups (Johnston and others 2008). Thus, the third lesson is that policy needs to pay increasing attention to long-term regulation of the distribution of resources between competing uses and users.

The experience across cities likewise shows the need to find strategies for engaging citizens in local adaptation action. Probably with the exception of Cape Town, attempts have been moderate, as has been the success. What adds to the task is that citizens do not correlate climate change and local effects with their own preferences and lifestyles. The lessons that follow is that the implementation of local climate action needs to consider communication much more prominently, perhaps needs to use a large variety of communication instruments, and might need to emphasize the links between the local effects of climate change, "mainstream" development, and individual consumption and lifestyles.

Finally, confronting the challenges of climate change will continue to face uncertainties about the direction and magnitude, the effect on levels of exposures, and the implications for policy despite attempts to bring climate models down to the local level. Thus, learning how to deal with uncertainty and to design processes that lead to "legitimate" action will be a major new challenge for local action.

References

Stand-alone Papers That Form the Basis for This Chapter

Aggarwal, R. 2009. "Adapting Cities to Climate Change: The Case of Delhi."
Barton, J. 2009. "Adapting Cities to Climate Change: The Case of Santiago de Chile."
·Bharucha, E., C. Butsch, and F. Kraas. 2009. "Adapting Cities to Climate Change: The Case of Pune."
Fragkias, M. 2009. "Adapting Cities to Climate Change: The Case of the Pearl River Delta."
Heinrichs, D., K. Krellenberg, and J. Vogel. 2009. "Adapting Cities to Climate Change: The Case of São Paulo."
Johnston, P. 2009. "Adapting Cities to Climate Change: The Case of Cape Town."
Lampis, A. 2009. "Adapting Cities to Climate Change: The Case of Bogotá."
Ooi, G. L. 2009. "Adapting Cities to Climate Change: The Case of Singapore."

Other References

Burch, S., and J. Robinson. 2007. "A Framework for Explaining the Links between Capacity and Action in Response to Global Climate Change." *Climate Policy* 7 (4): 314–16.
Haddad, B. 2005. "Ranking the Adaptive Capacity of Nations to Climate Change When Socio-Political Goals Are Explicit." *Global Environmental Change* 15 (3): 199–213.
IIED (International Institute for Environment and Development). 2007. "Reducing Risks to Cities from Climate Change: An Environmental or a Development Agenda." Environment and Urbanization Brief 15, IIED, London.

IPCC (Intergovernmental Panel on Climate Change). 2007. *Climate Change 2007: Synthesis Report. Contribution of Working Groups I, II and III to the Fourth Assessment Report of the Intergovernmental Panel on Climate Change.* Geneva: IPCC.

Johnston, P. A., D. B. Louw, O. Crespo, and T. B. Lumsden. 2008. "Quantifying the Costs, Benefits and Risks Associated with Planning and Management Alternatives Associated with Climate Risk for Water Resource Development—The Berg River Catchment Area Case Study (South Africa)." In *Building Adaptive Capacity—Mainstreaming Adaptation Strategies to Climate Change in African Transboundary River Basin Organisations (CCA-RBO).* Kampala: InWEnt Uganda.

Mukheibir, P., and G. Ziervogel. 2007. "Developing a Municipal Adaptation Plan (MAP) for Climate Change: The City of Cape Town." *Environment & Urbanization* 19 (1): 143–58.

Pielke, R., G. Prins, S. Rayner, and D. Sarewitz. 2007. "Lifting the Taboo on Adaptation." *Nature* 445: 597–98.

Tompkins, E., and N. Adger. 2005. "Defining Response Capacity to Enhance Climate Change Policy." *Environmental Science and Policy* 8 (6): 562–71.

UN (United Nations). 2008. *World Urbanization Prospects: 2007 Revision.* New York: UN Department of Social and Economic Affairs.

Yohe, G. 2001. "Mitigative Capacity: The Mirror Image of Adaptive Capacity on the Emission Side." *Climate Change* 49 (3): 247–62.

9

A Conceptual and Operational Framework for Pro-Poor Asset Adaptation to Urban Climate Change

Caroline Moser

This chapter introduces a new asset-focused framework whose objective is both analytically to understand and operationally to address the different phases of urban climate change as they impact on the lives of poor urban communities. The framework builds on earlier research on asset vulnerability, asset adaptation, and urban poverty reduction (see Moser 1998, 2007; Moser and Felton 2007, 2009), as well as preliminary climate change–related work (see Moser and Satterthwaite 2008).

By way of background, the chapter briefly reviews current approaches to climate change adaptation. It then describes the asset adaptation framework in terms of two components: first, an asset vulnerability analytical framework that appraises the types of socioeconomic vulnerability and groups most affected by climate change–related disasters, and, second, an asset adaptation operational framework that identifies a range of "bottom-up" climate change strategies at the individual, household, and community levels. Complementing this, it also highlights some of the "top-down" interventions of external actors such as municipalities, civil society organizations, and the private sector. These are discussed in terms of four closely interrelated "phases" of urban climate change, namely, long-term resilience, predisaster damage limitation, immediate

This chapter draws heavily on numerous recent papers, including Moser and Satterthwaite (2008) and Simatele (2009). I would like to express my gratitude to David Satterthwaite, Danny Simatele, Alfredo Stein, and Christine Wamsler for their generosity in allowing me to cite from these documents and for their substantive contribution to this chapter.

■ **225**

postdisaster response, and rebuilding. Given the importance of robust methodology for both research and practice, the chapter concludes with a brief description of the research methodology for an asset adaptation appraisal, as well as techniques associated with action-planning implementation strategies. Again these are contextualized within current methodological approaches to community-focused climate change research and practice.

The chapter is intended to provide a useful theoretical framework for researchers seeking to better understand the link between climate change adaptation and the erosion of assets of the poor in cities of the global South. In addition, the operational framework seeks to set out guidelines for the development of specific tools that can be used to support pro-poor adaptation strategies in urban areas. These may assist local authorities, community organizations, and other relevant institutions to design strategies to support the poor's existing coping strategies to protect assets, as well as to rebuild them after climate change–related disasters.

Background

This section briefly sets out the case for climate action in cities of the developing world and reviews some existing approaches to climate change adaptation.

The Urgency of Recognizing Climate Change in Cities of the Global South

Urban centers of low- and middle-income countries concentrate a large proportion of those most at risk from the effects of climate change—as lives, assets, environmental quality, and future prosperity are threatened by the increasing risk of storms, flooding, landslides, heat waves, and drought and by overloading water, drainage, and energy supply systems.[1] The evidence that demonstrates the vulnerability of urban populations to climate change is based on data collected over the past 30 years, showing a dramatic upward trend in the number of people killed or seriously impacted by extreme weather events (UN-Habitat 2007; see also Hoeppe and Gurenko 2007). Within cities and towns, almost all serious disaster-related injuries and deaths occur among low-income groups. The principal driver of increasing loss of life as well as social and economic vulnerability is poverty (limiting individual, household, and community investments) and exclusion (limiting public investments and services). Climate change not only exacerbates existing risks but also reveals new hidden vulnerabilities as more locations are exposed to more intense floods and storms (Moser and Satterthwaite 2008, 4).

Current Approaches to Climate Change and Their Associated Methodologies

To date, climate change mitigation has been the main focus of attention, given the importance of getting governments to accept the scientific evidence for human-induced climate change. Nevertheless, increasing concern with the complementary issue of adaptation has led to an increased focus on this aspect of climate change. Approaches have ranged from disaster risk reduction that broadened in scope to include climate change to the emergence of new specific climate change adaptation approaches. The diversity of approaches to climate change adaptation is complex, interrelated, and often overlapping and, therefore, difficult to disentangle.

Table 9.1 therefore seeks to summarize some of these different adaptation approaches in terms of the historical period when developed, the key objectives, and current emphases, as well as other characteristics. It shows, first, the critical importance that the disaster risk reduction (DDR) and disaster risk management (DRM) communities have played in addressing disasters over the past 30 years long before climate change per se had even become identified as a global development priority; second, the emergence of newer climate change–specific approaches such as climate risk management; and, third, the increasing convergences in disaster risk and climate change communities with approaches such as climate change vulnerability resilience. Although community-based approaches to poverty reduction have been widely implemented in the past few decades as a consequence of the work of community-based organizations (CBOs), nongovernmental organizations (NGOs), and participatory rural developmentalists such as Robert Chambers (see Chambers 1992), more recently this approach has also been applied to climate change adaptation.

As identified in table 9.1, all these approaches to varying extents focus on assets primarily from the perspective of vulnerability. The following section, as identified in the last row of table 9.1, elaborates on an approach that focuses primarily and directly on assets.

An Asset Adaptation Framework: From Asset Vulnerability to Asset Adaptation

The asset adaptation framework comprises two components that can be summarized as follows, with a brief description of each:

- An asset vulnerability analytical framework that identifies the types of socioeconomic vulnerability and groups most affected in four closely interrelated "phases" or "stages" that can occur during urban climate change.

TABLE 9.1
Summary of Selected Approaches to Climate Change Adaptation

Name of approach	Period of development	Key objectives and current emphasis	Examples of institutions using the approach	Origin	Focus on assets
DRR/DRM	1980s	Reduction of underlying factors of risk, intensity and/or frequency of disaster occurrence in the predisaster and postdisaster context (development, relief, and response) including climate-related and non–climate-related disasters. Current emphasis is on the integration of DRR into sustainable development through a management perspective.	Tearfund, Environment, Climate Change and Bio-energy Division of FAO, GTZ, IDS, SIDA, DFID, and others	DRM (emergency/relief organizations, social scientists)	In the context of strengthening capacities and resilience of households, communities' and institutions' assets are a major theme
CRM	1990s/2000s	Reduction of vulnerability to climate risk by maximizing positive and minimizing negative outcomes caused by climate change with the final aim to promote sustainable development.	IDS, Energy for Sustainable Development Africa, UN Secretariat of ISDR, ADPC	Climate change adaptation community/DRM	Due to its orientation toward community adaptation and institutional capacity building, assets are addressed

Climate change adaptation	1990s/2000s	Reduction of vulnerability to climate risk developed as a reaction to the 1990s GHG debate that promoted the mitigation agenda. Emphasis of adaptation is on dealing with physical impacts of climate change.	South North, Acclimatise, TCPA, IIED, ADPC, ACTS	DRM/climate change adaptation	Assets addressed through the interest in local knowledge and competence
Climate change vulnerability resilience	2000s	Increasing the ability of communities to withstand and recover from climate change–related external shocks and stresses with an emphasis on economic well-being, stability of a community, social and political factors, institutional capacity, global interconnectivity, and natural resource dependence.	IDS, Tyndall Research Centre, Acclimatise, IIED, Practical Action	DRM/climate change adaptation	Assets addressed implicitly as approach attaches significance to governance quality at municipal and local levels

continued

TABLE 9.1, *continued*

Name of approach	Period of development	Key objectives and current emphasis	Examples of institutions using the approach	Origin	Focus on assets
Community-based adaptation	2007 (adapted from poverty-focused programs of 1990s)	Support of knowledge and coping strategies of individuals and communities to reduce vulnerabilities to climate risk, based on individual and community knowledge of climate variability.	IDS, Eldis, ACTS, ADPC, IISD, IIED, Practical Action	DRM/climate change adaptation (influenced by development experts such as Robert Chambers)	Assets form a central theme due to the bottom-up approach emphasizing people's capabilities and abilities
Asset-based vulnerability and adaptation	2008 (building on asset vulnerability of 1990s)	Analysis of asset vulnerability and asset adaptation relating to the erosion and/or protection of human, social, physical, and financial assets at individual, household, and community levels for resilience, predisaster damage limitation, immediate postdisaster response, and rebuilding.	Global Urban Research Centre, IIED	Asset vulnerability and asset accumulation framework, climate change adaptation	Assets main basis of focus at different levels including role of external institutions such as municipalities, NGOs, and private sector

Source: Adapted from Simatele 2009.

Note: ACTS = African City for Technology; ADPC = Asian Disaster Preparedness Center; CRM = community risk management; : DFID = Department for International Development (U.K.); DRM = disaster risk management; DRR = disaster risk reduction; FAO = Food and Agriculture Organization; GHG = greenhouse gas; GTZ = German Agency for Technical Cooperation; IDS = Institute of Development Strategies; IIED = International Institute for Environment and Development; IISD = International Institute for Sustainable Development; ISDR = International Strategy for Disaster Reduction; NGO = nongovernmental organization; SIDA = Swedish International Development Cooperation Authority; TCPA = Town and Country Planning Association.

- An asset adaptation operational framework, linked to the analytical framework, identifies the range of "bottom-up" climate change adaptation strategies that individuals, households, and communities have developed to cope with the different phases of climate change. It also identifies the range of "top-down" interventions of external actors at city and national levels—such as municipalities, civil society organizations, and the private sector.

Asset Vulnerability

Analysis of the risks arising from climate change to low-income urban households and communities is grounded in the concept of vulnerability. This draws on an the development debate that recognizes poverty as more than income or consumption poverty and that captures the multidimensional aspects of changing socioeconomic well-being.[2] Moser (1998) in an urban study defines vulnerability as insecurity in the well-being of individuals, households, and communities, including sensitivity to change. Vulnerability can be understood in terms of a lack of resilience to changes that threaten welfare; these can be environmental, economic, social, and political, and they can take the form of sudden shocks, long-term trends, or seasonal cycles. Such changes usually bring increasing risk and uncertainty. Although the concept of vulnerability has focused mainly on its social and economic components, in applying it to climate change, vulnerability to physical hazards is often more important.

Also of climate change, operational relevance is the distinction between vulnerability and capacity or capability with its links to resilience. The emergency relief literature has shown that people are not "helpless victims," but have many resources even at times of emergency and that these should form the basis for responses (Longhurst 1994; see also ACHR 2005); there is also widespread recognition of the resources that grassroots organizations can bring to adaptation (Satterthwaite and others 2007; see also Huq and Reid 2007). When sudden shocks or disasters occur, the capabilities of individuals and households are deeply influenced by factors ranging from the damage or destruction of their homes and assets, to constraints on prospects of earning a living, to the social and psychological effects of deprivation and exclusion, including the socially generated sense of helplessness that often accompanies crises.

The fact that vulnerability can be applied to a range of hazards, stresses, and shocks offers a particular advantage to the analysis of climate change–related risks in urban contexts. Urban poor populations live with multiple risks and manage the costs and benefits of overlapping hazards from a range of environmental sources under conditions of economic, political, and social constraints. Climate change also brings a future dimension to understanding vulnerability. It highlights the uncertainty of future risk and, associated with this, an insecurity concerning the bundle of assets that will enable adaptation and greater resilience or lead to increased vulnerability. An asset-based vulnerability approach that incorporates social, economic, political, physical, human, and environmental resources allows for flexibility in the analysis and planning of interventions that is harder to maintain within a hazard-specific approach. It also highlights how many assets serve to reduce vulnerability to a range of hazards.

Vulnerability is closely linked to a lack of assets. The more assets people have, the less vulnerable they generally are; the greater the erosion of people's assets, the greater their insecurity. Therefore it is useful to define assets as well as to identify those of particular importance in the context of climate change. Generally, an asset is identified as a "stock of financial, human, natural, or social resources that can be acquired, developed, improved and transferred across generations. It generates flows of consumption, as well as additional stock" (Ford Foundation 2004, 9). In the current poverty-related development debates, the concept of assets or capital endowments includes both tangible and intangible assets, with the assets of the poor commonly identified as natural, physical, social, financial, and human capital.[3] In impact assessments after disasters, assets are shown to be both a significant factor in self-recovery and to be influenced by the response and reconstruction process. Where survivors participate in decision making, psychological recovery strengthens the recovery of livelihoods and well-being. Reconstruction is a period in which either entitlement can be renegotiated to improve the capacity and well-being of the poor or poverty and inequality can be entrenched through the corresponding reconstruction of vulnerability.

Asset-Based Adaptation

Asset-based approaches to development are not new, and, as with poverty, definitions are rooted in international debates of the 1990s. Assets are closely linked to the concept of capabilities. Thus assets "are not simply resources that people use to build livelihoods: they give them the capability to be and act" (Bebbington 1999, 2029). As such, assets are identified as the basis of agents' power to act to reproduce, challenge, or change the rules that govern the control, use, and transformation of resources (Sen 1997). Moser (2007) distinguishes between an asset-index conceptual framework as a diagnostic tool for understanding asset dynamics and mobility and an asset-accumulation policy as an operational approach for designing and implementing sustainable asset-accumulation interventions (see also Moser and Felton 2007, 2009).

To get beyond vulnerability and focus on strategies and solutions, this chapter introduces an asset-based framework of adaptation to climate change that identifies the role of assets in increasing the adaptive capacity of low-income households and communities to this increasing phenomenon. Asset-based frameworks include a concern for long-term accumulation strategies (see Moser 2007; see also Carter 2007). Clearly the asset portfolios of individuals, households, and communities are a key determinant of their adaptive capacity both to reduce risk and to cope with and adapt to increased risk levels. As will be discussed, they also influence capacity to make demands on, and work with, local governments.

An asset-based adaptation strategy in the context of climate change includes three basic principles. First, the process by which the assets held by individuals and households are protected or adapted does not take place in a vacuum. External factors such as government policy, political institutions, and NGOs all play important roles. Institutions include the laws, norms, and regulatory and legal frameworks that either block or enable access, or, indeed, positively facilitate asset adaptation, in various ways. Second, the formal and informal context within which actors operate can provide an enabling environment for protecting or adapting assets. The adaptation of one asset often affects other assets that are highly interrelated; similarly, insecurity and erosion in one can also affect other assets. Third, household asset portfolios change over time, sometimes rapidly, such as death or incapacity of an income earner. Thus households can quickly move into security or vulnerability through internal changes linked to life cycle as well as in response to external economic, political, and institutional variability.

An asset-based focus on climate change requires, first and foremost, the identification and analysis of the connection between vulnerability and the erosion of assets. Following this, an asset-based adaptation framework then seeks to identify asset adaptation or resilience strategies as households and communities exploit opportunities to resist, or recover from, the negative effects of climate change.

An Asset Vulnerability Analytical Framework

Hazards created or magnified by climate change combine with vulnerabilities to produce impacts on the urban poor's human capital (health) and physical capital (housing and capital goods) and their capacity to generate financial and productive assets. Some impacts are direct, such as more frequent and more intense floods. Those that are less direct include reduced availability of freshwater supplies. Finally, others that are indirect for urban populations include constraints on agriculture and thus on food supplies and increased prices that are likely in many places.

To assess the vulnerability of local population to climate change, it is necessary to identify the variation, in terms of both the hazards to which they are exposed and their capacity to cope and adapt. These include settlement variations in terms of the quality of physical capital and homes, the provision of infrastructure (much of which should reduce risks), and the risks from flooding or landslides. In addition, a local population's interest in risk reduction through building improvements will vary depending on ownership status, with tenants often less interested, especially if their stay is temporary, for example, as seasonal migrants (Andreasen 1989).

There may also be differences in people's knowledge and capacity to act. These include issues such as gender, with differences between women's and men's exposure to hazards, and their capacities to avoid, cope with, or adapt to them. Age is also important, with young children and older groups facing particular risks from some impacts and with reduced coping capacities. Individual health status is also crucial, regardless of age and gender (Bartlett 2008).

To systematize the broad range of vulnerability and "unpack" these generalizations, it is useful to identify different aspects or types of vulnerability to climate change in terms of four interrelated "phases."

Long-Term Resilience

First is long-term resilience, which requires identification of those who live or work in locations most at risk from the direct or indirect impacts of climate change, lacking the infrastructure necessary to reduce risk, or both. Among those most at risk are lower-income groups living in environmentally hazardous areas that lack protective infrastructure. These include concentrations of illegal settlements that often exist on hills prone to landslides. Risks faced in such sites have often been exacerbated by damage to natural systems, including the loss of mangroves or hillside vegetation and deforestation—yet areas constantly exposed to flooding still attract low-income groups because of cheaper land and housing costs. Extreme-weather impacts frequently relate more to the lack of protective infrastructure and services than to the hazards inherent to urban sites. The lack of attention to building long-term resilience (and thus disaster prevention) may simply be the result more of government inertia than of any policy.

Predisaster Damage Limitation

When discussing predisaster damage limitation, it is important to clarify who lacks knowledge and capacity to take immediate short-term measures to limit impact. Generally high-income groups with good-quality buildings and safe, protected sites do not require "emergency preparedness" measures in response to forecasts for storms and high tides. For groups living in less resilient buildings and more dangerous sites, risks to health and assets can be reduced by appropriate actions in response to warnings. However, to be effective, reliable information needs to reach those most at risk in advance—to be considered credible—and to contain supportive measures that allow them to take risk-reducing actions. This includes the identification of known safer locations and provision of transport to assist them to move.

Effective community-based predisaster measures to limit damage require levels of trust and cohesion—community social capital—that are often not present. Such social capital depends on a complex set of factors, including length of time in the settlement, pattern of occupation (including tenure), and state infrastructure-delivery mechanisms (see Moser and Felton 2007). Differences also exist in knowledge and the capacity to act to limit risk based on age, gender, and health status, including differentials as simple as the capacity to run or to swim, with speed variations among different groups; infants, younger children, adults caring for them, the disabled, and older people all move more slowly when responding to impending risks. In societies where women are constrained by social norms from leaving the home, they may move less rapidly to avoid floodwater, because many women take responsibility for young children.

Immediate Postdisaster Responses

Immediate postdisaster responses concern groups less able to cope with impacts. When disasters occur, they often separate communities, inhibiting responses by established community organizations. Particular groups, differentiated by age, gender, health status, and other forms of exclusion such as ethnicity or religion, face particular difficulties in coping with the immediate effects of extreme-weather-related disasters. Infants, young children, and older age groups are at greater risk from the disruption these events bring to, for instance, supplies of safe water and food. Disaster events can also endanger the personal safety of girls and women, with higher risk of gender-based violence, abuse, and maltreatment associated with displacement, household stress, or both (Bartlett 2008).

Rebuilding

Poorer groups not only get hit hardest by the combination of greater exposure to hazards and a lack of hazard-removing infrastructure, but they also have less capacity to adapt after disasters, generally receiving less support from the state and rarely having any insurance protection. Postdisaster reconstruction processes rarely allow the poorest groups and those most affected to take central roles in determining locations and forms of reconstruction. In many instances, the poorest groups fail to get back the land from which they were displaced, because this is acquired by commercial developers (ACHR 2005). When populations are forced to move, gender inequalities that exist before a disaster can manifest themselves in the resources and services available to support recovery and reconstruction.

Women's needs and priorities are rarely addressed in resettlement accommodation, with particular problems faced by women-headed households and widows (see Enarson 2004). Women generally assume most child-rearing and domestic responsibilities. At the same time they often "struggle in the fast-closing post-disaster 'window of opportunity' for personal security, land rights, secure housing, employment, job training, decision-making power, mobility, autonomy, and a voice in the reconstruction process" (Enarson and Meyreles 2004, 69). Equally problematic is the failure to recognize women's individual and collective capacities for recovery and reconstruction. Finally, children often experience greater physiological and psychosocial vulnerability to a range of associated stresses, as well as the long-term developmental implications of these vulnerabilities. Thus, many of the well-documented pathways between poverty and poor developmental outcomes for children are intensified by the added pressures of climate change.

Community Responses to Climate Change: An Asset-Based Adaptation Framework for Storms and Floods

Where city or municipal governments have proved unable or unwilling to provide the infrastructure, services, institutions, and regulations to reduce risks from extreme weather events for many of their people, they are unlikely to develop the capacity necessary to adapt to climate change. Therefore adaptation frameworks need to be developed to support household- and community-based responses, as well as supporting citizen capacity to negotiate and work with government—and, if needed, to contest government. This section outlines such an adaptation framework, focusing on one set of likely climate change impacts: the increased intensity, frequency, or both of floods and storms.

As in the earlier discussion of vulnerability, it is useful to distinguish between the four closely related aspects of adaptation: long-term resilience, predisaster damage limitation, immediate postdisaster response, and rebuilding. For each of these, asset-based actions and associated institutions or social actors at household, community, and government levels are identified. Obviously, the greater the success in building long-term resilience, the less is the need for intervention in the second, third, and fourth aspects; similarly, good predisaster damage limitation can greatly reduce the impacts (especially deaths and injuries) and reduce the scale of the required postdisaster response and rebuilding.

Asset-Based Adaptation to Build Long-Term Resilience

In most instances, the most effective adaptation in terms of avoiding disasters is establishing the infrastructure and institutions that prevent storms or floods from becoming disasters. For most urban centers in low- and middle-income countries, however, this is also the most difficult to implement, because of the lack of funding and government capacity and the large deficits in infrastructure provision that need to be remedied. This often relates to the way higher levels of government have retained the power, resources, and fundraising capacities that urban governments need.

It is important to start by recognizing that most low-income urban groups already have a range of measures by which they adapt to risk and to changing circumstances. At the same time, their survival needs and economic priorities often conflict with risk reduction.

Table 9.2 highlights the importance of a number of issues including the following:

- For poor urban households, housing is the first and most important asset they seek to acquire (see Moser and Felton 2007). The relocation of existing houses and settlements away from areas that cannot be protected from floods and storms, coupled with land-use management strategies to prevent new settlements in such areas, is an important component of an asset-based strategy.
- Homeowners and renters alike will often resist relocation, however, because it can result in a decline in financial capital and social networks, as well as the loss of the physical asset itself, the housing. Thus those who have built their own homes are more likely to opt for housing improvements and risk reduction rather than relocation.
- Home and possession insurance is one of the main means by which middle- and upper-income groups protect their asset base from extreme weather events. This is often not affordable, however, for low-income groups living in poor-quality housing at high risk. Although there is often scope for community-level action to build more resilience to extreme-weather events, this is difficult to manage without representative, inclusive community-based organizations.
- Community organizations cannot address some issues, however well organized and representative the groups are. Much of what is needed for

TABLE 9.2
Asset-Based Adaptation Framework for Long-Term Resilience against Floods and Storms

Asset-based actions	Institutions and actors
Household and neighborhood levels	
Households choose to move to safer sites (perhaps resulting in erosion of financial and social capital)	Households, housing finance agencies
Households improve housing (providing better protection against hazards); risk reduction through community space management to reduce local hazards (for example, install drains, keep drains clear)	Households, CBOs, NGOs
Households protect productive assets	Households
Households get insurance (property and possessions) with implications for financial capital	Insurance companies, NGOs, community-based microinsurance
Community-based disaster-response and preparedness training, including early-warning systems, safe sites, and routes to them identified as preventative measures for human capital and family first aid	NGOs, CBOs
Municipal or city level	
Local government provide or upgrade protective infrastructure and adjust official standards for building and land use	In partnership with CBOs and NGOs
Local/city government support for household and neighborhood action to improve dwellings and infrastructure (including slum and squatter upgrading)	Government agencies and households, CBOs, NGOs
City/municipal hazard mapping and vulnerability analysis as basis for identifying adaptation strategy; land-use planning so settlements do not end up in the most risky sites; and, where needed, wetlands and floodplains are retained and can fulfill their natural protective functions	Government agencies working with NGOs and CBOs
At regional and national levels	
Risk-reduction investments and actions that are needed beyond city boundaries (such as upstream or within watershed)	Local and extra-local government
State framework to support the above	Regional and national government

Source: Author.

Note: CBO = community-based organization; NGO = nongovernmental organization.

long-term resilience in cities is large-scale, expensive infrastructure that is part of citywide systems—for instance, storm and surface drains (and measures to keep them free of silt and solid waste) and components of an effective piped water system, which includes getting the bulk water for distribution and its treatment.

- In addition, most sites at high risk from extreme weather can have risks reduced if building quality is improved and infrastructure and services provided. This, however, requires government agencies to reach agreements with residents over the transfer of land tenure.
- Often those people require resettling will not want to move if the sites offered to them are too peripheral. Meanwhile, nonpoor groups will generally object to the resettlement of low-income groups close to them.
- Conflicts can develop with forced relocation, including standoffs, physical resistance, and even personal injury to those trying to defend informal property and associated livelihoods. This is exacerbated when alternative sites are inadequate or not provided at all.

Asset-Based Adaptation for Predisaster Damage Limitation

Turning to the second phase, the immediate period before an extreme event, well-conceived interventions can greatly reduce loss of life, serious injury, and loss of possessions, while also having the potential to moderate damage to homes. This is particularly important in cities at high risk from extreme weather events that lack the capacity to invest in the long-term resilience measures just mentioned. Households and communities may have well-developed immediate measures to cope with storms and flooding, based on past experience with these events and their timing. However, climate change can alter the frequency, timing, and severity and intensity of such events.

Table 9.3 summarizes an extensive range of interventions not only by households but also by local government, CBOs, and NGOs. One of the most important of these initiatives is an early warning system:

- One of the foundations of predisaster damage limitation is an early warning system that not only identifies the risk but also communicates information to all neighborhoods at risk.
- This is not something that low-income communities can provide for themselves but depends on government institutions. Many low-income countries do not have an adequate weather-monitoring system, although the importance of this is now more widely recognized.
- However, a warning system does not in itself necessarily generate the required response if local communities and households do not trust the information provided.

TABLE 9.3
Asset-Based Framework for Predisaster Damage Limitation

Asset-based actions	Institutions and actors
At household and neighborhood levels	
Social assets in place to facilitate the dissemination of early warning and knowledge of how to respond	CBOs, NGOs, coordination with state agencies for early warning and responses, including identification of safe sites and routes to them
Households temporarily move away from high-risk sites or settlements	State provides transport to safe sites to those without access to private transport; police and civil defense prepare to protect assets left behind after the disaster has passed (such as from looting)
Households prepare property to withstand event (protecting physical capital)	Households, CBOs, NGOs
Households protect or move productive assets	Households, CBOs
Community-based disaster-response and preparedness training, including early-warning systems, safe sites, and routes to them, identified as preventative measure for human capital and family first aid	CBOs, NGOs
At municipal or city level	
Preparation of safe spaces with services to which people can move temporarily	Government, NGOs, CBOs; oversight in early warning to ensure communication between state agencies and local focal points
Organizing corridors for mass evacuation	Police and civil defense clear main routes to enable fast evacuation and to prepare for the distribution of relief aid
At regional and national levels	
Flood management upstream	Private and state-owned flood-management infrastructure
Disaster early-warning system	State at national and regional levels

Source: Author.

Note: CBO = community-based organization; NGO = nongovernmental organization.

Asset-Based Adaptation for Immediate Postdisaster Response

After any disaster, two separate intervention points are the immediate response and then the longer-term follow-up. The two are separated largely because responsibility for them is generally divided between different institutions, both within low- and middle-income countries and within international agencies.

Table 9.4 illustrates the role of actors at different levels for immediate post-disaster response.

One of the main influences on low-income groups' capacity to address their postdisaster needs is the effectiveness of their predisaster efforts to protect their assets. In addition, growing awareness of the assets and capabilities of women, men, youth, and children affected by a disaster, and their importance in immediate postdisaster response, has resulted in more community-focused approaches, which include the following:

- Maternal and child health care and nutritional supplementation are among the first support mechanisms set up in the immediate aftermath of disaster.
- To address the needs of human capital, health interventions beyond the availability of health services and provision for personal safety and environmental health in postdisaster situations are often very inadequate, especially for children and girls and women. Awareness of the heightened potential for injury is also critical after an extreme event, especially where children are concerned, requiring careful assessment.

TABLE 9.4
Asset-Adaptation Framework for Immediate Postdisaster Response

Asset-based actions	Institutions and actors
At household and neighborhood levels	
Reducing risks in affected areas (such as draining flooded areas, clearing roads), recovering assets	Government (mainly agencies responsible for disaster response), perhaps international agencies
Adopt cash-based social protection measures	Donors, NGOs
Help restore infrastructure and services	Utilities, disaster-response agencies
Support for households to restore livelihoods with gender-disaggregated analysis	Local governments, NGOs
Planning and implementing repairs	Households, insurance companies, local contractors
At municipal or city level	
Rapid repairs to key infrastructure and services such as health care, safe water provision	Government and utilities
Human capital social protection of displaced especially for elderly and children	Government ministries of health/education/welfare, NGOs
Protection of physical capital to prevent looting and further erosion of assets	Police and security services
Support for community action	Local government, NGOs
At regional and national levels	Funding and institutional support

Source: Author.

Note: NGO = nongovernmental organization.

Many of the problems experienced after disasters are related to delivery systems for emergency and transitional assistance. Local people frequently feel little or no control over their lives and no role in decisions that affect them. The resources, skills, and social capital within local communities are often overlooked in the rush to assess risks and needs. Therefore, among the key guidelines for responses are the following:[4]

- The emergency response stage should be kept as short as possible, with a shift to cash transfers and microfinance projects rather than direct supply of goods and services.
- Where people are displaced, shelter should be organized with the aim of keeping family members and communities together, with a tracing service established to reunite people and families. Normal cultural and religious events should be maintained or reestablished.
- Adults and adolescents (both male and female) should participate in concrete, purposeful, common-interest activities, such as emergency relief activities. As soon as resources permit, school-aged children should have access to schooling and to recreational activities.
- The community should be consulted regarding decisions on where to locate religious places, schools, water points, and sanitation facilities. The design of settlements for displaced people should include recreational and cultural space.
- Where ethnic or other excluded groups are affected by disaster, they should be included in all postdisaster responses.

Asset-Based Adaptation for Rebuilding and Transformation

Although the reconstruction process can be an opportunity for transformation to address both short- and longer-term development issues, it frequently fails to do this, simply replacing old problems with new ones. One often finds limited understanding of how reconstruction can be turned to better advantage to rebuild social as well as physical assets. Table 9.5 outlines the key asset-based actions for rebuilding after a disaster. Various important interventions can be highlighted here:

- For poor households the most urgent issue is their housing—whether they can get back their previous home or the site on which to rebuild—but lack of land title, and government decisions that prevent rebuilding in affected areas, can both act as constraints.
- Solid gender analysis should be included in rebuilding. Often individual reconstruction does not work well, and community-led development works better.

TABLE 9.5.
Asset-Adaptation Framework for Rebuilding after a Disaster

Asset-based actions	Institutions and actors
At household and neighborhood levels	
Displaced households seeking land rights and titles associated with political capital, rebuilding physical capital	Households and government agencies, NGOs
Building/rebuilding homes and physical capital undertaken with community involvement that also rebuilds trust and collaboration relating to social capital	Households, NGOs, CBOs, government
Households rebuild productive capital relating to income-generating activities	Relatives sending remittances, financial service institutions
Building/rebuilding houses and neighborhood infrastructure such as transport links and water and sanitation infrastructure	Households, CBOs, and government
Securing provision of infrastructure to enhance well-being for affected and host populations where relocation has been necessary	Affected and host households, local government, NGOs
Recovering the household and local economy	Households, CBOs, NGOs, municipal and national governments
At municipal or city level	
Building/rebuilding infrastructure (to more resilient standards)	Government agencies working with CBOs, NGOs
Rebuilding of systems of safety and security in communities to ensure accumulation of assets	Police and security systems
Building/rebuilding livelihoods and productive capital	Government working with households
At regional or national level	
Rebuilding productive capital of region	Financial services and banks
Regional reconstruction of natural and physical capital—such as water systems	Contributions of state/provincial governments and national governments to reconstruction

Source: Author.

Note: CBO = community-based organization; NGO = nongovernmental organization.

- The location of rebuilt settlements has obvious implications for livelihoods as well as for access to such amenities as schools, markets, and health facilities.
- Housing in new settlements is often placed in a grid pattern on leveled land, which can fail to make optimal use of space from a social perspective.
- Recovering the household and local economy is a cornerstone of progressive adaptation after a disaster. Without this, recovery and reconstruction can

easily reproduce or even exaggerate the social inequality and asset poverty that led to disaster in the first place (see UNDP 2004).

- Where possible, local sourcing of materials and skills should be promoted, with decision-making powers transferred to survivors. The recovery of the local economy and landownership are interdependent. Loss of rights over land and forced resettlement during reconstruction, under the guise of "adaptation" or "risk reduction," serves to transfer land rights from the poor to the rich.

Given space constraints, this section has highlighted a few of the most important interventions during the four phases, prioritizing those focusing on local communities—even though, as shown in the tables, city and municipal governments play an equally important complementary role in adaptation. Obviously, effective adaptation strategies depend on more competent, better-resourced, accountable urban governments that are willing and able to work with poorer groups. This also means that urban governments need support from national governments and international agencies.

The Research Methodology for Testing an Asset-Based Adaptation Framework for Storms and Floods

To date, the asset adaptation framework described is largely hypothetical in nature. Although each phase is backed up by empirical evidence, as a holistic comprehensive framework, it still requires testing in practice. This final section, therefore, provides a description of one such potential methodology. By way of background, as with approaches to climate change, this is contextualized within a range of community-focused methodologies.

Current Community-Focused Methodologies

As shown in table 9.6, within community-focused methodologies, a range of different methods exist. Many originate in emergency or relief with objectives that are quite similar. Essentially they seek to map vulnerabilities and capabilities of local populations as the basis for then identifying risk-reduction measures and action plans. Equally they all use a range of participatory rural and urban appraisal tools, first developed for poverty analysis and the implementation of poverty reduction measures (see Chambers 1992, 1994). These range from communitywide vulnerability and capacity assessment (CVCA) to participatory vulnerability assessment (PVA) to participatory impact assessment (PIA), with the differences in names appearing to be more a question of institutional branding related to organizations such as the Red Cross, Action Aid, or Tearfund. The extent to which participatory methodologies are specifically adapted to focus on climate change as against being applied generically, as suggested in table 9.6, may ultimately be what distinguishes them (if at all). It should be noted that none of the methodologies appear to focus specifically on assets, which is the unique feature of the participatory methodology for asset adaptation described in this chapter.

Toward a Participatory Methodology for Climate Change Asset Adaptation

This methodology combines three components: first, "bottom-up" participatory research undertaken in poor communities in each research city; second, a rapid appraisal of policies, programs, and institutions; and, third, the triangulation of results using a microaction planning or consultation process.

Participatory Climate Change Adaptation Appraisal

The purpose of participatory climate change adaptation appraisal (PCCAA) is to appraise the mechanisms through which climate change directly or indirectly leads to the erosion of assets. It is undertaken with different social groups of the urban poor in research cities or towns. This process includes community, household, and individual perceptions of current policies, programs, and institutions that directly or indirectly constrain their adaptive capacity, as well as their recommendations concerning pro-poor adaptation policies. It comprises two parts.

First, an asset vulnerability analytical framework identifies the links between vulnerabilities and assets. These relate to both external shocks and stresses, as well as to internal capacities to resist or withstand them. This framework identifies the groups most affected and types of socioeconomic vulnerability in four closely interrelated phases or stages that can occur during urban climate change, namely, long-term resilience, immediate predamage limitation, immediate postdisaster (including disaster emergency), and rebuilding (long term).

Second, an asset adaptation operational framework identifies concrete measures to increase resilience and to reduce vulnerability in the face of long-term changes as well as immediate shocks that result from global climate change. This framework identifies the range of "bottom-up" climate change adaptation strategies that individuals, households, and communities have developed to increase their resilience to cope with the different phases of climate change (see the earlier discussion).

TABLE 9.6
Summary of Selected Community-Focused Methodologies Applied to Climate Change Adaptation

Method	Main users	Main objective	Priority tools
CVCA	Emergency/relief institutions, such as the Red Cross, city municipalities, NGOs, and CBOs	Analysis and mapping of vulnerabilities and capacities to identify risk-reduction measures and action plans (including non–climate-related risks)	Participatory methodologies for sustainable livelihoods including mapping, focus group discussion, needs assessment, key informants, and institutional and network analysis
PVA	Emergency/relief and development institutions, such as Action Aid International	Analysis and mapping of vulnerabilities to identify risk-reduction measures and action plans (including non–climate-related risks)	Participatory methodological tools including focus group discussion, historical profile, vulnerability maps, seasonal calendar, Venn diagrams, livelihood analysis
Vulnerability mapping	Emergency/relief and development institutions, such as Tearfund	Analysis and mapping of vulnerabilities to identify risk-reduction measures and action plans (including non–climate-related risks)	Participatory tools including focus group discussion, semistructured interviews, key informants, and ground truthing
Local options for communities to adapt and technologies to enhance capacity (LOCATE)	Emergency/relief and development institutions, such as African City for Technology (ACTS) and IDRC	Identification and implementation of context specificity adaptation action plans (part of methodology development for community-based adaptation to climate change, thus including only climate-related risks)	Participatory monitoring and evaluation tools including discussion groups, needs assessments, and mapping
PIA	Development institutions, NGOs and CBOs, and researchers	Identifying intervention measures and action plans	Participatory tools including needs assessments, well-being ranking, focus group discussion, key informants, historical profiling, mapping

continued

TABLE 9.6, *continued*

Method	Main users	Main objective	Priority tools
Asset adaptation	Research institution (GURC)	Identification of adaptation measures and implementation of community-focused action-planning processes to address climate-related risks	Participatory urban climate change asset adaptation appraisal tools including community maps, historical profiles, causal flow diagrams, Venn diagrams

Source: Adapted from Simatele 2009

Note: CBO = community-based organization; CVCA = communitywide vulnerability and capacity assessment; GURC = Global Urban Research Centre; IDRC = International Development Research Centre; NGO = nongovernmental organization; PIA = participatory impact assessment; PVA = participatory vulnerability assessment.

A range of PVA techniques (see Moser and McIlwaine 1999) are adapted specifically for use in the PCCAA that will be undertaken with a range of groups within communities, identified by age, gender, economic status, and other appropriate criteria. PCCAA tools include the following:

- Participatory community maps: to identify most vulnerable sites and households
- Historical profile or time lines: to list key historical events especially relating to past climate change–related events
- Seasonality calendars: to identify climate change issues such as patterns of severe droughts (water scarcity) and issues around food security, heat waves, floods, and peaks and troughs of diseases
- Well-being ranking: to enable local people to identify different social and economic categories in the community that will help identify the people most vulnerable to climate change within a community
- Listings and rankings: both general tools to see the prioritization of climate change issues as well as the climate change priority problems; these will help identify the assets different groups consider important in adapting to climate change as well as the major climate change issues that local people consider most severe
- Climate change, disaster, and community problem time lines: these will be essential to identify community perceptions of changing patterns in the weather (and whether these coincide with those identified here)
- Causal flow diagrams: to identify perceptions of causes and consequences of climate change asset-related problems (identified in the problem listing and ranking); causal flow diagrams will also be used to identify individual, household, and community solutions

- Institutional (Venn) diagrams: to identify institutions both within and outside the community that play a role in climate change adaptation strategies; these may be positive and negative and differentiated by level of importance
- Diagrammatic representations of strategies and solutions: identifying the type of danger, strategies, solutions, and institutions required.

The PCCAA is intended to be undertaken by two local research teams over a four-week period. Teams need to be selected in terms of their prior knowledge of participatory appraisal techniques, though almost certainly not on its application to climate change issues. As in other participatory appraisals, the following components need to be undertaken in this time frame: training, piloting (one community), PCCAAs in two communities, and analysis and report writing.

A Rapid Appraisal of Current Policies, Programs, and Institutions

Rapid appraisal of current policies, programs, and institutions includes an analysis of the institutional landscape; evaluation of relevant national, municipal, and institutional policies, regulations, and mandates, as well as scientific studies (such as weather forecasts, mapping, and research); and evaluation of relevant programs and practice from the perspectives of the stakeholders on different levels.

The asset adaptation operational framework mentioned in this chapter is used to identify institutions, policies, and programs that directly or indirectly constrain the adaptive capacity of the urban poor; are instrumental in designing, implementing, and monitoring pro-poor adaptation policies, or have the potential to do so.

Appraisal tools include a range of appraisal techniques, such as the following:

- Structured and semistructured interviews: these will be undertaken with officials, program managers, and operational and technical staff of different institutions. Chain or purposeful sampling will be used to select the interviewees working at the municipal level, such as Ministries of Housing, Environment, Education, and Health; local-level authorities; NGOs; multilateral and bilateral aid agencies; and the private sector (for example, construction and insurance companies). "Rapid Assessment Check Lists" will be used, followed up with more open questions guided by interview protocols.
- Focused interviews: these will be undertaken with identified key informants.
- Secondary data reviews: review of "gray" and "white" literature, including program documentation, national, municipal, and institutional policies, regulations, and mandates, as well as research studies. The aim is to identify key stakeholders and to analyze relevant policies and programs.
- Observation: identifying and analyzing key measures of selected programs. This will be carried out together with operational and technical staff of the

respective implementing institutions. Recording of data is in the form of pictures and field memos.

• Participatory research workshops: generating additional insights about inter-institutional cooperation and barriers in the interactions between selected key institutions; if possible, workshops will be organized with institutions working in the selected communities together with community groups participating in the PCCAA. These will use a range of participatory appraisal techniques.

This research is undertaken simultaneously as the PCCAA by one or two team members.

Triangulation and Validation

Triangulation and validation of results of the programs just discussed are undertaken through one of the two processes.

An action-planning exercise can be used to triangulate the results from the different actors. This is a participatory exercise that allows urban poor communities and public authorities together to articulate and identify common problems, to define and structure strategies and solutions, to reach consensus, and to negotiate collaboration (Hamdi and Goethert 1997).

The microplanning exercise involves, first, a general assembly of the community to explain the purpose of the workshop and to select participants for the exercise, and, second, a microplanning workshop; this takes one day, during which participants from the community and the local authority identify and prioritize problems, identify and prioritize solutions, and reach consensus on the major activities that could be executed to strengthen the asset adaptation strategies of the community. The results of the workshop can then be taken to both the municipal council and the general assembly of the community for ratification.

In other contexts, a formal consultation process may be appropriate. This will involve representatives of the communities in which the research took place, the local government as well as other local governments, NGOs, national authorities, and members of the international donor community. The results of the study will be discussed in groups.

Collaborative Partners to Undertake Participatory Climate Change Asset Adaptation Research

To undertake such research requires various research partners with comparative advantages in working at different levels. These may include the following:

Primary research counterpart: A national, regional, or local-level institution is needed to take responsibility for carrying out the research and administering resources. They will need to train and supervise local researchers who will carry out the PCCAA methodology research in the designated communities as well as the action-planning process. In addition, they will be responsible for systematizing and analyzing results of the participatory research, institutional analysis, and planning workshop results.

Research center with links with local communities: It may also be necessary to identify a local research center with community-level trust and contacts. Their physical installations may be used during the entire exercise: for the working session the first week, as a logistical center during the piloting and application of the PCCAA in two additional communities, and afterwards, for the week of systematizing the results.

Local government linkages: Personnel from the municipality are often needed to help identify the communities where the PCCAA and microplanning exercise can be undertaken. The action plan needs to identify potential concrete projects to be cofinanced by the municipality and the local community.

Scaling-up of research results and replication of methodology: To scale up research results it may be helpful to involve a second-tier organization whose staff undertakes the PCCAA so that, as a second-tier institution that works through local governments and microfinance institutions, it can replicate this methodology in other municipalities in which it works.

Concluding Comment

The Global Urban Research Centre as part of its research, teaching, and training program on "community empowerment and asset-based adaptation to urban climate change" is currently in the process of finalizing various case studies to test the research and action-planning framework in various southern African, Latin American, and Asian cities. As a whole, this comparative research project will undoubtedly modify the climate change asset adaptation framework described in this chapter. The outcome then is intended to be a more robust theoretical framework both for researchers seeking to better understand the link between climate change and the erosion of assets of the poor in cities of the global South as well as an operational framework that sets out guidelines for the development of specific tools and methods that can be used to support the development of pro-poor adaptation strategies in urban areas.

Notes

1. Although it is difficult to generalize about likely risks of urban climate change, the scale and nature of risk vary greatly between and within centers and between different population groups or locations. The following grouping, according to certain shared physical characteristics that relate to climate change risk, was identified by Moser and Satterthwaite (2008, 4). This includes cities already facing serious impacts from heavy rainstorms and cyclones (including hurricanes and typhoons) and heat waves, coastal location and thus impacted by sea-level rise, location by a river that may flood more frequently, and location dependent on freshwater sources whose supply may diminish or whose quality may be compromised.

2. Sen's (1981) work on famines and entitlements, assets, and capabilities, as well as that of Chambers (1992, 1994) and others on risk and vulnerability, influenced an extensive debate that defined concepts such as capabilities and endowments and distinguished between poverty as a static concept and vulnerability as a dynamic one that better captures change processes as "people move in and out of poverty" (Lipton and Maxwell 1992, 10).

3. In addition to these five assets, which are already grounded in empirically measured research, more "nuanced" asset categories have been identified. These include the aspirational (Appadurai 2004), psychological (Alsop, Bertelsen, and Holland 2006), and productive and political assets, increasingly associated with human rights (Ferguson, Moser, and Norton 2007; Moser, Sparr, and Pickett 2007).

4. See Batniji, van Ommeren, and Saraceno (2006) and Sphere Project (2004), cited in Bartlett (2008).

References

ACHR (Asian Coalition for Housing Rights). 2005. "Tsunami: How Asia's Precarious Coastal Settlements Are Coping after the Tsunami." *Housing by People in Asia* 16 (August).

Alsop, Ruth, M. Bertelsen, and Jeremy Holland. 2006. *Empowerment in Practice: From Analysis to Implementation.* Washington, DC: World Bank.

Andreasen, Jørgen. 1989. "The Poor Don't Squat: The Case of Thika, Kenya." *Environment and Development* 1 (2): 16–26.

Appadurai, Arjun. 2004. "The Capacity to Aspire: Culture and the Terms of Recognition." In *Culture and Public Action,* ed. V. Rao and M. Walton, 59–84. Stanford, CA: Stanford University Press.

Bartlett, Sheridan. 2008. "Climate Change and Urban Children: Implications for Adaptation in Low and Middle Income Countries." International Institute for Environment and Development (IIED) Working Paper IIED, London.

Batniji, R., M. Van Ommeren, and B. Saraceno. 2006. "Mental and Social Health in Disasters: Relating Qualitative Social Science Research and the Sphere Standard." *Social Science and Medicine* 62 (8): 1853–64.

Bebbington, Anthony. 1999. "Capitals and Capabilities: A Framework for Analysing Peasant Viability, Rural Livelihoods and Poverty." *World Development* 27: 2021–44.

Carter, Michael. 2007. "Learning from Asset-Based Approaches to Poverty." In *Reducing Global Poverty: The Case for Asset Accumulation,* ed. C. Moser, 51–61. Washington, DC: Brookings Institution Press.

Chambers, Robert. 1992. "Poverty and Livelihoods: Whose Reality Counts?" Discussion Paper 347, Institute of Development Studies, Brighton, U.K.

———. 1994. "The Origins and Practice of Participatory Rural Appraisal." *World Development* 22: 953–69.

Enarson, Elaine. 2004. "Gender Matters: Talking Points on Gender Equality and Disaster Risk Reduction." http://www.gdnonline.org/wot_cases.php.

Enarson, Elaine, and Lourdes Meyreles. 2004. "International Perspectives on Gender and Disaster: Differences and Possibilities." *International Journal of Sociology and Social Policy* 24 (10/11): 49–93.

Ferguson, Claire, Caroline Moser, and Andy Norton. 2007. "Claiming Rights: Citizenship and the Politics of Asset Distribution." In *Reducing Global Poverty: The Case for Asset Accumulation,* ed. C. Moser, 273–88. Washington, DC: Brookings Institution Press.

Ford Foundation. 2004. *Building Assets to Reduce Poverty and Injustice.* New York: Ford Foundation.

Hamdi, Nabeel, and Reinhard Goethert. 1997. *Action Planning for Cities: A Guide to Community Practice.* Chichester, U.K.: John Wiley.

Hoeppe, Peter, and Eugene Gurenko. 2007. "Scientific and Economic Rationales for Innovative Climate Change Insurance Solutions." In *Climate Change and Insurance: Disaster Risk Financing in Developing Countries,* ed. Eugene Guerenko, 607–20. London: Earthscan Publications.

Huq, Saleemul, and Hannah Reid. 2007. *Community Based Adaptation: A Briefing.* London: International Institute for Environment and Development.

Lipton, Michael, and Simon Maxwell. 1992. "The New Poverty Agenda: An Overview." Discussion Paper 306, Institute of Development Studies, Brighton, U.K.

Longhurst, Richard. 1994. "Conceptual Frameworks for Linking Relief and Development." *Institute of Development Studies Bulletin* 25 (4): 21–23.

Moser, Caroline. 1998. "The Asset Vulnerability Framework: Reassessing Urban Poverty Reduction Strategies." *World Development* 26 (1): 1–19.

———. 2007. "Asset Accumulation Policy and Poverty Reduction." In *Reducing Global Poverty: The Case for Asset Accumulation,* ed. C. Moser, 83–103. Washington, DC: Brookings Institution Press.

Moser, Caroline, and Andrew Felton. 2007. "Intergenerational Asset Accumulation and Poverty Reduction in Guayaquil Ecuador (1978–2004)." In *Reducing Global Poverty: The Case for Asset Accumulation,* ed. C. Moser, 15–50. Washington, DC: Brookings Institution Press.

———. 2009. "The Construction of an Asset Index: Measuring Asset Accumulation in Ecuador." In *Poverty Dynamics: A Cross-Disciplinary Perspective,* ed. A. Addison, D. Hulme, and R. Kanbur, 102–27. Oxford: Oxford University Press.

Moser, Caroline, and Cathy McIlwaine. 1999. "Participatory Urban Appraisal and Its Application for Research on Violence." *Environment and Urbanization* 11 (2): 203–26.

Moser, Caroline, and David Satterthwaite. 2008. "Towards Pro-Poor Adaptation to Climate Change in the Urban Centres of Low- and Middle-Income Countries." Human Settlements Discussion Paper Series, Climate Change and Cities 3, IIED/GURC Working Paper 1, University of Manchester, Global Urban Research Centre, London.

Moser, Caroline, Pamela Sparr, and James Pickett. 2007. "Cutting-Edge Development Issues for INGOs: Applications of an Asset Accumulation Approach." Asset Debate Paper 1, Brookings Institution, Washington, DC.

Satterthwaite, David, Saleemul Huq, Mark Pelling, Hannah Reid, and Patricia Lankao-Romero. 2007. "Adapting to Climate Change in Urban Areas: The Possibilities and Constraints in Low- and Middle-Income Nations." Climate Change and Cities Series, Discussion Paper 1, International Institute for Environment and Development, London.

Sen, Amartya. 1981. *Poverty and Famines: An Essay on Entitlement and Deprivation.* Oxford: Clarendon Press.

———. 1997. "Editorial: Human Capital and Human Capability." *World Development* 25 (12): 1959–61.

Simatele, Danny. 2009. "Urban Climate Change Adaptation and Assets: A Background Review of Current Community-Focused Conceptual and Methodological Approaches." Unpublished paper.

Sphere Project. 2004. *Humanitarian Charter and Minimum Standards in Disaster Response.* Geneva: Sphere Project.

UNDP. 2004. "Reducing Disaster Risk: A Challenge for Development." http://www.undp.org/cpr/disred/rdr.htm.

UN-Habitat. 2007. *Enhancing Urban Safety and Security: Global Report on Human Settlements 2007.* London: Earthscan Publications.

10

Epilogue: Perspectives from the 5th Urban Research Symposium

To do justice to the wealth of research and discussion that took place during the 5th Urban Research Symposium, this final chapter condenses the findings from a selection of 42 symposium papers.[1] Written by leading researchers and academics, this synthesis is organized into four sections, reflecting the five thematic clusters of the symposium: (1) models and indicators to measure impact and performance; (2) infrastructure, the built environment, and energy efficiency; (3) city institutions and governance for climate change; and (4) economic and social aspects of climate change in cities (this last section merged from two of the symposium clusters).

Models and Indicators to Measure Impact and Performance
Anu Ramaswami and Joshua Sperling

Scientific knowledge and accurate measurement techniques to address climate action in cities are only now catching up with the magnitude of the urban climate challenge. This thematic area reviews key gaps in our knowledge to date and summarizes available models, field measurement, and indicators in two main areas: (1) energy-use and greenhouse gas (GHG) emissions associated with cities and (2) understanding climate risks, vulnerabilities, and adaptation strategies in cities.

Significant transboundary exchange of energy and materials occurs between cities and surrounding hinterland areas. These exchanges are reflected in trade and transport among cities and in large-scale infrastructure such as the power plants that serve cities but are often located outside city boundaries.

Such transboundary activities confound measurements of GHG emissions at the city scale and raise many important questions, such as the following:

- What are the best methods to measure GHG emissions from cities when human activities in cities transcend the small geographic-administrative boundary of cities?
- What are the principles by which GHG emissions are allocated to urban residents? How is trade between cities, national and international, incorporated into GHG accounting?
- How can city-scale GHG accounting techniques be more policy relevant and compatible with existing methodologies established to promote carbon trading?
- Can city-scale GHG emissions be benchmarked and compared with national-scale GHG emissions and with other cities?
- What do we know about current baseline energy-use benchmarks in buildings and transport sectors in cities across the world?
- How can urban design—the layout and choice or urban materials—enhance GHG mitigation in the buildings sector?

In the commissioned research paper "Greenhouse Gas Emission Baselines for Global Cities and Metropolitan Regions," Kennedy, Ramaswami, Carney, and Dhakal address the question of GHG accounting to incorporate transboundary urban activities. The paper reviews key methodologies for measuring GHG emissions from cities and covers multiple activity sectors—energy use in stationary and mobile combustion addressing building and transport sectors, industrial nonenergy process emissions, waste emissions, and land-use change. A major breakthrough of this paper is to harmonize different methods in the literature for estimating GHG emissions associated with cities and to develop a resulting consistent methodology that is applied to 43 cities across the globe. The methodology distinguishes between energy-use and direct GHG emissions within urban boundaries (Scope 1 emissions) computed consistently with Intergovernmental Panel on Climate Change (IPCC) methods, transboundary contributions associated with electricity generation for use within cities (Scope 2), and emissions associated with marine and airline travel from cities (Scope 3). The paper demonstrates that data are available and that overall GHG emissions can indeed be computed in a consistent manner for numerous cities across the world. A key finding of the paper is that required reporting on Scope 1 and Scope 2 emissions, supplemented with optional reporting of Scope 3 items, offers a robust methodology for representing GHG emissions associated with urban activities.

Growing interest exists in assessing spatial variation in GHG emissions both within urban areas as a function of urban form and across the urban-rural gradient. For example, in the paper "Energy Consumption and CO_2 Emissions in Urban Counties in the United States," Parshall, Hammer, and Gurney have mapped direct fossil energy-use and GHG emissions associated with 157 urban areas in the United States; their paper enables analysis of geospatial variations in transportation-related GHG emissions with parameters such as population density in a case study of the New York City metropolitan area. Because the Vulcan data product used in the analysis does not track end use of electricity, overall energy use in the building stock could not be compared geospatially. However, the paper demonstrates the power of spatial visualization. Future work in this area of spatial mapping of GHG emissions will require more detailed utility-derived data on electricity use at higher resolutions, including the neighborhood level.

The commissioned paper by Gupta and Chandiwala, "A Critical and Comparative Evaluation of CO_2 Emissions from National Building Stocks," demonstrates the importance of benchmarks for understanding and mitigating GHG emissions from buildings. Their paper provides a comprehensive analysis of energy-use benchmarks and GHG emissions from the building stocks in India, the United Kingdom, and the United States as well as insightful comparisons between the three nations. The paper examines end uses of energy and reviews technology and policy strategies to reduce GHG emission from the urban building stocks in the three countries. Changes in energy consumption profiles are assessed from the 1990s into the 21st century, and quantitative metrics are developed to represent energy-use intensities in the three nations. Design and policy strategies applied in the three countries to reduce GHG emissions from the urban building stock are surveyed and compared.

In the construction of new buildings and neighborhoods, a variety of factors—including density and form of buildings, orientation, building materials, and landscape characteristics—all play an important role both in reducing energy use in buildings as well as mitigating the urban heat island effect. In "Mitigating Urban Heat Island Effect by Urban Design," Bouyer, Musy, Huang, and Athamena provide a synthesis of some of the research streams addressing how urban form (characterized by the spatial proportion and arrangement of buildings in a neighborhood or block) along with the selection of rooftop materials determines surface albedo, which in turn affects energy use in buildings and the urban heat island effect. The authors propose preliminary indicators of urban form and effective albedo as design guides for designing blocks or neighborhoods with reduced energy use and, hence, lower GHG emissions. The utility of the method is demonstrated qualitatively using simulations of two city blocks in France.

The same spatial scale issues that render GHG accounting in cities challenging also arise in assessments of climate-related vulnerabilities at the city scale. Currently, climate projections for the present century are provided by the IPCC, most recently in its Fourth Assessment Report, but these have several limitations that inhibit their application at the city scale. First, the projections are typically provided at coarse spatial (such as hundreds of kilometers) and temporal (such as monthly) scales, and decisions have to be made at finer regional or local scales and require information at submonthly time scales. Second, the projections provide average temperature and precipitation, whereas vulnerability assessments require a suite of climate information (such as wet or dry and hot or cold spells, extreme events, and the like). Last but not least, they do not capture urban features, and near-term decadal projections are less skillful than long-term projections. Furthermore, climate model projections have not been linked systematically with distribution of vulnerabilities and societal capacities for adaptive governance. Thus, key questions in the area of climate adaptation at the city scale include issues such as the following:

- What are the best methods to downscale climate models while integrating key urban features such as anthropogenic heat fluxes and urban surface characteristics?
- What is the range of extreme events that can be expected in cities as a consequence of climate change, and how are they different from larger-scale projections?
- What are the available frameworks for translating climate impacts into hazards, risks, and adaptive strategies in cities, as planners recognize the disproportionate impacts on the most vulnerable populations?

Climate change is expected to generate a range of impacts that cities must address in adaptation planning, including more frequent extreme heat events, droughts, extreme precipitation and storm events, sea-level rise, and changes in disease vectors. Such impacts can affect public health, ecosystems, and the many infrastructure systems, including water, energy, transportation, and sanitation systems, that serve cities. To better characterize these impacts, climate models downscaled to the urban scale are gaining more attention. McCarthy and Sanderson are leading the work in this arena, as presented in their paper "Urban Heat Islands: Sensitivity of Urban Temperatures to Climate Change and Heat Release in Four European Cities," on preliminary results from downscaling regional climate models using an improved urban surface scheme (MOSES2). Their results indicate that when finer-scale urban layers are included—particularly anthropogenic heat fluxes and surface characteristics of urban areas—more extreme temperature impacts may be seen in cities than previously projected. For example, the number of hot nights in London for the decade of 2050 is projected to be three times greater if urban areas and anthropogenic heat release are included in model simulations, when compared with rural areas.

A holistic framework that integrates climate impacts with associated climate hazards in cities, resulting vulnerabilities, and society's adaptive capacity is offered in the commissioned paper by Mehrotra and others, "Framework for City Climate Risk Assessment." The paper presents a detailed review of the body of literature on hazards, risks and vulnerabilities, and adaptive capacity, woven together in a comprehensive framework for climate adaptation in cities. The three-component framework is developed and tested in four case study cities—Buenos Aires, Delhi, Lagos, and New York City—and covers a range of hazards, including sea-level rise for coastal cities and extreme heat events for landlocked tropical cities such as Delhi. The authors note that the vulnerabilities identified in each city suggest differential impacts on poor and nonpoor urban residents as well as sectorally disaggregated implications for infrastructure and social well-being. In response, they highlight successful policies and programs at the city level that aim to reduce systemic climate risks, especially for the most vulnerable populations. A four-track approach to risk assessment and crafting of adaptation mechanisms is proposed (including assessment of hazards, vulnerability, adaptive capacity, and emerging issues) so that city governments can respond to climate change effectively and efficiently.

Although the papers in this thematic area represent recent developments in the field, research is progressing fast. Knowledge sharing among researchers and between researchers and practitioners is needed as new knowledge, measurement tools, and appropriate indicators are developed. Currently, there is no single place where city-scale climate change indicators and metrics are located. A first attempt at putting such information together in one database is discussed by McCarney in the last commissioned paper in this thematic area, "City Indicators on Climate Change." McCarney describes the process of developing a standardized set of city indicators, which includes a full range of city-scale climate-related metrics, addressing GHG emissions, mitigation, adaptation, vulnerability, and resilience, while also measuring city services and quality of life. The outputs of the Global City Indicators Program can be expected to respond continuously to new and improved methods of measuring city-scale GHG emissions, sectoral energy use, climate impact projections, and climate adaptation capacity.

Infrastructure, the Built Environment, and Energy Efficiency
Sebastian Carney and Cynthia Skelhorn

Cities are both large energy consumers and large GHG emitters. The energy consumption of a city is due, in part, to its infrastructure, building stock, culture, economic makeup, and population densities. In addition to the energy directly consumed by cities, we should recognize a wide range of emissions associated with the production of the goods and services that are consumed within cities but that may have been produced elsewhere.

This thematic area brings together examples of research from around the world on how cities may decarbonize over the coming years and decades. When planning for reducing GHG emissions, cities must recognize their current emissions sources and how they may seek to reduce these emissions, without increasing emissions elsewhere. With the global population expected to increase further in coming decades, and with much of this growth expected to take place in cities, how future populations live, work, and travel will determine the energy used to perform these tasks and, therefore, the significant part of their potential emissions.

The application of mitigation policies at the city scale remains in its infancy. Although targets for GHG reductions and (or through) renewable energy implementation are regularly touted, the policy linked to delivering the targets does not always enjoy the same clarity. As a consequence, it is important to learn from those cities that have begun to implement change. This is taken forward in "A Comparative Analysis of Global City Policies in Climate Change Mitigation" by Croci, Melandri, and Molteni and in "A Comparative Study of Energy and Carbon Emissions Development Pathways and Climate Policy" by Phdungsilp. The former considers a range of the world's global cities, whereas the latter concentrates on Southeast Asian cities.

These analyses are particularly complemented by the detailed work of van den Dobbelsteen and others in their paper on the REAP (Rotterdam Energy Approach and Planning) methodology, "Towards CO_2 Neutral City Planning— The Rotterdam Energy Approach and Planning (REAP)." This team modeled the current and potential future energy requirements of Rotterdam and combined it with available renewable energy resources within the city. The methodology follows established principles of mitigation, namely, measuring energy consumption, establishing areas for reduction, and minimizing waste flows. This structured approach, when considered with the wider documentation that exists online, affords a variety of graphical ways to communicate to wide audiences the types of changes necessary to deliver emissions reductions over differing time scales.

A city-level mitigation strategy is inevitably a function of its parts, with buildings contributing a sizeable component of a city's energy consumption. This requires investigating options for reducing energy consumption in the buildings sector in different contexts and creating a situation where buildings, both existing and future, may be considered "more sustainable." The transition to this point will vary across cities. The future energy consumption of a building is likely to be driven by a series of factors, including behavior, building design, and future climate. Kershaw and Coley demonstrate the impact of the latter point by applying a set of existing climatic scenarios to a set of differing building designs in "Characterizing the Response of Buildings to Climate Change." Their research demonstrates the need for building designs to be able to control their internal temperatures with a variable outside temperature and highlights the importance of existing policies on building design on both near-term (2020) and long-term (2080) energy consumption and wider climatic resilience.

The amount of energy consumed by a building should not necessarily be considered in isolation. A building has wider impacts associated with its upkeep that are not always included in energy balances, water being a particular example. With water becoming scarcer, using rainwater for particular functions in buildings may lead to an overall reduction in energy consumption. Schmidt presents four demonstration projects in Berlin and provides wider insights with respect to rainwater use in "A New Water Paradigm for Urban Areas to Mitigate the Urban Heat Island Effect." This wider impact of buildings is taken further in "Indicators to Assess the Sustainability of Building Construction Processes" by Floissac and others, who consider the emissions impact of a building's entire life, from construction to demolition. Taken together, the papers in this area reaffirm our understanding of the key role of future building design and retrofitting of the existing building stock when considering both mitigation and adaptation—as well as the synergies between the two.

After buildings, the transport sector is a key user of energy in cities. The energy consumption of both sectors is influenced by how a city is designed. A variety of approaches may be taken to reduce emissions from road transport within cities, which pertain to both demand- and supply-oriented measures. Bertaud, Lefevre, and Yuen consider both types of measures as they present a study on the relationships between GHG emissions, urban transport policies and pricing, and the spatial form of cities in the commissioned paper "GHG Emissions, Urban Mobility, and Efficiency of Urban Morphology." They suggest that price signals are the main driver of technological change, transport modal shifts, and land-use regulatory changes. The use of road transport within cities is also affected by other forms of available transportation, as well as travel to and from a city. Recognizing this, the paper by Ravella and others, "Transport Systems, Greenhouse Gas Emissions, and Mitigation Measures," analyzes GHG emissions mitigation measures for different modes of land transport within cities and wider interurban networks in Argentina.

Individual aspects of a city will each provide part of the mitigation solution, but they must be consistent with one another to deliver the best outputs. This potentially requires a framework for assessing the current emissions sources and how each may contribute to a city's emission reduction. In "Getting to Carbon Neutral," Kennedy and others establish measures of cost effectiveness for reducing GHG emissions from 22 city case studies.

The issue of adaptation is perhaps deemed "closer to home" than mitigation, because it has a clear local impact rather than a more global impact. Penney, Ligeti, and Dickison, in their paper "Climate Change Adaptation Planning in Toronto," document Toronto's process for creating an adaptation strategy and framework document and reflect on barriers to integration with existing city plans and programs. They note the specific departments and programs involved as well as the process by which adaptation strategies were incorporated into these, but they also note barriers to implementation. In a very captivating example related to addressing urban form, Carbonell and Meffert assess large-scale ecosystem restoration, flood protection, jurisdictional advocacy and oversight, and land policies that promote climate change adaptation and mitigation for New Orleans and the wider regional ecosystem in "Climate Change and the Resilience of New Orleans." They make a series of recommendations regarding the restoration of ecosystem services and the potential benefits for urban systems.

Although we cannot accurately predict the specific long-term consequences of a changing climate for a particular city, we should embrace this uncertainty; it is important to move forward with the current state of knowledge and for cities to determine how best to mitigate GHG emissions in their own context—taking due care of national and international policies. Although uncertainty remains on the impacts of climate change, particularly at fine spatial scales, the research presented here and elsewhere demonstrates that new insights are being made available to others and are developing at a rapid pace. It is important for these to be translated into useful policy-making tools.

City Institutions and Governance for Climate Change
Shobhakar Dhakal and Enessa Janes

Appropriate forms of governance and institutional involvement are critical for achieving successful urban climate change mitigation and adaptation. The papers in this thematic area explore a unique aspect of governance and provide insights on current institutional considerations in the context of climate change. Together, they address a set of important questions, including the following:

- What are the motivations of cities to address climate change?
- What types of climate-related governance systems are currently being developed, and what are the institutional mechanisms that have emerged?

- What roles do nonstate and other stakeholders play in the governance process?
- What factors have enabled local institutions to become early adopters of climate change mitigation and adaptation strategies?
- What are the major institutional barriers to successful climate change mitigation and adaptation in cities?
- How can we improve upon institutional capacity to enhance preparedness to the impacts of climatic change?

Numerous important themes emerge from the discussion of urban climate change and governance. First is the analysis of factors that motivate cities to act and their willingness to make explicit commitments to build climate resilient cities. We have observed that the discourse on the urban impacts of climate change has been historically led by municipalities and municipal networks, associations, and organizations such as the Mayor's Climate Summit, ICLEI, C40 Cities, and the Climate Alliance. Recently, other regional initiatives and multilateral organizations have joined the discussions.

The growing role of city governments in climate change can best be attributed to the following major factors: national mandates for cities to shoulder climate targets, lack of leadership on the part of some national governments, the willingness of some cities to participate on global issues without making serious commitments, expectations of new technology and funding related to climate initiatives, and new business prospects for local economies. Moreover, it is not uncommon for cities, often in developing countries, to make climate mitigation commitments without developing a clear idea of the ramifications for policy and implementation.

For these reasons, local knowledge, capacity, and governance are important for achieving successful adaptation and mitigation approaches. Carmin, Roberts, and Anguelovski show in the commissioned paper "Planning Climate Resilient Cities" that the enabling factors for early-adapter cities such as Durban and Quito are largely internal. These factors include local incentives, ideas, and knowledge generated through local demonstration projects and local networks, linking adaptation to ongoing programs, and the ability to enlist the support of diverse stakeholders from within the city. These dispel the prevalent notion that external factors are always the main drivers of action and help us to understand how a city's internal needs and priorities act as powerful agents for institutional responses to adaptation.

The second theme in the climate change and governance discussion has to do with the various forms of climate change governance, many of which are path dependent and reflect priorities and characteristics that are unique to each city. We observe that strong political leadership, very often by a mayor, is a key component to the development of appropriate city actions. This is especially true in cities in developing countries where international donors, local scholars, and civil society groups can help advance the climate agenda at a rapid pace. It is clear that the ability of local governments to gather resources and to muster the legislative power needed to devise and enforce plans is a crucial factor for successful climate change governance. The commissioned paper "Cities and Climate Change: The Role of Institutions, Governance, and Planning for Mitigation and Adaptation by Cities" by Bulkeley and others points out that local governments can govern climate change mitigation in four ways: self-governing (reducing GHGs from municipal actions and activities), governing through legislation, governing by provisioning, and governing by enabling.

The rising interest of local governments in assuming more responsibility on the issue of climate change governance is a positive trend for cities around the globe. Nevertheless, policy debates often overemphasize the role of municipal governments and fail to take into account the limited ability of municipal governments to induce substantial levels of emissions reductions. This limitation is due in part to structural factors in cities, such as the city's dominant role as a facilitator rather than an actor, the provisioning of municipal utility services by the private sector, and deteriorating financial performance.

Local governments, nongovernmental organizations, and other urban institutions (including state and national governments, scholarly communities, and local stakeholders) have their own impacts on fostering climate-resilient cities. Although the role of municipal government is absolutely necessary for implementing urban climate change mitigation and adaptation strategies, it is not the only responsible institution. It is evident that the most successful model for building urban climate resilience is a multilevel system of governance. Key issues associated with multilevel climate change governance include how to integrate a city's climate agenda into existing institutions (and vice versa), how to allocate responsibilities and actions across scales of governance in ways that allow capacity and resources to match policy influence, and how to foster collaboration and communication between various organizations and stakeholders. The paper by Bulkeley and others, mentioned earlier, as well as "Governance and Climate Change" by Gore, Robinson, and Stren and "Viral Governance and Mixed Motivations" by Warden, address these issues with several examples, the last two papers focusing on Canadian and U.S. cities.

A third theme is that of governmental policy frameworks and the positioning of policy instruments (economic, fiscal, regulatory, information and voluntary, and the like) into the prevailing socioeconomic and cultural contexts of cities. The ability to formulate sound, implementable policies and to ensure effective, efficient results both relate to urban capacity and context. In "Adapting Cities to Climate Change," Heinrichs and others show us that early action requires strong leadership, risk awareness, interpersonal and interinstitutional interaction, dedicated climate teams, and enhanced financial capacity. In "Understanding and Improving Urban Responses to Climate Change," Sanchez Rodriguez emphasizes the role of urban planning in cultivating climate-resilient cities and questions whether planning institutions currently have the vision, capacity, and flexibility to guide future urban growth in resilient directions. He notes that collaboration among scientists, planners, policy makers, and urban stakeholders is paramount. Overall, the papers in this area have perhaps weakly addressed the issue of policy instruments and their implementation. However, several papers illustrate that institutional capacity, forms of governance, and other factors are fundamental to the success of policy instruments.

Current discussions about climate change mitigation and adaptation take place in a range of forums and involve different sets of stakeholders and institutions. Mitigation is often seen as a globally salient topic and is typically an intensely political issue. In contrast, adaptation is usually undertaken at the local scale and is less politically sensitive. Both strategies, however, should be integrated through the concept of urban resilience building. The shortcomings associated with planning separately for mitigation and adaptation include missed opportunities for developing efficient infrastructure and financially optimal climate solutions. Certainly there are no silver bullets for governance and institutional solutions. Every city is different, and each requires different sets of solutions suited to its social, economic, institutional, and cultural context. Ultimately, we should strive for an integrated approach to resilience, characterized by better coordination and coherent planning and governance.

Economic and Social Aspects of Climate Change in Cities
Chris Kennedy and Elliot Cohen

The papers in this area, discussing the social and economic dimensions of climate change, provide several key findings. In particular, the papers demonstrate the enormous social challenges faced by the urban poor in adapting to climate change and the inadequacy of current financing mechanisms to address these challenges. Some approaches to meet these financial demands are proposed, highlighting the specific roles of the private sector, community organizations, and local governments. Broader economic issues also are associated with climate change, such as potential changes to industry strategy and consumer preferences.

The uneven social impacts of climate change in urban areas and the distribution of risks among populations is stressed by Bartlett and others in their commissioned paper "Social Aspects of Climate Change in Urban Areas in Low- and

Middle-Income Nations." Hundreds of millions of urban dwellers in low- and middle-income nations are at risk from current and likely future impacts of climate change. The risks, however, are distributed very unevenly because of differences in the magnitude and nature of hazards in different locations; the quality of housing, infrastructure, and services; measures taken for disaster risk reduction; the capacity and preparedness of local governments; and the social and political capital of vulnerable populations. The authors emphasize that vulnerabilities can be overcome by removing the hazards to which people are exposed, noting that measures taken to address climate change–related risks can be pro-poor, but many are antipoor and increase poverty. They stress that pro-poor development has strong synergies with helping the poor adapt to climate change.

An asset-based framework for both understanding and operationally addressing the impacts of climate change on poor urban communities is presented by Moser in "A Framework for Pro-Poor Asset Adaptation to Urban Climate Change." This framework has two components. First, the asset vulnerability of groups most affected by climate change–related disasters is appraised for four interrelated phases: long-term resilience, predisaster damage limitation, immediate postdisaster response, and rebuilding. Second, bottom-up and top-down strategies for climate change adaptation that individuals, households, and communities have developed to cope with the four phases are identified.

In looking at the funding available for local governments to address mitigation and adaptation to climate change, Paulais and Pigey in their paper "Adaptation and Mitigation" find there is a "mismatch between needs and financing tools." Existing funding sources are found to be insufficient, highly fragmented, and generally not designed for local government use. They note that an integrated approach to investment in urban areas is required, and they are concerned that carbon finance through the Clean Development Mechanism in part may be substituting for, rather than adding to, traditional official development assistance. Moreover, though estimation is difficult, Paulais and Pigey suggest that the investment needs for mitigation and adaptation are one to two orders of magnitude greater than the funds available.

Several different approaches to meet the financial demands of climate change may be taken. To get more funding to local governments where it is needed, Paulais and Pigey consider cases with and without national intermediation agencies that can support or pool borrowers. To create more leverage and incentives for local governments, they suggest that climate change and pure development investment mechanisms be consolidated. They also suggest that incentives such as hybrid loans, credit enhancement, buy-down loans, and various tax incentives for the private sector be used. The authors also encourage a more prominent role for wealthy industrialized cities to partner with cities that are at low-income levels.

In contrast, Dodman, Mitlin, and Co in "Victims to Victors, Disasters to Opportunities" examine the potential for community-based initiatives to help the urban poor adapt to climate change. They draw upon the experiences of the Homeless People's Federation of the Philippines in responding to disasters. At the center of the organizing methodology are community savings programs, which provide a versatile means for acquisition of and relocation to less vulnerable areas, thereby enhancing disaster preparedness and risk reduction. The examples from the Philippines show how appropriate responses to some aspects of climate change can be implemented through partnerships among local organizations, professionals, and city officials.

The private sector has a substantial role to play in mobilizing resources to address climate change adaptation and mitigation. In "Mobilizing Private Sector Resources toward Climate Adaptation and Mitigation Action in Asia," Park explores this role, particularly in Asia. He suggests that increased investment could be achieved using institutional structure and public policy that can facilitate and create business-led innovation. Park also notes that it is challenging to ensure that climate solutions help, or at least do not harm, poor, energy insecure, and economically marginalized groups. He proposes a triple bottom-line strategy for financing climate change action in Asia. This involves the following: (1) investing in sector-based carbon mitigation strategy for industries, encouraged, for example, by reduction of fuel subsidies; (2) financing of community-based ecosystem and clean energy microenterprises; and (3) building resilience to climate change through market-based adaptation strategies, such as catastrophe bonds, contingent surplus notes, exchange-traded catastrophe options, catastrophe swaps, and weather derivatives.

Whether as part of market-based approaches to address climate change or otherwise, the cost of carbon is likely to rise, which will have substantial impacts on municipal finances. The paper by Annez and Zuelgaray, "High Cost Carbon and Local Government Finance," examines the financial impacts of rising carbon costs using case studies from the Indian state of Maharashtra and from Spain. They note that local government revenues are generally not dependent on the price of energy, and therefore local governments see negligible fiscal gain from increasing energy prices. However, many public services that local governments provide, such as garbage collection, are energy intensive. Consequently, higher energy prices will create an adverse fiscal shock for local governments. Hardest hit will be smaller, less diversified governments currently operating at low levels of service because the most basic services tend to be most energy intensive. Annez and Zuelgaray suggest that the appropriate policy response will be for higher levels of government, which generate surpluses from taxing energy, to compensate local governments hard hit by high energy bills. This is to protect the financial integrity of local governments and to ensure reasonable service delivery.

Climate change also has broader economic implications for cities, a few of which are addressed by other papers in this section. With respect to economic strategy, Zhang asks in her paper "Does Climate Change Make Industrialization an Obsolete Development Strategy for Cities in the South?" whether industrialization still represents a viable development strategy in the context of climate change. Through considering the development experiences of Shanghai, Mumbai, and Mexico City, Zhang argues that climate change makes industrialization an even more important strategy than before. Nonetheless, for the sake of local and national prosperity, as well as the global sustainability, it is critical that developing cities decarbonize their industries. Zhang suggests that the experience of Shanghai shows that this can be achieved. In "The Price of Climate," Cavailhès and others demonstrate that economic benefits to climate change may be found, albeit in an industrialized country context. The authors use a hedonic price method to study consumer preferences in the face of climate change in France. Although very hot days are not desirable, the research shows that French households value warmer temperatures. Gross domestic product is calculated to rise by about 1 percent for a 1 degree Celsius rise in temperature.

The research findings presented here and discussed in the symposium demonstrate the interest of the research community and the rapid pace of production of new insights. At the same time, the symposium also revealed numerous areas where further work is required to strengthen diagnosis and policies. As mentioned in the introduction, the areas where most urgent research is required include adaptation in general, economic and social analysis broadly, and the specific needs and circumstances of developing country cities. Meanwhile, despite considerable uncertainty on the specific long-term consequences of a changing climate in any particular city, it is important to move forward with the current state of knowledge. Cities need to determine how best to mitigate GHG emissions in their own context—in the context of national and international policies—and how best to respond and adapt to a changing climate. It is important for knowledge and research insights to be translated into useful policy-making tools, which we hope will follow from the 5th Urban Research Symposium.

Note

1. Apart from the papers included in this printed volume, more than 30 other edited papers are available as a companion, online publication at the symposium website, accessible through http://www.worldbank.org/urban. Titles and abstracts of these papers are in the appendix to this volume. The full versions of all papers presented at the symposium are also available through the symposium website.

Appendix: Titles and Abstracts of Papers Not Included in Full in This Volume

A Critical and Comparative Evaluation of CO$_2$ Emissions from National Building Stocks of Developed and Rapidly-Developing Countries — Case Studies of UK, USA, and India
Rajat Gupta and Smita Chandiwala

The IPCC's Fourth Assessment Report (2007) on greenhouse gas (GHG) emission mitigation potential identified buildings as a sector where the fastest and deepest cuts are likely to be made in the period up to 2030. Given such a context, this paper answers the questions: What can be done to achieve significant reductions in CO$_2$ emissions from the existing building stock of developed and rapidly developing countries to reduce the worst impacts of climate change? How can we measure, benchmark, reduce, and manage CO$_2$ emissions from energy use in the existing building stock? What are the barriers in implementing appropriate CO$_2$ reduction measures in buildings, and how can these barriers be reduced? A critical and comparative evaluation is undertaken of the approaches and policies to measure, benchmark, reduce, and manage energy consumption and CO$_2$ emissions from the existing building stocks in India, the United Kingdom, and the United States, to share the lessons learned in implementing CO$_2$-reducing policies in each of these countries. A comparative analysis is also undertaken of environmental rating methods, BRE Environmental Assessment Method/Code for Sustainable Homes (BREEAM/CSH) in the United Kingdom, Leadership in Energy and Environmental Design (LEED) in the United States, and the Energy and Resources Institute's Green Rating for Integrated Habitat Assessment (TERI-GRIHA) and LEED-India in India. Robust performance-based standards (in terms of kWh/m^2/year or kg CO$_2$/m^2/year) are proposed for reducing the energy consumption in existing buildings, which could be adopted by any developed or developing country. It is realized that, although the United Kingdom is at the forefront of developing standards and methodologies for reducing the environmental impact of existing buildings, there is a lack of good-quality bottom-up data sets of real energy consumption in buildings. However, in the United States, there are good building energy datasets available, but CO_2-reduction policies seem more fragmented in the absence of legal national-level targets for CO_2 reduction. In India, work is ongoing on target setting, policy evaluation, and initial data collection to provide baseline energy consumption in buildings.

Framework for City Climate Risk Assessment
Shagun Mehrotra, Claudia E. Natenzon, Ademola Omojola, Regina Folorunsho, Joseph Gilbride, and Cynthia Rosenzweig

Estimation of spatially and temporally disaggregated climate risks is a critical prerequisite for the assessment of effective and efficient adaptation and mitigation climate change strategies and policies in complex urban areas. This interdisciplinary research reviews current literature and practices, identifies knowledge gaps, and defines future research directions for creating a risk-based climate change adaptation framework for climate and cities programs. The focus is on cities in developing and emerging economies. The framework unpacks risk into three vectors—hazards, vulnerabilities, and adaptive capacity. These vectors consist of a combination of physical science, geographical, and socioeconomic elements that can be used by municipal governments to create and carry out climate change action plans. Some of these elements include climate indicators, global climate change scenarios, downscaled regional scenarios, change anticipated in extreme events, qualitative assessment of high-impact and low-probability events, associated vulnerabilities, and the ability and willingness to respond. The gap between existing responses and the flexible mitigation and adaptation pathways needed is also explored. To enhance robustness, the framework components have been developed and tested in several case study cities: Buenos Aires, Delhi, Lagos, and New York City . The focus is on articulating differential impacts on poor and nonpoor urban residents as well as sectorally disaggregating implications for infrastructure and social well-being, including health. Finally, some practical lessons are drawn for successful policies and programs at the city level that aim to reduce systemic climate risks, especially for the most vulnerable populations. Additionally, a programmatic response is articulated with a four-track approach to risk assessment and crafting of adaptation mechanisms that leverages existing and planned investments in cities so that city governments can respond to climate change effectively and efficiently.

City Indicators on Climate Change: Implications for Policy Leverage and Governance
Patricia McCarney

Risks associated with climate change are increasingly finding expression in cities. Issues of greenhouse gas emissions; sea temperature change; sea-level change; land and air temperature adjustments; air quality deterioration; shifting rain, wind, and snow patterns; and other unstable climate shifts, while global in nature, find particular expression in the world's cities. These phenomena serve to introduce new layers in our interpretation of urban risk, new complexities in governing cities, and new research challenges to measure and monitor these risks in order to inform policy, planning, and management. How do we address this multiple layering and new complexity? The vulnerability of cities to climate change is largely underestimated. There is no established or standardized set of city indicators that measures the effects of climate change on cities and assesses those risks, nor is there a comprehensive set of indicators with a common, accepted methodology designed to measure the impact that cities have on climate change and the role that cities play, for example, in contributing to greenhouse gas emissions.

Effective and long-term solutions must be anchored in an empowered city governance approach that acknowledges the respective roles and contributions of a wide array of actors. Addressing climate change risk in cities must also be considered in a broader framework of risks confronting cities. Cities in the 21st century are facing unprecedented challenges. The world's urban population is likely to reach 4.2 billion by 2020, and the urban slum population is expected to increase to 1.4 billion by 2020, meaning one out of every three people living in cities will live in impoverished, overcrowded, and insecure living conditions. Social cohesion, safety, security, and stability are being tested by social exclusion, inequities, and shortfalls in basic services.

While the literature on urban governance is extensive and the research field of city indicators has grown and strengthened in very recent years, there is little work to date on how city indicators can be used for improved governance. It is the intersection of city indicators and city governance that this paper begins to address.

Detecting Carbon Signatures of Development Patterns across a Gradient of Urbanization: Linking Observations, Models, and Scenarios
Marina Alberti and Lucy Hutyra

Urbanizing regions are major determinants of global- and continental-scale changes in carbon budgets through land transformation and modification of biogeochemical processes. However, direct measurements of the effects of urbanization on carbon fluxes are extremely limited. In this paper, we discuss a strategy to quantify urban carbon signatures (spatial and temporal changes in fluxes) through measurements that can more effectively aid urban carbon emissions reduction scenarios and predictive modeling. We start by articulating an integrated framework that identifies the mechanisms and interactions that link urban patterns to carbon fluxes along gradients of urbanization. Building on a synthesis of the current observational studies in major U.S. metropolitan areas, we develop formal hypotheses on how alternative development patterns (that is, centralized versus sprawling) produce different carbon signatures and how these signatures may in turn influence patterns of urbanization. Finally, we discuss the fusion of observations, scenarios, and models for strategic carbon assessments.

Energy Consumption and CO₂ Emissions in Urban Counties in the United States with a Case Study of the New York Metropolitan Area
Lily Parshall, Stephen A. Hammer, and Kevin Gurney

Urban areas are setting quantitative, time-bound targets for emissions reductions within their territories; designing local policies to encourage shifts toward cleaner energy supply, higher energy efficiency, and transit-oriented development; and exploring ways to participate in local carbon markets. These efforts require systematic estimates of energy consumption and emissions presented in a format and at a spatial resolution relevant for local governance. The Vulcan data product offers the type of high-resolution, spatial data on energy consumption and CO_2 emissions needed to create a consistent inventory for all localities in the continental United States. We use Vulcan to analyze patterns of direct fuel consumption for on-road transportation and in buildings and industry in urban counties. We include a case study of the New York City Metropolitan Area.

Mitigating Urban Heat Island Effect by Urban Design: Forms and Materials
Julien Bouyer, Marjorie Musy, Yuan Huang, and Khaled Athamena

This paper provides a synthesis of three complementary research works that contribute to the same objective: proposing solutions to reduce building energy consumption by modifying local climate. The first work explores urban forms: It proposes methods to describe them and analyze the climatic performances of classified urban forms. The second work focuses on one parameter of direct relevance to urban heat island phenomenon: the surface albedo. The albedo of a city or a district depends on surfaces' arrangement; materials used for roofs, paving, coatings, and the like; and solar position. The third work proposes a simulation tool that permits one to evaluate the impact of the outdoor urban environment on buildings' energy consumption. This analysis permits us to propose morphology indicators to compare the relative efficiencies of different typologies. The conclusion discusses the relevance of using indicators (based on physics or morphology, related to site or to built form) in the urban design process and proposes a methodology to produce indicators.

Towards CO_2 Neutral City Planning—The Rotterdam Energy Approach and Planning (REAP)

Andy van den Dobbelsteen, Nico Tillie, Marc Joubert, Wim de Jager, and Duzan Doepel

By the year 2025, the city of Rotterdam, with the largest port in Europe, aims to reduce its CO_2 emissions by half, an ambitious plan that will require a revolutionary approach to urban areas. One proactive response to this challenge is an exploratory study of the Hart van Zuid district. An interdisciplinary team has investigated how to tackle CO_2 issues in a structured way. This has resulted in the Rotterdam Energy Approach and Planning (REAP) methodology. REAP supports initial demand for energy, propagates the use of waste flows, and advocates use of renewable energy sources to satisfy the remaining demand. REAP can be applied at all levels: individual buildings, clusters of buildings, and even whole neighborhoods. Applying REAP to the Hart van Zuid district has shown that this area can become CO_2 neutral. Most important, REAP can be applied regardless of location.

An Investigation of Climate Strategies in the Buildings Sector in Chinese Cities

Jun Li

About 60 percent of Chinese people will be living in cities by 2030. Energy consumption and GHG emissions could increase exponentially with unprecedented urban expansion and constant rise in living standards as a result of lifestyle change without drastic policies being undertaken immediately. Because of its long lifetime characteristics, the quality of large-scale urban infrastructure is critical to the achievement of long-term GHG emissions mitigation objectives in the next decades given the spectacular pace of urban development (for example, China will build the equivalent of the whole EU's existing housing area of the European Union [EU] by 2020). Here we investigate the role of urban infrastructure in shaping the long-term trajectory of energy and climate securities protection and sustainable urban development prospects in China. Based on a quantitative analysis in a selected case city (Tianjin), we demonstrate how China can set its large cities on a sustainable energy supply-and-demand track by building climate-resilient-buildings infrastructure in cities, and we also discuss the implications for financing policy and institutional change.

A Comparative Study of Energy and Carbon Emissions Development Pathways and Climate Policy in Southeast Asian Cities
Aumnad Phdungsilp

The United Nations has estimated that about half of the 6.5 billion world population currently lives in cities. Moreover, an additional 1.8 billion people will move to urban areas by the year 2030. Understanding the relationships between energy-use patterns and carbon emissions development is crucial for estimating future scenarios and can facilitate mitigation and adaptation of climate change. This paper investigates the development pathways on selected Southeast Asian cities, including Bangkok, Hanoi, Jakarta, and Manila, which are major cities in the region in terms of energy consumption, carbon emissions, and climate policies. The paper investigates the development of energy and carbon emissions and climate change mitigation strategies of the selected case studies. In addition, the paper attempts to estimate the energy consumption and associated carbon emissions. Then, it compares overall patterns of selected cities and analysis of their climate policies.

Characterizing the Response of Buildings to Climate Change: The Issue of Overheating
Tristan Kershaw and David Coley

Many buildings currently demonstrate levels of overheating close to the maximum allowed by the building regulations of the countries in which they are located. Therefore there is the potential that such buildings will clearly breach the regulations under the climatic conditions predicted as a result of climate change. To examine the problem, weather files indicative of possible future climate were created and applied to a variety of buildings. Using numerous combinations of buildings and weather scenarios, the modeling demonstrated that the projected levels of climate change engender a linear response in the internal temperature of the buildings. The resulting constant of proportionality that this implies has been termed the "climate change amplification coefficient." This paper demonstrates that optimization of the climate change amplification coefficient during the design process of a new building will promote the adaptation of architectural design to the effects of climate change and thereby improve resilience.

Opportunities and Challenges to Electrical Energy Conservation and CO_2 Emissions Reduction in Nigeria's Building Sector
John-Felix Akinbami and Akinloye Lawal

Using an energy demand model, MADE-II (Model for Analysis of Demand for Energy), the electrical energy demand for household, commercial, and industrial buildings over a long-term period was estimated for Nigeria based on the concept of useful energy demand. This analytical tool uses a combination of statistical, econometric, and engineering process techniques in arriving at the useful electrical energy demand projections. The associated CO_2 emissions were also estimated. These projections reveal that the electrical energy growth is enormous, especially considering the associated financial cost, and the estimated CO_2 emissions are also substantial. This study therefore discusses the potentials for efficient energy use in the buildings sector in Nigeria. In addition, obstacles to the full realization of energy-saving potentials in the nation's building sector are discussed. Finally, a framework of strategies to overcome these obstacles, to promote energy conservation, and thereby to enhance sustainable development in the nation's built environment is suggested.

Indicators to Assess the Sustainability of Building Construction Processes
Luc Floissac, Alain Marcom, Anne-Sophie Colas, Quoc-Bao Bui, and Jean-Claude Morel

This paper proposes a way to assess the sustainability of building construction processes. The impacts of building materials, energy and material consumption, waste and nuisance generation, management of materials at end of life, building construction organization, and social impacts are used to evaluate sustainability. Indicators are proposed for each of these areas, and the results from applying these indicators are assessed.

The case study presented here concerns the construction of three private houses in a developed country (France). These houses have the same architecture, but each one uses a different building process: local materials, standard industrial productions, or "fashionable" industrial materials. This paper shows that the proposed indicators can help to facilitate the choice of construction materials with respect to sustainability.

Transport Systems, Greenhouse Gas Emissions, and Mitigation Measures: A Study in Argentina
Olga Ravella, Cristian Matti, Nora Giacobbe, Laura Aon, and Julieta Frediani

This paper aims to present the results of the analysis of greenhouse gas emissions mitigation measures for different modes of land transport in Argentina. It traces efforts to analyze different transport patterns by applying a bottom-up analysis from the study of interurban corridors and urban areas. This type of analysis as well as the collection and organization of disaggregated information is the first attempt of this type in the country. The methodology comprises two sets of activities: (1) the estimations of indicators on transport patterns and their related emissions and (2) the formulation of scenarios to analyze the potential impact of different mitigation measures. Information related to interurban corridors includes data on highways and geography recorded at intervals with different levels of activity, while several studies of urban areas rely on contrasting compact and dispersed areas of the baseline city and the extrapolation of data obtained to five cities in the country. The study analyzes four potential measures: mode transfer, lower speed, changes in cargo transportation schedule, and good practices. Finally, limitations and recommendations related to the study and application of the analyzed measures as well as further research required to improve this type of study are suggested.

The Role of Intelligent Transport Systems for Demand Responsive Transport
Robert Clavel, Elodie Castex, and Didier Josselin

Demand Responsive Transport (DRT) is a public transport system that provides the user with the advantages of both public transport and taxi services. It was often considered as a marginal mode of transport reserved for areas with low population densities. Since the end of the 1990s, the number of DRT systems been increasing consistently, with new investments in urban, suburban, and rural spaces and with varying degrees of operational flexibility. The flexibility and efficiency of DRT systems are influenced by several factors, the most important being technological. Most of these technological developments are in the field of information and communication technologies (ICT). This paper illustrates the use of technology to improve DRT efficiency with two case studies from France (Pays du Doubs Central and Toulouse). The type and level of ICT used is strongly dependent on the type of DRT service, its level of flexibility, and its specific optimization problem.

The examples of Doubs Central and Toulouse, two different areas, show that technology can play a key role to optimize DRT trips and to bring quality service to the population in a large area or when the patronage is high. Technology offers the potential for achieving real-time demand responsiveness in transport services, particularly in complex networks, to a level far in advance of manual systems.

Urban Sprawl and Climate Change: A Statistical Exploration of Cause and Effect, with Policy Options for the EU
Istvan Laszlo Bart

The EU should get involved in regulating the growth of cities. The great impact of sprawling urban development on greenhouse gas emissions makes this inevitable. Governments cannot afford to watch idly as the hard-earned gains in reducing emissions elsewhere are obliterated by cities built to require ever-greater car use.

The growing demand for urban, car-based transport is a main driver in the growth of transport emissions. As the ever greater demand for automobile use is rooted in the car-centric way cities are being built today, these emissions cannot be checked alone by technical solutions that reduce per-kilometer CO_2 emissions. Because people want maximum comfort, this can be achieved only by building cities where not having a car is an advantage, not an impediment.

Urban planning is no longer just a local or national issue; its impact on climate change makes it a matter for the EU to regulate. It is also clear that in most places local governments are unable to prevent an ever-greater sprawling of cities. The objective of regulation should be to make sure that new urban development is not exclusively car oriented, thus minimizing the increase of transport-related greenhouse gas emissions. EU-level regulation may be done through establishing minimum standards of certain indicators, but emissions trading with the participation of parking space providers is also a possible method of controlling transport emissions and at the same time ensuring that future urban development is not exclusively car oriented.

This study provides a brief evaluation of the relationship between trends in transport emissions and urban land use. It concludes that the growth of transport emissions is a result of specific urban planning and land-use policies (or their absence). These policies can cause an increase in transport emissions even if the population size remains the same and there is no economic growth. This implies that governments need to implement sensible land-use policies. Such policies may not be very visible, but they have a huge impact on transport emissions.

Finally, the study outlines a few possible measures that could control transport emissions by addressing land-use issues. It explores ideas related to benchmarks, mandatory plans, and the possibility of using the concept of emissions trading in connection with land-uses causing transport emissions.

Getting to Carbon Neutral: A Review of Best Practices in Infrastructure Strategy
C. Kennedy, D. Bristow, S. Derrible, E. Mohareb, S. Saneinejad, R. Stupka, L. Sugar, R. Zizzo, and B. McIntyre

Measures of cost effectiveness for reducing GHG emissions from cities are established for 22 case studies, mainly involving changes to infrastructure. GHG emissions from cities are primarily related to transportation, energy use in buildings, electricity supply, and waste. A variety of strategies for reducing emissions are examined through case studies ranging from $0.015 million to $460 million of capital investment (U.S. dollars). The case studies have been collected to support a Guide for Canadian Municipalities on Getting to Carbon Neutral (G2CN). The cost effectiveness, given by annual GHG emissions saved per dollar of capital investment, is found to vary between 3 and 2,780 tons eCO_2/year/$million for the G2CN database. The average cost effectiveness of the database of 550 tons eCO_2/year/$million is significantly exceeded by solid waste projects in Canada (FCM) and by developing world projects under the Clean Development Mechanism. Five case studies in the G2CN database with GHG savings of over 100,000 tons eCO_2 are highlighted. Yet, cities need to start planning projects with reductions on the order of more than 1 million tons eCO_2/year in order to substantially reduce emissions below current levels for smaller cities (1 million people) and megacities.

Climate Change and the Resilience of New Orleans: The Adaptation of Deltaic Urban Form
Armando Carbonell and Douglas J. Meffert

Using New Orleans, Louisiana, as the departure point, this paper discusses emergent trends of climate change and hurricanes, along with policies and practice representing adaptive land use, mitigation, and governance. The role of urban form in adapting to and mitigating climate change will be addressed, including an emphasis on natural wetland and water "ecostructures." The New Orleans case study offers information that can inform international sites, particularly historic, vulnerable port delta cities.

Vulnerability and Resilience of Urban Communities under Coastal Hazard Conditions in Southeast Asia
Vilas Nitivattananon, Tran Thanh Tu, Amornrat Rattanapan, and Jack Asavanant

Most coastal cities are facing complex interrelated problems associated with greater intensity and frequency of climate extremes. Often times, these challenges require adaptation strategies that bring together comprehensive vulnerability assessments and implementation actions. The main objective of this paper is to apply the concept of vulnerability and resilience to coastal communities facing climate hazards in Southeast Asia. Southern Vietnam and Thailand are chosen as representative regions for the purpose of this study. The results show that flood risk has several consequences at different urbanization levels under increased climate variability. The main factors influencing the vulnerability of coastal communities are related to economics, institutional capacity, and the accessibility of knowledge for local community-based organizations.

Climate Change Adaptation Planning in Toronto: Progress and Challenges
Jennifer Penney, Thea Dickinson, and Eva Ligeti

The city of Toronto is one of the first Canadian cities to establish a citywide process to respond to its vulnerability to climate change. In 2008, Toronto developed Ahead of the Storm, a climate change adaptation strategy. This case study describes past, current, and potential future impacts of climate change on Toronto, along with the steps taken to develop the adaptation strategy. These steps include the creation of an Adaptation Steering Group and the development of an initial framework document. The strategy was underpinned by existing programs that provide protection from current weather extremes and included short-term actions as well as a longer-term process for developing a comprehensive strategy. The city is in the early stages of implementing the strategy. This paper also reflects on some of the barriers to the integration and mainstreaming of adaptation into the city's plans and programs.

Planning Climate Resilient Cities: Early Lessons from Early Adapters
JoAnn Carmin, Debra Roberts, and Isabelle Anguelovski

Climate change is expected to place increasing stress on the built and natural environments of cities as well as to create new challenges for the provision of urban services and management systems. Minimizing the impacts of climate change requires that cities develop and implement adaptation plans. Despite the imperative, only a small number of cities have initiated the adaptation planning process. Drawing on theories of diffusion and capacity and empirical assessments of initiatives in Durban, South Africa, and Quito, Ecuador, this paper examines two questions: What is driving cities to initiate climate adaptation planning? and What is enabling the efforts of early adapters to take root? Scholars argue that incentives from external sources such as regulations and funder requirements, the diffusion of international knowledge and norms, and the presence of sufficient capacity are critical drivers of subnational change in the policy and planning arenas. However, rather than being driven by external pressures, the early adapters examined in this study were motivated by internal incentives, ideas, and knowledge generated through local demonstration projects and local networks and the means to link adaptation to ongoing programs and to enlist the support of diverse stakeholders from within the city.

Governance and Climate Change: Assessing and Learning from Canadian Cities
Christopher Gore, Pamela Robinson, and Richard Stren

Canada hosted one of the first international meetings to address climate change in 1988. The Toronto Conference on the Changing Atmosphere helped focus the attention of national governments on the emerging international challenge presented by rising concentrations of greenhouse gases in the atmosphere. But in Canada, this event did not translate into national leadership to address climate change. Many pragmatic reasons exist to explain why Canada has been ineffective at reducing emissions, particularly the size of the country and the associated use of automobile and truck transportation to cover long distances, as well as its cold climate. Political and intergovernmental reasons are also significant.

Though national leadership on climate change action has been lacking, Canadian cities are national and international leaders in climate action. This paper examines and explains why Canadian cities have taken action to reduce GHG emissions, while also adapting to and mitigating climate change. The paper also inventories the activities of select medium to large Canadian cities (populations between 300,000 and 2.5 million). The paper offers a simple yet unique approach to analyzing action. Action is classified as an initiative, output, or outcome.

Using this approach to understand the climate action of Canadian cities provides an opportunity to draw lessons about the character of these early and ongoing leaders and to identify the specific actions of Canadian cities. The initiatives documented include shorter-term technical actions and medium- and longer-term actions that require more complex coordination with citizens and the private sector. The goal of the paper is to highlight how and why cities in a country with limited national leadership have chosen to act. This provides an opportunity for cities starting to initiate action, both in states that are actively engaged in national GHG emission reduction efforts and in those that are not, to understand how cities in Canada have independently taken action and how future collaborations with other cities and levels of government might evolve to better mitigate and adapt to climate change.

Understanding and Improving Urban Responses to Climate Change. Reflections for an Operational Approach to Adaptation in Low- and Middle-Income Countries
Roberto Sanchez Rodriguez

This article reflects on the construction of an operational approach for adaptation to climate change in low- and middle-income countries. I depart from the assumption that climate change is a development challenge for urban areas and that adaptation to its impacts needs to be considered a learning process rather than a single product. I argue that an operational approach to climate change needs to address the formal and the informal process of urban growth in order to be efficient. This requires attention to the balance between structure and agency in the construction of the urban space and the combination of top-down and bottom-up actions. The article considers the role of urban institutions and the collaboration among scholars and local governments and stakeholders as part of an operational approach for adaptation.

City Health System Preparedness to Changes in Dengue Fever Attributable to Climate Change: An Exploratory Case Study
Jostacio M. Lapitan, Pauline Brocard, Rifat Atun, and Chawalit Tantinimitkul

City health system preparedness to changes in dengue fever attributable to climate change was explored in this collaborative study by Imperial College London and World Health Organization Kobe Centre. A new toolkit was developed, and an exploratory case study in Bangkok, Thailand, was undertaken in 2008. This study found that there is a clear lack of research in this area, as most research looked at impacts and not at responses and preparedness for effective response. There is also a clear need to develop and scale up national capital city efforts to assess and address the implications of climate change for health systems. It recommends further case studies to validate the toolkit and generate guidelines on how to develop effective response plans.

Climate Change and Urban Planning in Southeast Asia
Belinda Yuen and Leon Kong

The challenge of climate change is real and urgent in Southeast Asia. Southeast Asia is one of the world's fastest growing regions. This paper presents a desk review of the state of climate change research and policy in Southeast Asia. It highlights the challenges, knowledge gaps, and promising practices, with a specific focus on urban planning interventions to increase cities' resilience to climate change. The discussion reflects on how urban form and planning can support people's sustainable choices in terms of transportation, housing, and leisure activities and conveys the drivers and barriers to urban planning as a strategy of climate proofing. Issues that can be addressed through appropriate urban policy, planning, design, and governance are highlighted.

Social Aspects of Climate Change in Urban Areas in Low- and Middle-Income Nations
Sheridan Bartlett, David Dodman, Jorgelina Hardoy, David Satterthwaite, and Cecilia Tacoli

This paper discusses the implications of climate change for social welfare and development in urban areas in low- and middle-income nations, especially for those people with low incomes and those who are particularly vulnerable to climate-change impacts. Hundreds of millions of urban dwellers in these nations are at risk from the direct and indirect impacts of current and likely future climate change—for instance, more severe or frequent storms, floods and heat waves, constraints on fresh water and food supplies, and higher risks from a range of water and food-borne and vector-borne diseases. But these risks are distributed very unevenly between nations, between urban areas within nations, and between populations within urban areas. This is underpinned by differentials in the following:

- The scale and nature of hazards by site and location
- The quality of housing, infrastructure, and services·
- The extent of measures taken for disaster risk reduction (including postdisaster response)
- The capacity and preparedness of local governments to address the needs of low-income groups and to work with them
- The social and political capital of those who face the greatest risks

Does Climate Change Make Industrialization an Obsolete Development Strategy for Cities in the South?
Le-Yin Zhang

This paper attempts to explore the implications of climate change for economic development strategies in cities in the global South. In particular, it examines whether climate change makes industrialization an obsolete development strategy for these cities. It starts by examining the effects of climate change and the challenges posed for the cities concerned, followed by a discussion of the role of industrialization in economic development and climate change. It then investigates how these issues affect Southern cities by considering the experiences of Shanghai, Mumbai, and Mexico City. In conclusion, the paper hypothesizes that climate change will make industrialization a more, not less, important development strategy, even for those cities that are currently affected by premature deindustrialization.

The Price of Climate: French Consumer Preferences Reveal Spatial and Individual Inequalities
Jean Cavailhès, Daniel Joly, Hervé Cardot, Mohamed Hilal, Thierry Brossard, and Pierre Wavresky

We use the hedonic price method to study consumer preferences for climate (temperature, very hot or cold days, and rainfall) in France, a temperate country with varied climates. Data are for (1) individual attributes and prices of houses and workers and (2) climate attributes interpolated from weather stations. We show that French households value warmer temperatures while very hot days are a nuisance. Such climatic amenities are attributes of consumers' utility function; nevertheless, global warming assessments by economists, such as the Stern Review Report (2006), ignore these climatic preferences. The social welfare assessment is changed when the direct consumption of climate is taken into account: from the estimated hedonic prices, we calculate that GDP rises by about 1 percent for a 1 degree Celsius rise in temperature. Moreover, heterogeneity of housing and households is a source of major differences in the individual effects of climatic warming.

Adaptation and Mitigation: What Financing Is Available for Local Government Investments in Developing Countries?
Thierry Paulais and Juliana Pigey

This article reviews specific funding available for adaptation and mitigation investments of cities and discusses the mismatch between needs and financing tools. These funding sources are insufficient, highly fragmented, and not really tailored to local governments. They are narrowly sector based and risk being counterproductive in the urban context. Furthermore, they are complex and costly to access or else targeted to sovereign borrowers. The article makes proposals to adapt these finance tools, to reintroduce local authorities in mechanisms from which they are presently excluded, and to create incentives in their favor. Finally, it proposes an initiative for cities in fragile states, based on greater involvement of wealthy Northern cities and the recourse to a specific financing mechanism.

Mobilizing Private Sector Resources toward Climate Adaptation and Mitigation Action in Asia
Jacob Park

This paper will explore the current state of and future outlook for mobilizing private sector resources in the Asian post-2012 climate policy context, with a special emphasis on the energy-poor and environmentally fragile urban population. Two issues and questions will be explored in this paper. First, what is the current state of and future outlook for public and private investments to address global and Asian climate change concerns? Second, what new triple bottom-line strategy of financing climate change action is required to respond more effectively to the urban climate change dilemma in Asia?

High-Cost Carbon and Local Government Finance
Patricia Clarke Annez and Thomas Zuelgaray

Global climate change has certain unique features in terms of optimal policy. Some of these have been discussed already at the global level and some at the national level. But what is the impact of these features on local government finance? This paper examines the impact of high-cost carbon on municipalities' finances. We compare municipalities' finances in India (State of Maharashtra) and in Spain. We conclude that raising energy prices will create an adverse fiscal shock for local governments, the magnitude of which will depend on the structure of spending. Smaller, less diversified governments currently operating at a low level of service and with a very small operating deficit will be harder hit, precisely because the most basic services tend to be energy intensive, and their energy bill is high in relation to their scope for borrowing to weather the shock. However, all municipalities would appear to be hard hit, and a system of compensation from national governments would be needed to avoid disruption to essential services.

Victims to Victors, Disasters to Opportunities: Community-Driven Responses to Climate Change in the Philippines
David Dodman, Diana Mitlin, and Jason Christopher Rayos Co

Advocates of community-based adaptation claim that it helps to identify, assist, and implement community-based development activities, research, and policy in response to climate change. However, there has been little systematic examination of the ways in which existing experiences of dealing with hazard events can inform community-based adaptation. This paper analyzes the experience of the Homeless People's Federation of the Philippines Incorporated (HPFPI) in respect to community-led disaster responses, with the aim of informing future discussions on the role of planning for climate change adaptation in low- and middle-income countries.

The Urban Poor's Vulnerability to Climate Change in Latin America and the Caribbean
Lucy Winchester and Raquel Szalachman

Cities in Latin America and the Caribbean (LAC) currently face many environmental and sustainable development challenges, with significant impacts on human health, resource productivity and incomes, ecological "public goods," poverty, and inequity. In this context, climate change impacts in the region will exacerbate and create additional complexity, particularly in urban areas. For hundreds of millions of urban dwellers in LAC, most of the risks from the impacts of climate change are a result of development failures. For the urban poor, this fact is disproportionately true. This paper seeks to contribute to the limited body of knowledge regarding climate change, cities, and the urban poor in the region and to inform how institutions, governance, and urban planning are keys to understanding the opportunities and limitations to possible policy and program advances in the area of adaptation.

Built-in Resilience: Learning from Grassroots Coping Strategies to Climate Variability
Huraera Jabeen, Adriana Allen, and Cassidy Johnson

It is now widely acknowledged that the effects of climate change will disproportionately increase the vulnerability of the urban poor in comparison to other groups of urban residents. While significant attention has been given to exploring and unpacking "traditional" coping strategies for climate change in the rural context—with a focus on agricultural responses and livelihoods diversification—with few exceptions, there is less work on understanding the ways the urban poor are adapting to climate variability. The central argument of this paper is that significant lessons can be drawn from examining how the urban poor are already coping with conditions of increased vulnerability, including how they respond to existing environmental hazards such as floods, heavy rains, landslides, heat, and drought. Knowledge of these existing coping capacities for disaster risk reduction can help to strengthen planning strategies for adaptation to climate change in cities because they draw on existing grassroots governance mechanisms and support the knowledge systems of the urban poor.

Index

ECO-AUDIT
Environmental Benefits Statement

The World Bank is committed to preserving endangered forests and natural resources. The Office of the Publisher has chosen to print *Cities and Climate Change: Responding to an Urgent Agenda* on recycled paper with 50 percent postconsumer fiber in accordance with the recommended standards for paper usage set by the Green Press Initiative, a nonprofit program supporting publishers in using fiber that is not sourced from endangered forests. For more information, visit www.greenpressinitiative.org.

Saved:

- 11 trees

- 4 million BTUs of total energy

- 1,116 pounds of net greenhouse gases

- 5,035 gallons of waste water

- 320 pounds of solid waste